CRADLES OF CIVILIZATION

EGYPT

EGYPT

General Editor: Jaromir Malek

ANCIENT CULTURE, MODERN LAND

University of Oklahoma Press
Norman, Oklahoma

ABOVE: Ramesses III (1184–1153 BC) welcomed by the god Shu, in the tomb of his son, Prince Khaemwese, in the Valley of the Queens. THE IMAGE BANK/TOM OWEN EDMUNDS

ABOVE: Detail of an astronomical ceiling, depicting various constellations, in the burial chamber of Sethos I (1294– 1279 BC) in the Valley of the Kings. AUSTRAL/CAMERA PRESS

Published by the University of Oklahoma Press, Norman, Publishing Division of the University

Produced by Weldon Russell Pty Ltd
107 Union Street North Sydney NSW 2060 Australia

Copyright © 1993 by Weldon Russell Pty Ltd

ISBN 0-8061-2526-8
LC 92-50718

Managing editor: Dawn Titmus
Project coordinator: Yani Silvana
Copy-editor: Susan Stone
Picture researcher: Jane Lewis
Designer: Kathie Baxter Smith
Illustrator: Jan Smith
Indexer: Garry Cousins
Production: Jane Hazell/Di Leddy

Printed by Tien Wah Press, Singapore

FRONT COVER: Head of a colossal statue and an obelisk of Ramesses II (1279–1213 BC) in front of the pylon of the Luxor temple. AUSTRALIAN PICTURE LIBRARY/D. & J. HEATON

BACK COVER: Modern Cairo is an interesting blend of the old and the new. Ancient landmarks such as the Ramesses II obelisk stand beside the modern Cairo Tower. PETER CLAYTION

PAGE TWO: The hawk associated with the god Horus stands in front of the hypostyle (columned hall) of the temple of Horus at Edfu. THE IMAGE BANK/DAVID W. HAMILTON

PAGE THREE: Graywacke sculpture from the valley temple of King Menkaure (2488–2460 BC) at Giza, showing the king accompanied by the goddess Hathor and a deity personifying one of the administrative districts into which Egypt was divided. MUSEUM OF FINE ARTS, BOSTON

PAGE FIVE: Baked clay statue of a lion from c. 2600 BC, found in the temple at Kom el-Ahmar (Hierakonpolis). ASHMOLEAN MUSEUM, OXFORD/WERNER FORMAN ARCHIVE

PAGE SIX: The houses in Nubia, the area south of the First Nile Cataract, were renowned for their beautifully painted facades. Sadly, Nubian villages were flooded when Lake Nasser was created. AUSTRALIAN PICTURE LIBRARY/D. & J. HEATON

PAGE SEVEN TOP LEFT: Traditional means of transport in rural Egypt. THE IMAGE BANK/ BRETT FROMER

PAGE SEVEN BOTTOM LEFT: The Step Pyramid of King Netjerikhet Djoser (2628–2609 BC) at Saqqara. H. CHAMPOLLION

PAGE SEVEN RIGHT: Cairo is one of the busiest cities in the world, full of energy and vitality. AUSTRAL/CAMERA PRESS LONDON

PAGE EIGHT: Larger than life head of a quartzite statue of a Middle Kingdom ruler, almost certainly Senwosret III (1878–1859 BC) NELSON-ATKINS MUSEUM OF ART, KANSAS

PAGE NINE: Gold statuette of the god Osiris, second half of the first millennium BC. ANCIENT ART AND ARCHITECTURE COLLECTION/RONALD SHERIDAN

SERIES PREFACE

Timothy Potts

Cradles of Civilization is a new series which provides the readers with a reliable, up-to-date, and well-illustrated account of the world's great civilizations. Each volume is written by a team of leading international experts, providing an authoritative review of the cultures which have played a leading role in shaping the course of human history. Brought to light in modern times through the discoveries of archaeology, the piecing together of the patterns of the past represents one of the major scientific and humanistic achievements of our age.

Unlike other ancient history series, *Cradles of Civilization* brings together geographers, anthropologists, archaeologists and historians to form a broader picture of life in ancient times, one that seeks not only to describe the past but also, as far as possible, to explain it. Taking as its theme the juxtaposition of "Ancient Culture, Modern Land", each civilization is examined in the context of its environment — the physical and cultural landscape which molded lifestyles and formed the foundation upon which empires were to rise and fall — while special features examine the arts, sciences and great personalities of history.

The legacy of the past is very much apparent in the way we live today, and each volume traces the history and culture of a particular region up to modern times, building into a concise but comprehensive overview of human achievement through the ages. Both individually and as a series, *Cradles of Civilization* will form a valuable guide to the cultures which not only represent the highpoints of antiquity around the globe but have also done most to shape the face of the modern world today.

CONTENTS

SERIES EDITOR

TIMOTHY POTTS

Former Research Lecturer and British Academy Post-doctoral Fellow in Near Eastern archaeology,
University of Oxford, UK

GENERAL EDITOR

JAROMIR MALEK

Editor of the *Topographical Bibliography of Ancient Egyptian Hieroglyphic Texts, Reliefs and Paintings* and
Keeper of the Archive at the Griffith Institute, Ashmolean Museum, Oxford, UK

CONTRIBUTORS

M. L. BIERBRIER
Assistant Keeper, British Museum, London, UK

JANINE BOURRIAU
Fellow of the McDonald Institute for Archaeological Research,
University of Cambridge, UK

ALAN K. BOWMAN
Student and tutor in ancient history, Christ Church, University
of Oxford, UK

WALTRAUD GUGLIELMI
Associate Professor of Egyptology, Eberhard-Karls University,
Tübingen, Germany

FAYZA M. H. HAIKAL
Visiting Professor, American University, Cairo, Egypt

JANE JAKEMAN
Research student, St John's College, Oxford, UK

JAC J. JANSSEN
Emeritus Professor in Egyptology, University of Leiden, the
Netherlands

PENELOPE JOHNSTONE
Tutor in Arabic, Oriental Institute, University of Oxford, UK

C. A. KELLER
Associate Professor of Egyptology, Department of Near Eastern
Studies, University of California, Berkeley, USA

KENNETH A. KITCHEN
Professor of Egyptology, University of Liverpool, UK

ARIELLE P. KOZLOFF
Curator of Ancient Art, the Cleveland Museum of Art,
Ohio, USA

JOHN D. RAY
Herbert Thompson Reader in Egyptology, University of
Cambridge, UK

D. S. RICHARDS
Lecturer in Arabic, University of Oxford, UK

IAN SHAW
Research Fellow in Archaeology, New Hall, Cambridge
University, UK

COLIN C. WALTERS
Tutor, Department of Extended Education, University of
Oxford, UK

INTRODUCTION

Jaromir Malek

OURS IS THE age of package tours — jumbo jets and passenger planes, air-conditioned buses, boats, and hotels, bland food that does not unduly upset our stomachs, and carefully organized sightseeing trips. The image of Egypt that visitors take home is also a package, a package of neatly wrapped-up memories: Tutankhamun's treasures in the Egyptian Museum, the pyramids and the Sphinx, the temples at Karnak and Luxor, the Valley of the Kings, perhaps the Cairo Citadel and the mosque of Muhammad Ali, and a few chance impressions that nobody could plan in advance. And most of the books on Egypt are packaged in the same way: many color illustrations of the best-known monuments, a few atmospheric and picturesque views so that we do not forget that we are in an Islamic country, and an undemanding text. Indeed, one might be forgiven for thinking that the sword of Alexander the Great stopped the clock of history in 332 BC and that not much has happened since. The reader of the typical book on Egypt may be offered a lot of facts but is usually given few opportunities to understand.

The book in your hands tries to avoid the packaged approach. It has been written by a team of specialists from different parts of the world, and although it is intended for a reader without detailed knowledge of the country, it will also be interesting to those previously initiated into the study of Egypt. In addition to who, what, and when, this book tries to explain why. It is thought-provoking and will encourage a search for characteristics common to all humankind, and it does not shy away from the controversial. All the stages of Egyptian civilization are explored: ancient, Greco-Roman, Coptic, and Islamic — from pharaonic times right down to the recent Gulf war. The book is unabashedly and contagiously enthusiastic about Egypt, and the authors hope to communicate to their readers some of their feeling for the country, its civilization, and its people.

AN ENDURING LAND

THE BLACK LAND, THE RED LAND

Ian Shaw

OVER THE COURSE of millions of·years, a series of dramatic geological events produced the four distinct physical regions of Egypt: the Nile valley and delta, the Western Desert, the Eastern Desert, and the Sinai peninsula. The uncomplicated geography of the country could hardly have been better suited to the ancient Egyptians' strong sense of symmetry. They were able to divide their environment into a series of carefully balanced pairs and opposites. So the dry Red Land of the desert contrasted sharply with the fertile Black Land of the Nile Valley. The Black Land itself could then be subdivided into the northern and southern kingdoms of the Delta (Lower Egypt) and the Valley (Upper Egypt). Foreigners outside Egypt tended to be characterized as "northerners" (Asians) or "southerners" (Africans), leaving the Egyptians as a race apart.

Egypt is in an unusual geographical position at the junction of three continents, with its northern border facing Europe across the Mediterranean, its southern and western borders in Africa, and its eastern border separated from Western Asia (the ancient Near East) only by the Red Sea and the Sinai peninsula. The physical geography of Egypt has remained constant in many respects for at least 5,000 years, but,

although the fundamental topography and climate have altered little since the Neolithic (or Predynastic) period (*c.* 5000–3000 BC), a rich variety of human adaptive strategies have developed within these familiar constraints. The nature and scale of agricultural exploitation in the Nile valley, delta and oases have undergone numerous changes, as dependence on the resources of the surrounding deserts has also varied enormously from one period to another, tending to reflect dramatic fluctuations in demand for different commodities and raw materials. Similarly, the different routes taken by hunting, trading, and mining expeditions over the centuries have imprinted on the landscape a record of the changing patterns of exploitation.

Although it may seem that Egypt's modern shape and political boundaries are almost indistinguishable from those that prevailed throughout the earlier periods, this geographical continuity is difficult to assess from the archaeological record alone. The Neolithic inhabitants of the Nile Valley seem to have been more open to foreign interference than their successors, since during the Neolithic period the Libyan and Eastern deserts were less arid and therefore more hospitable to travelers from central Africa

TOP: Detail from David Roberts's "Ascent of the lower range of Mount Sinai" painted in 1839. VICTORIA & ALBERT MUSEUM, LONDON/PETER CLAYTON

ABOVE: Modern methods of crop cultivation and new irrigation techniques are being tried under the relentless pressure for increased agricultural production. THE IMAGE BANK/GUIDO ALBERTO ROSSI

OPPOSITE: Nilotic landscape on a Roman mosaic pavement found in the Italian town of Palestrina (Praeneste), probably from the first century BC. PALESTRINA NATIONAL MUSEUM/JOHN G. ROSS

PREVIOUS PAGE: A landscape typical of the area just below the First Cataract, near Aswan. In the foreground is the island of Elephantine. THE IMAGE BANK/NEIL FOLBERG

and the Near East. The late Predynastic cultures of Egypt show indications of outside influences both in the iconography of artifacts and the physical appearance of the people.

During the dynastic (pharaonic) period (after *c.* 3000 BC) most of the population was concentrated in the vicinity of the Nile, as it is now, and the surrounding deserts were controlled only to the extent that the routes of trading and mining expeditions could be protected. At this time the desert regions would not have been considered parts of Egypt proper but regarded instead as threatening marginal lands into which forays were made only when necessary. When the pharaohs of the New Kingdom (1540–1069 BC) began to boast of "extending the borders" of Egypt, they were thinking primarily in terms of victories over the settled peoples to north and south rather than over the "sand-dwellers" of the Eastern and Western deserts. The borders with Nubia and Syria–Palestine regularly expanded and contracted in more or less direct relation to the strength of the central power in Egypt. In the Libyan Desert the main oases were probably always dominated by the Egyptians, but the population derived largely from the area now occupied by modern Libya rather than from the Nile Valley.

THE CLIMATE AND NATURAL HISTORY

Modern Egypt has only two seasons: a hot summer (May–October) and a cool winter (November–April), with temperatures ranging from about 43°F (6°C) at night in winter up to a maximum of around 115°F (46°C) at the height of summer. There is now a growing body of archaeological evidence concerning the

LEFT: Crocodiles were a common sight in ancient Egypt and were regarded as manifestations of certain deities, in particular the god Sobek of the Faiyum Oasis in Middle Egypt. Cemeteries of mummified crocodiles are known from several places, for example Kom Ombo. In the course of the nineteenth century crocodiles disappeared from Egypt proper and their sightings in Nubia became rare in the twentieth century. The situation may now be changing again as the result of the creation of Lake Nasser. Photograph by E. Béchard taken in the 1870s or 1880s. GRIFFITH INSTITUTE, ASHMOLEAN MUSEUM, OXFORD

climate of Egypt in earlier times, based primarily on the results of paleobotany and radiocarbon dating. The first Egyptians of the Paleolithic period (before *c.* 10,000 BC) appeared in the grasslands of northeastern Africa in about 250,000 BC, but it was not until the onset of a drier climate in about 25,000 BC that these populations were forced into the Nile Valley. This gradual process of desiccation eventually led to the formation of the Eastern and Western deserts. During the Mesolithic period (*c.* 10,000–5000 BC), a number of seminomadic cultures inhabited the immediate area of the Nile Valley, relying on hunting and fishing for their subsistence. More settled Neolithic communities along the Nile, primarily relying on animal and plant domestication, appeared in about 5000 BC.

There was a surprising degree of innovation in animal husbandry during the pharaonic period (after *c.* 3000 BC). In addition to rearing cattle, sheep, goats, and pigs, the Egyptian farmers of the Old Kingdom (2647–2124 BC) experimented with the domestication of the gazelle, oryx, hyena, and ibex. In the Middle Kingdom (2040–1648 BC) the indigenous fleeceless sheep began to be replaced by a new wool-bearing species from Western Asia, and by the New Kingdom

(1540–1069 BC), both the horse and the zebu had also been introduced. The principal domesticated animals in modern Egypt are sheep, goats, poultry, water buffalo, horses, donkeys, and camels.

The detailed pictograms of the hieroglyphic script and the scenes on the walls of the ancient tombs and temples provide abundant evidence of the rich animal and plant life of the late Predynastic and pharaonic periods. Numerous species that have now become extinct or retreated farther south into tropical Africa, such as the hippopotamus and the crocodile, are portrayed with considerable accuracy and detail. As early as about 2600 BC the elephant, rhinoceros, giraffe, and gerenuk gazelle ceased to be found north of Aswan, and the number of lions and leopards was greatly reduced. It is not clear to what extent this change was due simply to overhunting by humans or to the gradual desiccation that took place during the early pharaonic period. Certainly the complete lack of forests in Egypt means that modern wildlife is correspondingly limited, with only a few surviving ibex in the Eastern Desert and the Sinai and a scattering of wild boars, jungle cats, and lynx in the Delta.

As far as the vegetation of ancient Egypt is concerned, the once prolific

CONTROLLING THE NILE

ABOVE: *The shadoof is a simple water-lifting device that consists of a long wooden pole with a bucket at one end and a counterweight at the other. It is usually operated by one man, occasionally two, but the height to which water can be raised (about 5 feet/1.5 m, although several can be combined to obtain greater lift) and its volume are limited. The water is scooped from the river, a canal, or a pond. The earliest representation of a shadoof is known from the reign of Akhenaten (1353–1337 BC) but it probably was not an Egyptian invention and may have been imported from Mesopotamia. Shadoofs are still used for irrigation of gardens or small plots, but modern technology is quickly replacing them.* MACQUITTY INTERNATIONAL COLLECTION

ABOVE: *The saqiya (water wheel) was introduced in Egypt during the Ptolemaic period (305–30 BC). Its main components are a large, vertically positioned wheel with containers to hold water, placed over a well (and thus not necessarily in the immediate vicinity of surface water), and another wheel, placed horizontally, turned by a buffalo, a camel, or a donkey. Depending on the sophistication of the design, water can be raised to a height of several yards and the effectiveness of the saqiya is considerably greater than that of the shadoof. Modern saqiyas, made of metal, some engine-driven, are fast replacing old wooden wheels with large pottery jars used as scoops.* SONIA HALLIDAY PHOTOGRAPHS

BELOW LEFT: *A screw-pump ("Archimedean screw," tunbur) is an irrigation device that raises water by the rotation of a screw inside a water-tight cylinder. It was introduced during the Ptolemaic period (305–30 BC) and Archimedes (c. 287–212 BC), an Alexandrian scholar, is credited with its invention. Human force is employed to operate it so the height to which water can be raised is limited, but it is still occasionally used.*

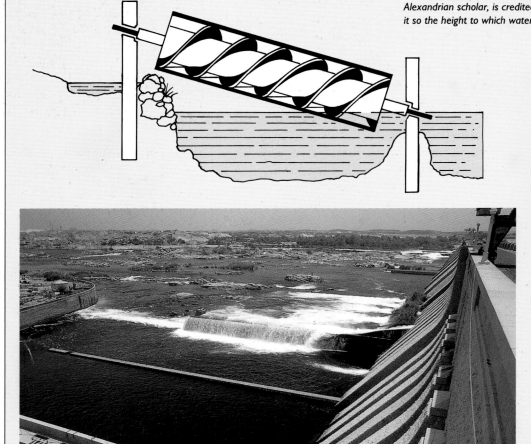

ABOVE: *The building of El-Sadd el-Aaly (High Dam) at Aswan and the creation of Lake Nasser may have had some adverse side effects on the country's agriculture, ecology, and antiquities, but there is little doubt that without these projects the hugely increased energy demands and the recent series of barely adequate Nile inundations would have had a disastrous effect on Egypt's economy.* MACQUITTY INTERNATIONAL COLLECTION

LEFT: *The first dam built at Aswan was the largest in the world when completed in 1912. It has undergone further modifications and is now 2340 yards (2140 m) long and 55 yards (50 m) high. It was constructed mainly in an attempt to regulate the flow of the Nile, particularly during inundation, for agricultural purposes.* ALASTAIR SCOTT/ROBERT ESTALL

LEFT: *The landscape at Thebes is picturesque, but the area's agricultural potential has always been limited. In antiquity, the importance of the city of Weset was mainly ideological. Its advantages lay in its proximity to natural resources (gold, copper, and minerals), commercial routes (across the Eastern Desert and to Nubia), manpower sources (Nubia), and its distance from the northern power centers during crises.* THE IMAGE BANK/PAUL TRUMMER

papyrus plant has virtually disappeared, while recently introduced species of eucalyptus, cypress, and elm are thriving in the modern climate. The main crops grown in the pharaonic period were barley, wheat, and flax. The sheer fertility of the Egyptian soil seems to have discouraged innovation in this area, although a few new varieties of grain and vegetables were eventually introduced in the course of the Greco-Roman period (after 332 BC).

THE NILE AND THE DELTA

The Egyptian section of the Nile Valley descends for 500 miles (800 km) from the Sudan border to Cairo and then flows for a further 150 miles (240 km) along each of its major Delta branches down to the Mediterranean coast. In the first century AD there were still seven Delta branches of the river, but natural and constructed blockages have now reduced the number to two major tributaries: the Rosetta and the Damietta branches. Egypt without the River Nile is almost inconceivable. Numerous other civilizations have grown up around rivers and floodplains, but the influence of the northernmost stretch of the Nile on the society and economy of the people of Egypt from the Paleolithic period through to the present day has been extreme. Unlike other rivers in the ancient world, the waters of the Nile rose every year between July and September, flooding the surrounding valley and depositing new layers of fertile silt. This apparently miraculous phenomenon, known as the annual "inundation" of the Nile, was the most crucial factor in the Egyptian economy until modern times, since the success of the annual harvest was directly related to the size of the flooding (which was ultimately dependent on the monsoon rains of the Ethiopian highlands far to the south).

The gradual accumulation of fertile Nile alluvial deposits — carried down every summer for millennia — has not only prevented the Mediterranean Sea from eroding away Egypt's northern coastline but also transformed the fan-shaped Delta region from a succession of prehistoric swamps and "turtleback" islands into some of the richest farming land of modern Egypt. Rainfall in the Nile Valley is almost nonexistent (although there has been a slight increase since the creation of Lake Nasser), and even in the Delta it amounts to an annual figure of only between four and eight inches (100–200 mm). Since prehistory, therefore, the rise and fall of the Nile has been the most significant variable in the environment of Egypt.

Many facets of the so-called "hydraulic civilization" of ancient Egypt, from religious myths to social and

ABOVE: *Some agricultural methods have not noticeably changed since antiquity and seem to have been taken straight from ancient Egyptian tomb walls.* H. CHAMPOLLION

economic cycles, inevitably hinged on the annual inundation. Throughout all periods there was an understandable preoccupation with the measurement of the fluctuating height of the Nile. The techniques ranged from simple rock carvings in the Early Dynastic period (c. 2950–2647 BC), particularly in the region of Aswan, to specially constructed stone-lined pits such as the ninth century Nilometer on Roda Island.

THE ASWAN DAM AND THE SUEZ CANAL

From the beginning of Egyptian history, the major challenge for the country's rulers — and perhaps the initial basis of their power — has been the effective control and exploitation of the rivers, lakes, and canals. Two major problems have been confronted repeatedly: the regulation and diversion of the flow of the Nile, and the provision of a link between the Red Sea and the Mediterranean.

Until the last 200 years the human response to the annual Nile inundation consisted primarily of small, localized projects. The Egyptians' exploitation of the Nile environment has shown remarkable continuity throughout the different phases of their history, gradually evolving with the appearance of more sophisticated technology. In the Middle Ages — just as in pharaonic times — local irrigation mostly took the form of dredging, ditch digging, and the construction of small dams to retain the water once the annual floods had subsided. This type of artificial basin irrigation, which is almost certainly represented on the late Predynastic mace head of King "Scorpion" (*c.* 3000 BC), allowed Egyptian farmers to expand the available cultivable area and sometimes to obtain a second or third crop from the land by prolonging the benefits of the flooding.

From 1830 onward large canals were excavated beside the Nile in an attempt to gain a more fundamental form of control over the process of inundation itself. Unfortunately, these canals were choked rapidly by the vast amounts of silt carried by the annual floods, and eventually most of them had to be abandoned. By the late nineteenth century French and British engineers had begun to experiment instead with various large barrages, including one just north of Cairo that allowed the flow into the Delta to be regulated. The completion of the first Aswan Dam and the barrages at Asyut, Esna, and Nag Hammadi in the first half of the twentieth century enabled the upper waters of the Nile to be subjected to the same level of control. But the culmination of these manipulations of the Nile was undoubtedly the completion in 1971 of the Aswan High Dam — the largest dam in the world — which superseded the earlier British-built dam

and completely transformed the Egyptians' relationship with the Nile by preventing the annual floodwaters from passing to the north of the First Cataract. The major immediate effect of the High Dam was the tragic flooding of the ancient sites of northern Nubia, when the vast reservoir of Lake Nasser was created. This situation could only be partially remedied by the ambitious UNESCO-backed rescue excavations of the 1960s, which included the complete removal and reconstruction of such temples as Abu Simbel, Kalabsha, and Philae.

By making water available all year round rather than in one seasonal flood, the High Dam has enabled hundreds of thousands of acres of land to be reclaimed from the desert through perennial irrigation. Through its hydroelectric plant the dam also supplies the whole country with cheap electricity. However, the damaging effects of the new dam on the environment of Egypt have still not been properly assessed. Since the flood plain is no longer "cleansed" annually by the inundation, there have been increases in the waterlogging and salination of topsoils,

LEFT: Lake Nasser, the second largest artificial reservoir in the world, is 317 miles (510 km) long. Economic gains have, however, been dearly paid for in human terms by the loss of Nubian villages and dispersal of Nubian communities in the early 1960s. The inhabitants were resettled but their way of life, which was quite unlike anywhere else in Egypt, is gone forever. MACQUITTY INTERNATIONAL COLLECTION

RIGHT: *The natural resources of the Sinai peninsula and its strategic position gave it a special role in both ancient and modern Egyptian history. The earliest recorded expedition to the turquoise mines at Wadi Maghara, in southern Sinai, was sent by King Sekhemkhet (2609–2603 BC). In recent times, it was in the Sinai desert where some of the most bitter fighting took place during Egyptian–Israeli conflicts.* THE IMAGE BANK/ GUIDO ALBERTO ROSSI

BELOW: *Siwa, some 370 miles (600 km) southwest of Alexandria by road, is much larger than the generally held image of an oasis: it measures 50 miles (80 km) from east to west.* DR K. P. KUHLMAN, GERMAN INSTITUTE OF ARCHAEOLOGY, CAIRO

BELOW: *A palm grove is a most unusual sight in the inhospitable wilderness of the Sinai desert.* THE IMAGE BANK/DAVID W. HAMILTON

apparently threatening both the viability of agricultural land and the continued preservation of antiquities (particularly the vulnerable painted walls of temples and tombs). Furthermore, since the banks of the Nile are no longer being enriched by new layers of silt each year, chemical fertilizers have to be widely used on the fields, and there are major problems with erosion at various points along the banks of the Nile. Although all of these problems were anticipated before the construction of the new dam, there have been additional unexpected drawbacks, including the proliferation of vegetation,

mosquitoes, and snails (carriers of the disease bilharzia) in Lake Nasser and an overall increase in the river's temperature.

Compared with the control of the inundation, the problem of linking the Red Sea with the Mediterranean to provide a lucrative new trade route has generally been a less crucial issue in Egypt. Nevertheless, a great deal of resources have been expended in seeking to achieve this goal since at least as early as the sixth century BC, when the Twenty-sixth Dynasty king Necho II attempted to construct a canal along the Wadi Tumilat. This canal was eventually completed by the Persian kings Darius I (521–486 BC) and Xerxes I (485–465 BC), thus connecting the Gulf of Suez with the Pelusiac branch of the Nile and providing a rapid and convenient conduit for trade from countries to the south and east of Egypt (particularly from ancient Punt). The same waterway was later reopened by Ptolemy II Philadelphus in about 280 BC and by the Roman emperor Trajan in AD 98. It is not clear how long it then continued in use, but it had evidently silted up completely by the eighth century AD.

Over the next thousand years schemes were occasionally proposed for a new canal, but the trade link was not to be successfully reopened until the mid-nineteenth century, when the French diplomat and engineer Ferdinand de Lesseps managed to obtain financial backing for a direct canal between the Gulf of Suez and Port Said on the Mediterranean coast. The Suez Canal, stretching for a hundred miles (160 km), was constructed at great cost between 1859 and 1869, finally allowing Egypt to capitalize on the growing trade between Asia and the European imperial powers. However, it was not until after President Nasser had nationalized the canal in 1956 that the financial rewards of the trade began to be enjoyed by the Egyptian government rather than by Britain and France. The revenue from the canal was then used to help finance the Soviet-built High Dam at Aswan, thus neatly linking together the two principal hydraulic achievements of modern Egypt.

THE DESERT ZONES AND OASES

To the south of Cairo, the Nile divides Egypt into two sections: the relatively mountainous Eastern Desert and the flat low plateau of the Libyan Desert, in which the dunes of the Great Sand Sea slope down northward from the heights of Gilf Kebir to the Libyan plateau in northwestern Egypt. The central tract of the Libyan Desert is punctuated by seven major depressions, starting with the uninhabitable saltwater lake of the

Qattara Depression farthest to the north, followed by six oases (Siwa, Faiyum, Bahariya, Farafra, Dakhla, and Kharga) that have been settled for as long as the Nile Valley itself. The vast resources of water beneath the oases derive partly from groundwater and partly from the Nile. They currently form the basis of a vast land reclamation project intended to transform the area into a "New Valley." The third Egyptian desert is the Sinai peninsula, which separates the Red Sea from the Mediterranean. During the pharaonic period the Sinai had a string of fortresses along its northern edge and turquoise and copper mines in its more southerly regions (particularly in the region of Serabit el-Khadim and Wadi Maghara).

The Egyptian desert zones acquired a new significance when the early Christian hermits chose to retire to the wilderness in order to devote themselves to meditation and prayer. Monastic communities were soon founded in the vicinity of these hermits' caves, usually located either in the cliffs at the edge of the cultivation or beside natural springs and oases in the desert. Some, such as the Coptic monasteries of St Antony and St Paul in the Eastern Desert, the community of St Macarius in the Wadi Natrun, and the Greek Orthodox monastery of St Catherine in the Sinai, have survived into modern times, despite

ABOVE: Although modern Egypt has made tremendous strides toward becoming a fully industrialized country, peasants working in the fields still hold the key to the country's prosperity. H. CHAMPOLLION

LEFT: The Greek Orthodox monastery of St Catherine is situated below Gebel Musa ("Mount of Moses") or Mount Sinai, at the spot where, according to tradition, Moses saw the burning bush. The original foundation of a church and a fort for the protection of the monks goes back to the Roman emperor Justinian in c. AD 530. The entry used to be through a trapdoor some 30 feet (9 m) above ground. The main feature of the still-functioning monastery is the Church of the Transfiguration; next to it there is a small mosque. The monastery is famous for its library, which has a large collection of manuscripts. STOCKSHOTS/J. BORTHWICK

QUARRIES AND MINES

Over the centuries the exploitation of the extensive mineral resources of the Eastern and Western deserts and the Sinai peninsula has helped to compensate for the low agricultural potential of these arid zones. From the Paleolithic quartzite quarries of Umm Shagir (in Dunqul Oasis, about 90 miles/150 km southwest of Aswan) to the modern oil wells in the Gulf of Suez and phosphate mines in the Libyan Desert, the Egyptians have employed a tremendous variety of strategies to extract and utilize the natural geological wealth of their country. One of the earliest surviving maps is an Egyptian papyrus, now in the Museo Egizio in Turin, bearing a schematic depiction of the route through a set of gold mines and siltstone quarries in the Eastern Desert. Dating to the Ramessid period (c.1150 BC), the map has been tentatively identified as a representation of the central part of the Wadi Hammamat area.

Since prehistoric times Egyptian mineral prospectors have been successful in locating a huge variety of valuable materials, ranging from the numerous isolated pockets of semiprecious stones in the Red Sea hills to the rich gold deposits of Nubia and the Eastern Desert. In each phase of Egyptian history a different array of resources was required: in the Old and Middle kingdoms there was an insatiable demand for limestone, granite, and basalt, primarily for the construction of funerary monuments, whereas in the New Kingdom other materials such as sandstone began to be exploited on an equally large scale. Many of these pharaonic mines and quarries continued to be used during the Roman period, when extensive new gray granite and "imperial porphyry" quarries were

also opened up at Mons Claudianus and Mons Porphyrites in the Eastern Desert, allowing fine stone to be exported throughout the Roman empire.

It was not only the raw materials for building or jewelry that were extracted from the ground: the Gebel el-Zeit mines on the Red Sea coast provided galena (lead sulfide), one of the principal ingredients of Egyptian cosmetics from the Predynastic period; and malachite, another substance used extensively in cosmetics, was mined from the Middle Kingdom (2040–1648 BC) onward at a number of sites in the Sinai and the Eastern Desert. The natural deposits of natron (sodium carbonate) at Wadi Natrun and el-Kab provided the embalmers with the necessary desiccating agent for mummification and the glass makers with one of the essential constituents of glass. Both natron and salt were considered sufficiently important commodities during the Greco-Roman period for there to be a royal monopoly on their extraction.

The quarry surfaces at some sites, such as the Gebel el-Silsila sandstone quarries, bear several different types of chisel marks that can be dated stylistically to periods from the Old Kingdom (2647–2124 BC) to as recently as the nineteenth century. Many of the leaders of pharaonic quarrying expeditions also left carved or painted inscriptions on the walls of the quarries or neighboring outcrops describing their achievements in extracting and transporting the stone. At most Egyptian quarrying or mining sites, such as the travertine (or "Egyptian alabaster") quarries of Hatnub and Wadi Gerrawi, the gypsum quarries of Umm el-Sawwan, and the amethyst mines of Wadi el-Hudi, there are also extensive remains of ancient stone

ABOVE LEFT: A Ramessid papyrus showing a gold-mining area of the Wadi Hammamat. The ancient Egyptian method of representing structures and landscape features in their most characteristic views either seen from above (in ground plan) or from one side (in elevation), was ideally suited for map-making. EGYPTIAN MUSEUM, TURIN/WERNER FORMAN ARCHIVE

ABOVE: Limestone quarries in western Thebes. JOHN ROMER

causeways and encampments, that provide some indication of the degree of organization involved in the mounting of long-distance quarrying expeditions.

Although quarrying was usually a seasonal activity, with military expeditions being sent whenever supplies of particular materials were needed by the king or a provincial governor, some of the more important sites appear to have included permanent quarry-workers' settlements occupied for centuries. The turquoise mines at Serabit el-Khadim in the Sinai, for instance, were accompanied by a temple dedicated to Hathor that was founded in the Middle Kingdom (c. 1950 BC) and then repeatedly refurbished and enlarged until it was finally abandoned, about 800 years later, in the reign of Ramesses VI (1143–1136 BC). The basalt quarries of Gebel Qatrani in the northwestern Faiyum were linked by a road with a considerable community of Middle Kingdom quarry workers housed in a walled mud-brick village at the site of Qasr el-Sagha.

There are no surviving paintings or reliefs of the dynastic period documenting the actual process of quarrying or mining, but the tomb of the provincial governor Djehutihotpe at Deir el-Bersha in Middle Egypt, dating to the

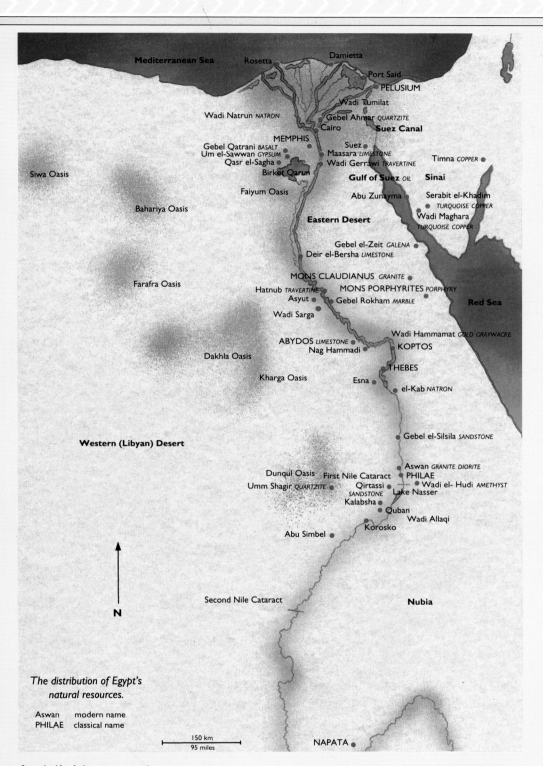

The distribution of Egypt's natural resources.

Aswan — modern name
PHILAE — classical name

150 km
95 miles

extracting veins of gold from quartz, describing how the quartz was smashed with hammers and then ground with mortars and hand mills, leaving a fine-grained powder that was then washed to separate out the gold from the quartz. The accuracy of this account is borne out by the frequent remains of such mortars and hand mills found at a number of gold-mining sites in the Eastern Desert and Nubia. The contemporary Egyptian accounts of gold-mining expeditions may be short on technical detail but they leave a distinct impression of the heroism displayed by the workers. An inscription of Ramesses II (1279–1213 BC) from the Nubian fortress of Quban describes the king's solution to the problems of an expedition along the Wadi Allaqi: "Ramesses heard of the richness in gold of Akita and determined to supply water along the roads. Animals and men in charge of gold convoys died of thirst or endured great hardship from lack of water, and for this reason gold ceased to come from the desert. The king summoned his council, and a well was ordered to be dug. At Akita water came in abundance, fields were cultivated, and fish ponds were established."

In the later periods the surviving pharaonic buildings themselves acted as fruitful "quarries" for building stone, but there was also a certain amount of genuine quarrying for particular materials, as in the case of the Islamic marble quarries at Gebel Rokham in the Eastern Desert. Although most of the Egyptian sources of gold and semiprecious stones had been completely exhausted by the mid-twentieth century, some of the sites exploited earlier are still at the center of commercial operations. The area around Hatnub, for instance, was quarried during the 1980s to supply chips of travertine for floor tiles manufactured in Cairo. In the same way the harbor of Abu Zunayma in southern Sinai, which was once the transit point for the ancient copper and turquoise mines, now serves as the main port for the modern manganese mines in the region. Pharaonic quarrying probably began with the extraction of limestone in the area of the Memphite necropolis (southwest of Cairo), and it is limestone that is still the most widely quarried material in Egypt, providing stone both for building purposes and for the lucrative cement industry. Quarrying and mining may no longer be the dangerous military expeditions that they used to be, but they are still crucial components of the modern Egyptian economy.

first half of the nineteenth century BC, contains a detailed portrayal of a colossal stone statue being dragged by lines of men from the travertine quarries at Hatnub to the Nile Valley. In addition, there is a fragment of an early New Kingdom stela (inscription on stone) from the Maasara limestone quarries (on the east bank of the Nile, south of Cairo)

showing a stone block being pulled along by three oxen under the supervision of several non-Egyptian workers — but again there is no indication of the methods by which the stone was extracted.

It was not until the second century BC that the Greek writer Agatharchides provided a written record of the Egyptian techniques for

RIGHT: *Sugar cane was not known in Egypt in antiquity and was only introduced in medieval times. Nowadays, much of it is cultivated in Middle Egypt.* ANCIENT ART AND ARCHITECTURE COLLECTION/RONALD SHERIDAN

repeated attacks by the Bedouin during the early medieval period. Many others, including the monasteries of St Simeon (at Aswan), St Thomas (at Wadi Sarga), and Apa Jeremias (at Saqqara), are now ruined and abandoned, but the remains of their granaries and church buildings clearly show that they were once thriving settlements in which thousands of monks practiced intensive agriculture and produced a diverse range of craft products.

In modern Egypt the deserts have gained a new importance both through the extensive land reclamation projects, which are gradually extending the limits of the Nile Valley, and through a policy of constructing new towns (such as Sadat City near Wadi Natrun, about 46 miles/ 75 km northwest of Cairo) in the desert rather than on valuable cultivable land.

POPULATION AND SUBSISTENCE

The human geography of the modern Arab Republic of Egypt is one of its most remarkable characteristics — the modern nation covers an area of about 400,000 square miles (or a million square kilometers), but less than 5 percent of this territory is under cultivation. Despite the overall size of Egypt, more than 96 percent of the country's population of over 57 million is squeezed into an area of only about 15,000 square miles (40,000 km^2) — roughly the size of Denmark.

A number of calculations have been made for the fluctuations in the size of the Egyptian population since prehistoric times, using the evidence for the quantity and quality of agricultural exploitation as a rough guide. The area of cultivable land in the late Predynastic period (*c.* 4000 BC) has been estimated at about 6,000 square miles (16,000 km^2) and the population is thought to have been no more than 350,000. But by the late second millennium BC, after the development of various irrigation techniques (particularly the introduction of the water-raising device, the shadoof), the available agricultural land had increased to about 8,500 square miles (22,500 km^2) and the population was perhaps as high as 3 million.

The agricultural potential of the Nile valley and delta seems to have reached unprecedented heights in the Greco-Roman period (probably as a result of higher annual flooding and the introduction of the *saqiya* water wheel and the "Archimedean screw"), and the amount of land under cultivation perhaps even surpassed 10,000 square miles (27,000 km^2). The extent of

LEFT: Most Egyptians still live in villages and are involved in agricultural production, but the number of town dwellers is increasing all the time. H. CHAMPOLLION

agricultural land in the Faiyum region was trebled during the Ptolemaic period (305–30 BC) by reducing the size of the main lake (the Birket Qarun) and creating an irrigation network radiating out from it. During the Roman period, when Egypt was supplying Rome with a great deal of its food, Egypt's agricultural output continued to rise. The ancient population appears to have peaked in the first century AD at about 5 million (it is unlikely to have even approached the 8 million reported by the historian Josephus) — a figure that was not to be reached again until the time of Muhammad Ali in the early nineteenth century AD. During the first millennium AD Egypt's agricultural production and population seem to have gone into a slow decline. The supportive capacity of the land was evidently still impressive, but the economy appears to have been badly affected by such factors as epidemics, wars, and poor land management.

The geographical distribution of the population gradually transferred northward during pharaonic times, so that by the Ptolemaic period the Delta was both more populous and more powerful than Upper Egypt. The Cairo region, at the apex of the Delta, was the site of Egypt's capital for much of its history, acting as a convenient fulcrum between the northern and southern zones of the country. Over 12 million Egyptians are currently estimated to be living in modern Cairo, making the density of population in the capital city almost unbearably high.

LEFT: Irrigation canals distribute Nile water locally and bring it closer to the fields, just as they did in antiquity. Most Egyptian villages are situated near such canals. JOHN G. ROSS

WITNESS TO
THE PAST

AN ANCIENT CIVILIZATION

Jaromir Malek

THE EARLIEST EGYPTIAN hieroglyphs appeared shortly before 3000 BC, and if the existence of a script and the ability to record events is to be the deciding criterion, that was when Egypt entered its historic age. The emergence, only slightly later, of a unified state was no accident but the outcome of a long and complicated process that would have been impossible without the unusually favorable environmental conditions prevailing in the northeastern corner of Africa at the time.

Archaeologists, physical anthropologists, and linguists agree that there was nothing homogeneous about the origins of the Egyptians. The earliest inhabitants of the Nile Valley lived by hunting, fishing, and plant collecting before an influx of people from the drought-stricken Sahara encouraged the adoption of plant cultivation and stock herding around 5000 BC. There probably also was immigration and certainly cultural influences from the northeast (the Levant or Western Asia, the ancient Near East). The first permanent settlements date from about 4000 BC, and contemporary tombs and their contents reflect the beginnings of social stratification of Egyptian prehistoric (Predynastic) society. Social stratification was in due course accompanied by

attempts to form larger geographical units, prompted by economic considerations (advancing aridity and varying local conditions) and fueled by rising expectations of the privileged members of the original communities.

Among the earliest "inscriptions" are names of several rulers who reigned before the kings belonging to the "dynasties" defined by the Ptolemaic historian Manetho. The extent of territory that these shadowy kings controlled is uncertain, but their successor Narmer (*c.* 2975 BC) probably ruled the whole of Egypt. There were cultural and artistic borrowings from abroad, mainly the Mesopotamian region, during the late Predynastic period, but it is no longer considered acceptable to explain the rise of Egyptian "dynastic" civilization as the result of the arrival of a "master race." Indeed, during the preceding millennium Egyptian society had remained remarkably stable. The rapid progress that followed demonstrated the economic superiority of a centrally managed state enjoying safety from outside interference.

During the reign of Narmer's successor, King Aha (*c.* 2950 BC, perhaps Menes, the legendary first king), a new capital, Ineb-hedj, "White Wall" (later Memphis), was founded not far from the apex of the Delta, between the two

TOP: A Predynastic vase found in a grave at Nagada in Upper Egypt and dating to about 3600 BC. ASHMOLEAN MUSEUM, OXFORD

ABOVE: The "Two Dogs Palette" was presented by a late Predynastic (c. 3000 BC) king to the temple of Horus at Kom el-Ahmar (Hierakonpolis) in Upper Egypt. ASHMOLEAN MUSEUM, OXFORD/WERNER FORMAN ARCHIVE

OPPOSITE: A colossal statue of Ramesses II (1279–1213 BC), with a smaller figure of a princess, has been reerected in front of the second pylon of the temple of Amun at Karnak. APL/D. & J. HEATON

PREVIOUS PAGE: The hill of Qubbet el-Hawa ("Windy Dome"), on the west bank of the Nile opposite the modern city of Aswan, with rock-cut tombs of local administrators of the late Old Kingdom and the Middle Kingdom (c. 2300–1850 BC). THE IMAGE BANK/PAUL TRUMMER

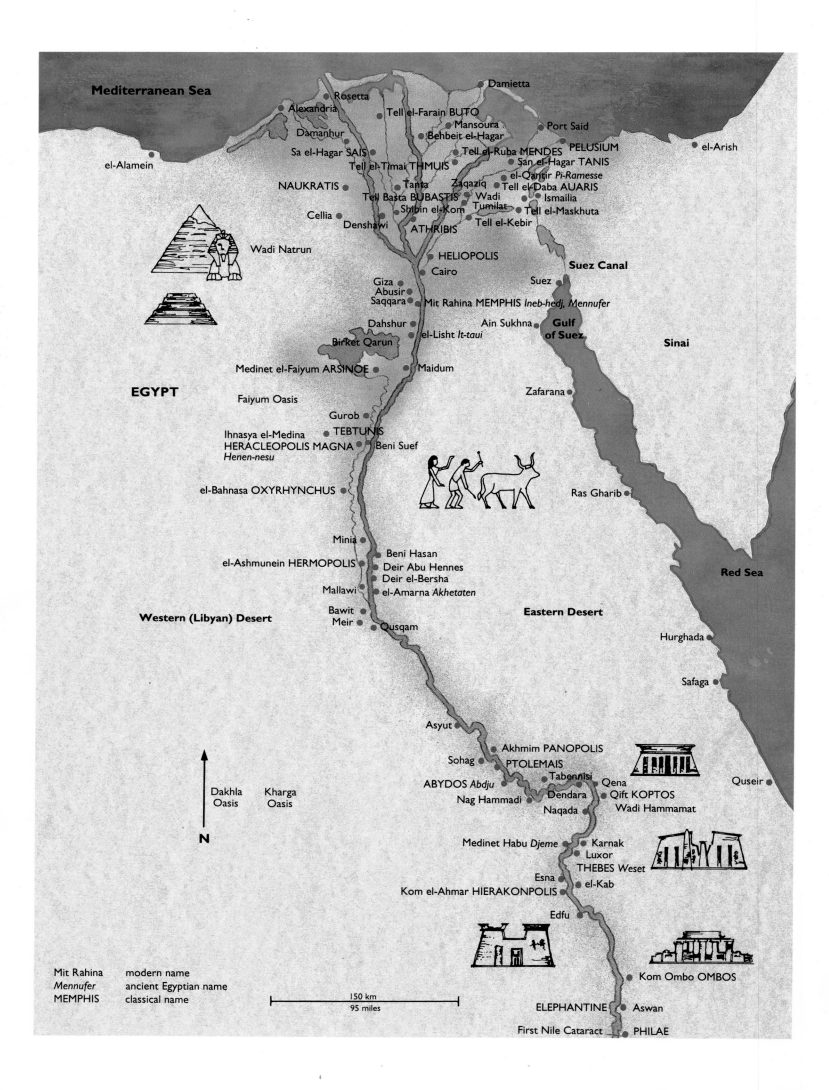

Mediterranean Sea

el-Alamein

Alexandria
Rosetta
Damanhur
Tell el-Farain BUTO
Damietta
Mansoura
Behbeit el-Hagar
Sa el-Hagar SAIS
Tell el-Ruba MENDES
Port Said
PELUSIUM
el-Arish
Tell el-Timai THMUIS
San el-Hagar TANIS
NAUKRATIS
Tanta
Zaqaziq
el-Qantir *Pi-Ramesse*
Tell el-Daba AUARIS
Tell el-Basta BUBASTIS
Wadi
Tumilat
Ismailia
Cellia
Shibin el-Kom
Tell el-Maskhuta
Denshawi
ATHRIBIS
Tell el-Kebir

Wadi Natrun

HELIOPOLIS
Cairo

Suez Canal

Giza
Abusir
Suez
Saqqara
Mit Rahina MEMPHIS *Ineb-hedj, Mennufer*
Dahshur
Ain Sukhna
**Gulf
of Suez**
Birket Qarun
el-Lisht *It-taui*

Sinai

EGYPT

Medinet el-Faiyum ARSINOE
Maidum

Faiyum Oasis
Zafarana

Gurob
Ihnasya el-Medina
TEBTUNIS
HERACLEOPOLIS MAGNA
Beni Suef
Henen-nesu

el-Bahnasa OXYRHYNCHUS
Ras Gharib

Minia
Red Sea
Beni Hasan
el-Ashmunein HERMOPOLIS
Deir Abu Hennes
Deir el-Bersha
Mallawi
el-Amarna *Akhetaten*
Bawit
Western (Libyan) Desert
Meir
Eastern Desert
Ousqam
Hurghada

Safaga

Asyut

Akhmim PANOPOLIS
Sohag
PTOLEMAIS
Dakhla
Oasis
Kharga
Oasis
Tabennisi
Qena
Quseir
ABYDOS *Abdju*
Dendara
Qift KOPTOS
Nag Hammadi
Naqada
Wadi Hammamat

N

Medinet Habu *Djeme*
Karnak
Luxor
THEBES *Weset*
Esna
el-Kab
Kom el-Ahmar HIERAKONPOLIS

Edfu

Mit Rahina   modern name
Mennufer   ancient Egyptian name
MEMPHIS   classical name

150 km
95 miles

Kom Ombo OMBOS

ELEPHANTINE
Aswan

First Nile Cataract
PHILAE

natural geographical parts of Egypt (Upper, or southern, and Lower, or northern). This move, dictated by economic and administrative considerations, marked the beginning of a long period of prosperity (some 800 years, usually divided into the Early Dynastic period, *c.* 2950–2647 BC, and the Old Kingdom, 2647–2124 BC). Tombs with massive brick superstructures for high officials of state were built nearby at Saqqara. A large work force was required for their construction, and such projects provided a perfect training ground for the officials of the emerging state bureaucracy. The basic methods of agricultural production changed little but benefited from increased stability and improved organization. Administration ran along simple patriarchal lines. The growing prosperity of the upper stratum of Egyptian society soon became apparent and created new opportunities for craftworkers and artists.

The gradual accumulation of experience in labor management and the growing mastery of materials (stone and metal) produced a sudden architectual flowering during the reign of Netjerikhet Djoser (2628–2609 BC). The king's tomb at Saqqara was built as a huge stone step pyramid, the first such monumental building in the world. The first true, straight-sided pyramid was introduced during the reign of Snofru, some 55 years later. Massive state-sponsored building enterprises, almost exclusively connected with the funerary cult, accelerated centralization of the administrative apparatus and helped to refine land management. Maintenance of the funerary cult of the deceased kings and other prominent members of society played an important part in the economic affairs of the country through the system of redistribution of goods. The vizier, at first one of the royal princes, was the highest official. The cult of the sun-god Re of On (Heliopolis) gained importance and was acknowledged by the building of sun temples. Advances in arts accompanied the astonishing progress in stone architecture. The script became a sophisticated method of communication for administrative and other purposes.

For reasons inherent in the system but compounded by unfavorable climatic changes, Egypt experienced different political, economic, and cultural conditions following the long reign of Pepy II (2236–2143 BC). The circumstances of the downfall of the ruling house of Memphis and the taking of power by rulers residing at Henen-nesu (Heracleopolis Magna, modern Ihnasya el-Medina in Middle Egypt) are not known. Only a few of the eighteen Heracleopolitan kings (2123–*c.* 2040 BC) enjoyed even a moderately long reign, and the effectiveness of the control they exercised over the country was suspect. Soon a rival claimant to the Egyptian throne appeared at Weset (Thebes, in southern Egypt), where the family of local administrators turned into a line of kings called Inyotef and Mentuhotpe. Around 2040 BC one of these, Mentuhotpe II, asserted his rule over the whole of Egypt. The 400 years that followed are usually described as the Middle Kingdom.

The two immediate successors of Mentuhotpe II continued to rule from Weset, but Amenemhet I (1980–1951 BC) established a new residence, It-taui (el-Lisht), near the economically important Faiyum Oasis. The main achievement of the first group of kings (all called Amenemhet or Senwosret) of It-taui, between *c.* 1980 and 1801 BC, was a

ABOVE: The Great Sphinx at Giza is the largest statue (c. 80 yards/73.5 m long and 22 yards/20 m high) known from Egypt. It combines a lion body with the likeness of King Khephren (2518–2493 BC).
JOHN G. ROSS

ABOVE: Two dismantled wooden boats were deposited near the southern face of the pyramid of Khufu (2549–2526 BC) at Giza. One has been reassembled, the other, less well preserved, is still in the rectangular pit where it has been resting for more than 4,500 years. The boats were for the king's use in the celestial journeys in the next world.
WERNER FORMAN ARCHIVE

EGYPTIAN KINGDOMS AND DYNASTIES

Every field of research develops its own terminology, and Egyptology is no exception. References to "kingdoms," "intermediate periods" and "dynasties" abound in books on ancient Egypt, that for a nonspecialist are confusing and not easy to understand.

Ancient Egyptians observed historical events in a way not dissimilar to ours, recording events accurately, producing compilations of such records, and comparing one state of affairs with another. Yet interpretation of what was happening over a longer period of time remained limited,

BELOW: Ramesses III (1184–1153 BC) carrying a ceremonial ram-headed staff sacred to the god Amun. This granite statue is one of many found in the temple at Karnak in 1903–06. THE EGYPTIAN MUSEUM, CAIRO/JÜRGEN LIEPE

because they did not see events as parts of a continuous process. The Egyptians regarded the reign of each king as a new beginning, a ritual reenactment of the events that led to the "unification" of the country and the creation of one Egyptian state. This typically Egyptian way of thinking manifested itself in other aspects of Egyptian civilization, including the arts, literature, and mathematics. History writing as we understand it today was not known, and there was nothing to encourage it.

The remains of the Palermo Stone, so called because of the present location of the largest fragment of the broken-up monument, contain yearly records (annals) of the earliest Egyptian kings. The recorded events, however, are mainly of a ceremonial and ritual nature. Fragments of "annals" of Amenemhet II (1918–1884 BC) found at Memphis are much more detailed. There were also lists of the rulers of the past. The most informative is a Ramessid papyrus now known as the Royal Canon in the Museo Egizio in Turin. Somewhat less complete lists have been found inscribed on the walls of temples at Karnak and Abydos and in a Ramessid tomb at Saqqara. Because of the large number of kings, compilers sometimes

had to be selective and include only those regarded as particularly important. Detailed lists also recorded how long each king ruled, inserting chronological totals at certain places and separating groups of rulers. Such lists were the closest the Egyptians came to historical evaluation and analysis. Egyptologists similarly make divisions of groups of rulers, but the two views do not always correspond.

The "kingdoms" are terms introduced by Egyptologists to describe the periods of the greatest achievement (as judged by them) of ancient Egypt. The division into Old, Middle, and New, now consecrated by usage, owes a great deal to the old-fashioned concept of the young, mature, and old stages of civilizations. The "intermediate periods" fill the gaps between the kingdoms; the "Early Dynastic" period provides a convenient introduction, and the "Late" period a conclusion. An ancient Egyptian scribe would recognize the kingdoms as the reigns of some of the most famous kings, but the division of history into larger periods was not known and would not be understood by him.

The commonly used system of dynasties derives from the Ptolemaic historian Manetho. The Egyptians grouped their rulers

ABOVE: *The head of a granite statue of Taharqa (690–664 BC). The king is wearing a "cap" (originally gilded) characteristic of the Kushite rulers. The royal crown is now broken off.* THE EGYPTIAN MUSEUM, CAIRO/JOHN G. ROSS

of the past according to the place of the royal residence rather than by chronological considerations (two or more kings may be contemporary) or even family ties. When the residence changed, a new line of rulers was started in the lists, for example, the kings of Ineb-hedj (Manetho's First through Fifth dynasties), Memphis (Sixth through Eighth), Heracleopolis (Ninth and Tenth), Thebes (Eleventh), It-taui (Twelfth), and so forth. Because Manetho used Egyptian sources, his system works well in some cases, and the definition of the dynasties is historically justified. In other cases, particularly the earlier part of Egyptian history, Manetho's divisions are arbitrary and sometimes misleading. For example, it seems that Manetho mistook additional notes accompanying the names of the early kings of Ineb-hedj and the formal arrangement of the lists for dynastic delineations. Thus, it is doubtful whether his divisions between the First through Fifth dynasties (and also the modern distinction between the Early Dynastic period and the Old Kingdom) are justified. The same doubts apply to the Sixth through Eighth and Ninth and Tenth dynasties.

Manetho's dynastic division is widely used for convenience. It provides a means of dating

ABOVE: *King Nectanebo I (380–362 BC) on a basalt intercolumnar slab (intended to fill the space between two columns).* BRITISH MUSEUM, LONDON

that avoids references to years BC. Exact dates are still disputed, and chronological charts give a somewhat spurious notion of accuracy. Nevertheless, it must be remembered that the basis of Manetho's dynasties is not faultless, and that to use them as significant dividing lines in the discussion of Egyptian history, economy, or arts is not always correct. Egyptology, however, is a conservative subject and is unlikely to abandon the system soon despite its many flaws.

LEFT AND FAR LEFT: *The temple built by Sethos I (1294–1279 BC) at Abydos contains a list of Egyptian kings that starts with the legendary Menes and is the most complete example of this genre known from an Egyptian temple. Altogether 76 names, written in cartouches (oval frames), are recorded for the period of some 1,700 years but rulers of the less memorable periods were disregarded. Sethos I and his son, the future Ramesses II, are shown on the far left.* GRIFFITH INSTITUTE, ASHMOLEAN MUSEUM, OXFORD

ABOVE: *The same artistic conventions governed the making of statues in various materials, but wood enabled the artist to free arms and legs from the original mass of material and lent greater softness to the modeling of the body. This statue was found at Sidmant in Middle Egypt and dates to c. 2250 BC. BRITISH MUSEUM, LONDON/WERNER FORMAN ARCHIVE*

ABOVE: *Wall-painting in the tomb of Nakht at Sheikh Abd el-Qurna (Thebes) showing men picking grapes. Nakht was an "hour-watcher" (astronomer) of the (temple of the) god Amun and probably lived under Tuthmosis IV and Amenophis III (between 1401 and 1353 BC). WERNER FORMAN ARCHIVE*

rigorous reorganization of the country's administration. This reorganization was needed to correct the anomalies of the preceding period during which local princes had gained a considerable degree of autonomy. The move introduced an efficient system based on centrally appointed local administrators. The country prospered and coregencies (that is, joint rules) ensured political stability. The cult of the god Amun of Thebes was in ascendance, while Osiris now achieved total dominance in funerary beliefs. Abydos became the most celebrated place of pilgrimage.

A less prosperous phase of the Middle Kingdom followed. There was no spectacular collapse, and the kings continued to rule from It-taui. Although their nominal authority remained unaffected, problems of succession and declining economy resulted in rapidly changing reigns and a reduction in state-sponsored building activities. The grip of the central authority on the districts was slackening. A challenge to the rulers in It-taui was rising in the northeast. The eastern Delta had always contained a proportion of non-Egyptians who, in the past, had been tolerated and absorbed into the Egyptian population. During the late Middle Kingdom the influx of immigrants from the Palestinian region steadily increased. These immigrants eventually became so powerful that around 1648 BC the suzerainty of their leaders, the Hyksos (an Egyptian term meaning "the rulers of foreign countries"), was acknowledged throughout the land.

The six Hyksos kings (c. 1648–1540 BC) were much vilified by their Egyptian successors, but their rule was a logical outcome of a process that had started in the late Middle Kingdom. They resided at Auaris (near Tell el-Daba) in the northeastern Delta and adopted the external trappings of Egyptian kingship. The Hyksos, perhaps following their tribal tradition, ruled the country as a coalition of self-governed districts that recognized Hyksos overlordship and rendered taxes, apparently collected by Egyptian officials in the rulers' service. Commercial, technological, and cultural contacts with the Syro-Palestinian region

and the Aegean were strengthened.

The advantages of distance from the power center were demonstrated when a reaction to the Hyksos overlordship came from Thebes. Although later portrayed in nationalistic terms, this reaction took the form of an expansionist (or "unifying" in Egyptian terms) move by an ambitious local ruler, as had been witnessed before and was to be seen on a number of later occasions. The challenge to Hyksos rule was brought to a head by Seqenenre Teo II and Kamose, and the process was successfully completed by King Amosis when he took Auaris around 1540 BC.

The reign of Amosis (1550–1525 BC) introduced a new period of a tightly centralized rule, the New Kingdom. The country was administered along the traditional division into districts ("nomes") but the bureaucratic complexity was acknowledged in the creation of a dual administration, each part headed by a vizier. Vigorous military campaigns in Palestine and Syria, initially perhaps a follow-up of the Hyksos wars, brought Egyptian soldiers to the banks of the Euphrates in Syria in the reign of Tuthmosis I (1504–1492 BC). Egyptian efforts to maintain and periodically to regain hold over the Syro-Palestinian territory and its mélange of city states in the face of opposition from the Syro-Mesopotamian kingdom of Mitanni and later the Anatolian Hittites formed much of the military history of the next 300 years.

Economically and culturally flourishing at home, supremely confident abroad, and with energetic and competent kings (mostly called Amenophis or Tuthmosis) at the helm, Egypt during the fifteenth and fourteenth centuries BC can only be viewed with awe and its achievements with admiration. With hindsight, the eventual approach of a crisis would not be totally unexpected. Egyptian religion and state ideology had always been a complex multilayered and multifaceted affair. The Hyksos episode and the profound changes in Egyptian society, such as the unprecedented growth of wealth and influence of institutions and individuals and the creation of empire, resulted in tensions, frictions, and demands that the traditional ideological

old forms reasserted themselves. Akhenaten's second successor, Tutankhaten, abandoned Akhetaten, changed the Aten element of his name for the name of a traditional god, and became known as Tutankhamun (1336–1327 BC).

The short-lived "Amarna period" seriously undermined the Egyptian economy and administration, and steps had to be taken to undo its effects. The confused issue of royal succession was resolved when Ramesses I ascended the throne in 1295 BC. His son, Sethos I (1294–1279 BC), was able to turn his attention abroad and successfully campaigned in Libya, Palestine, and Syria. In this he was followed by his son, Ramesses II (1279–1213 BC). A new capital of the country, Pi-Ramesse, was established in the northeastern Delta (near modern el-Qantir). The king was an enthusiastic builder and during his long reign (over 66 years) almost every temple in the land benefited from his attention. Formally, at least, the memory of the Amarna period was thoroughly exorcised. The god Amun (or Amun-Re) of Karnak, now with his cult centers all over the country, reigned supreme.

Successors of Ramesses II, Merneptah (1213–1203 BC) and Ramesses III

LEFT: The delicate pleating of the garment of this woman, probably Nefertiti, the queen of Akhenaten (1353–1337 BC) and the sensuous modeling of the body are hallmarks of the art of the Amarna period. LOUVRE MUSEUM, PARIS

BELOW: The Ramesseum is the traditional name given to the mortuary temple of Ramesses II (1279–1213 BC) on the west bank of the Nile at Thebes. One of the broken colossal statues lying there is Shelley's Ozymandias (this is a corruption of Usimare, one of the names of Ramesses II). THE IMAGE BANK/GUIDO ALBERTO ROSSI

set-up was unable to resolve or satisfy. A tendency toward a universal deity, with the sun-god Re (or Re-Harakhty) as the obvious candidate, had been noticeable for some time, but it was during the reign of King Amenophis IV (1353–1337 BC) that events unfolded with startling rapidity. The king promoted the worship of an impersonal aspect of the sun-god, the Aten ("sun disk"). The traditional gods and their temples were at first tolerated, then ignored or proscribed, and eventually persecuted. Amenophis IV changed his name to Akhenaten ("Radiance of the Aten") and moved to a new capital, Akhetaten ("Horizon of the Aten") in Middle Egypt (near el-Amarna, hence the term "Amarna period"). Changes in all spheres of Egyptian life, such as economy and arts, followed. Never before had the country witnessed a religious upheaval of this magnitude. Yet the reforms, however profound, petered out after the death of the king and his chief consort, Queen Nefertiti, and the

THE LANGUAGE AND WRITING

Ancient Egyptian belongs to the Afro-Asiatic (or "Hamito-Semitic") languages and is related to, among others, Akkadian, Hebrew, and Arabic. It is usually divided into Archaic (before *c.* 2600 BC, little known), Old (*c.* 2600–2100 BC), Middle (or "classical," spoken *c.* 2100–1500 BC, but used for monumental and religious purposes throughout the rest of pharaonic history), Late (spoken *c.* 1500–700 BC), demotic (from *c.* 700 BC), and Coptic (written from *c.* second century AD, died out in the sixteenth century). The hieroglyphic script was used for monumental inscriptions, and the hieratic (cursive) script for documents and religious texts. Demotic and Coptic had their own scripts.

RIGHT: Hieroglyphs are written from right to left or left to right, horizontally or vertically. Hieratic and demotic are written only from right to left, Coptic only from left to right. This is a hieroglyphic text from the tomb of Udjahateti, in Old Egyptian, in columns from left to right, at Saqqara, c. 2300 BC. JAROMIR MALEK

BELOW: The "alphabetic" sign for the glottal stop (not a separate consonant in English, a breathing pause that can be heard, for example, in "coopt"), representing the Egyptian vulture (Neophron percnopterus), compared with the real bird, below. Drawing by Howard Carter. GRIFFITH INSTITUTE, ASHMOLEAN MUSEUM, OXFORD

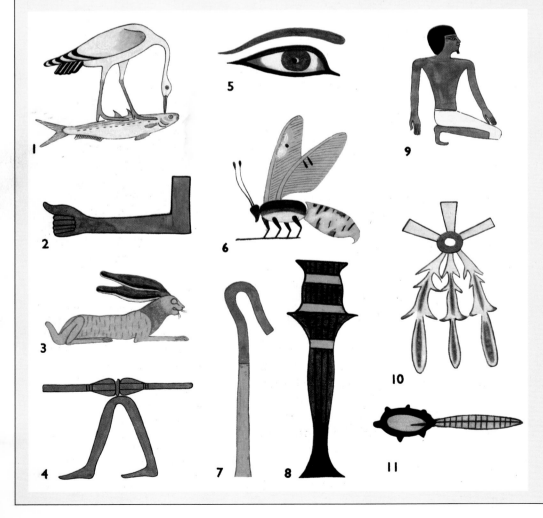

LEFT: Egyptian hieroglyphs are not picture writing but a system based on a combination of sound-signs to represent one or more consonants, as well as logograms, taxograms, and others. Sound-signs can be "alphabetic," for example (2) where the arm records the sound/letter "Ayin" (not known in English), and (11) where "the belly of a long-tailed animal" represents a type of "h." Hieroglyphs (1), (3), (8), and (10) each represent more than one consonant. Logograms are "sense-signs" showing the actual object, for example (6), a bee, and (7), a scepter. Taxograms are category indicators, for example (5), the eye, is added to words associated with seeing, and (9), to those describing a man performing a rite. Hieroglyph (4) records verbs of motion containing the "alphabetic" sign "s," represented by door-bolt. From Beni Hasan, c. 1980–1850 BC, copied by N. de Garis Davies. GRIFFITH INSTITUTE, ASHMOLEAN MUSEUM, OXFORD

(1184–1153 BC), were called upon to counter the threat of incursions by the "Sea Peoples." Although momentous from the Egyptian point of view, these incursions were but isolated episodes in the dramatic ethnic movements taking place in the Eastern Mediterranean around 1200 BC. For Egypt they heralded the beginning of much closer involvement with the other nations in the region. Even within the country a completely different political scene was ushered in. Ramesses XI (1099–1069 BC) was the last ruler of the Ramessid line and, in our eyes, brought the New Kingdom to a close. After his death the reins of authority were seized by Smendes (1069–1043 BC) and his successors residing at Tanis (San el-Hagar), in the northeastern Delta, although a semi-independent administration centered on the Theban temple of Amun was allowed to exist in the south. From the middle of the tenth century BC, the decisive political power in Egypt was wielded by rulers whose names (Shoshenq, Osorkon, and Takelot) confirm their Libyan origin.

Some 200 years later, events were set in motion that turned the territory of the politically, economically, and militarily weakened Egypt into a stage on which the confrontation between the regional superpowers of the day was to be played out. Kashta, the ruler of the Nubian kingdom of Kush, invaded the southern part of Egypt. His successors Piye (747–716 BC) and Shabako (716–702 BC) eventually gained control of the whole country and ruled over a huge African empire that stretched from the confluence of the White and Blue Niles in the Sudan to the shores of the Mediterranean. The capital was at Napata, near the Fourth Cataract, but the Nubian kings now eagerly adopted the paraphernalia of pharaonic kingship and actively embraced Egyptian religion and culture. Unfortunately, it was too late for Egypt to benefit from this development. King Shebitku (702–690 BC) encountered the military might of Assyria in Palestine, and his successor Taharqa (690–664 BC) had to face Esarhaddon and Assurbanipal on Egyptian soil. Nobody could resist Assyria at the peak of its power, and the

defeated Kushites had to withdraw into the safety of their faraway homeland. However, Psammetichus, the local ruler of Sais in the western Delta, obtained through shrewd diplomacy and favorable developments abroad at first nominal and then real control over Egypt (as Psammetichus I, 664–610 BC).

Under the "Saite" kings, ruling from Memphis, Egypt staged a spectacular economic recovery. A canal through Wadi Tumilat, started by Necho II (610–595 BC), was intended to allow ships to sail from the Nile to the Red Sea. Amasis (570–526 BC) regulated the important trade with the Aegean by confining Greek traders to the city of Naukratis in the western Delta. Foreign relations were of paramount importance. The Saite kings successfully campaigned in Palestine and Syria (this time as Assyria's allies), but Egypt's destiny was now largely determined by the rise or decline of the superpowers abroad. In 525 BC Egypt succumbed to the onslaught of the Persians under Cambyses and became a satrapy (province) of the Persian empire.

The last period of Egyptian independence, during the fourth century BC, owed much to the temporary internal disarray of the Persian empire and its preoccupation with the Aegean. In 342 BC Artaxerxes III reoccupied Egypt, and the Persians held it for a decade until they in their turn were unable to resist the military genius of Alexander the Great in 332 BC.

ABOVE: A small shrine built by Taharqa (690–644 BC) in the hypostyle (columned hall) of the temple of Amun at Kawa, south of the Third Nile Cataract, deep in Sudanese Nubia.
ASHMOLEAN MUSEUM, OXFORD

ABOVE: The theme of "protection," with the figure of a king or a private individual sheltering under the zoomorphic image of a deity, was a favorite topic in Egyptian art. Psamtek (this is the same name as Psammetichus, the Graecised version of the names of the three "Saite" kings) was a "Chief Steward" who probably lived under King Amasis (570–526 BC) and his graywacke statue comes from his tomb at Saqqara.
THE EGYPTIAN MUSEUM, CAIRO/JÜRGEN LIEPE

REDISCOVERING EGYPT

M. L. Bierbrier

IN THE RUE MAZARINE, Paris, on the morning of 14 September 1822, a brilliant flash of inspiration enabled Jean-François Champollion to read the hieroglyphic names of the Egyptian pharaohs Tuthmosis and Ramesses. In his excitement, he gathered his notes, rushed to the library of the Institut de France where his brother Jacques-Joseph was working, threw the papers on the desk in front of him, and exclaimed, *"Je tiens l'affaire!"* (I have got it!). Then he promptly fainted. This dramatic event can be regarded as the start of modern Egyptology. Champollion had rediscovered the principle of the hieroglyphic script of the ancient Egyptians.

The knowledge of the history and language of ancient Egypt among the native population disappeared under the impact of the new religions of Christianity and Islam. The ability to read the hieroglyphic script, which had been kept alive by the priesthood in the Greco-Roman period, was lost. The last hieroglyphic inscription dates from AD 394. The temples and tombs were despoiled and left in ruins. Even the native language, Coptic, the last phase of ancient Egyptian, was eventually replaced by Arabic and died out as a spoken tongue. In the course of the Middle Ages, a few European pilgrims to and from the Holy Land passed through Egypt, marveled at the ancient ruins near Alexandria and Cairo, and connected them with incidents in the Bible. The local inhabitants sought to exploit the ruins either by largely vain searches for treasure or by the powdering of ancient human remains into the drug *mummia*, thought to have medicinal properties.

It was during the Renaissance that European scholars rediscovered the accounts of ancient Egypt in the texts of the classical authors of Greece and Rome. The rebuilding of Rome also revealed a number of Egyptian monuments that had been brought there by the Roman emperors. These discoveries stimulated an interest in Egyptian hieroglyphs, which were seen as the product of an advanced civilization. Misled by the classical authors, scholars such as Athanasius Kircher (1602–80), who pioneered the study of Coptic, came to believe that the hieroglyphic signs were purely symbolic and mystic in nature. At the same time, European travelers began to visit Egypt in small numbers and to bring back Egyptian antiquities as curiosities. In the course of the seventeenth and eighteenth centuries,

TOP: *Portrait of Jean-François Champollion "le Jeune" (1790–1832), the decipherer of Egyptian hieroglyphs, painted by L. Cogniet.* LOUVRE MUSEUM, PARIS/ AUSTRAL / SYGMA

ABOVE: *The manuscript of Champollion's* Grammaire égyptienne, *which appeared in 1836. Its publication was supervised by Champollion's elder brother Jacques-Joseph Champollion-Figeac.* BIBLIOTHEQUE NATIONAL, PARIS

OPPOSITE: *The two "Cleopatra's Needles" when they were still at Alexandria, painted by Dominique Vivant Denon in 1798.* VICTORIA & ALBERT MUSEUM, LONDON/SEARIGHT COLLECTION

RIGHT: *In the vicinity of the village of Mit Rahina, south of Cairo, the French scholars accompanying Napoleon's expedition came across a fist of a colossal pink granite statue of Ramesses II (1279–1213 BC). This was one of the pieces that had to be surrendered to the British and can now be seen in the British Museum, London. Engraving from* Description de l'Égypte. ASHMOLEAN LIBRARY, OXFORD

BELOW: *The sanctuaries in the complex dominated by the temple of Isis at Philae may have been the last in which ancient Egyptian and Nubian gods were worshiped on Egyptian soil (the last hieroglyphic inscription at Philae dates to AD 394, the last demotic text to AD 452). Hector Horeau's painting shows it in 1839, well before the clearances carried out at the end of the nineteenth century.* GRIFFITH INSTITUTE, ASHMOLEAN MUSEUM, OXFORD

they were able to penetrate farther up the Nile and gradually to identify sites mentioned by classical authors. Père Claude Sicard (1677–1726), a French Jesuit resident in Egypt, made extensive trips throughout the countryside from 1712. He was the first to recognize Luxor as ancient Thebes, and he reached as far south as Aswan, but his explorations were not published. Later travelers such as Richard Pococke (1704–65) and Frederik Norden (1708–42), who were in Egypt in the 1730s, provided detailed accounts of their observations, but access to the country remained uncertain and dangerous.

The Napoleonic invasion of Egypt in 1798 was organized from its inception not only to exert French political control over the country but also to extend French knowledge of the newly conquered territory. Napoleon brought with him a team of French scholars in all disciplines who were soon busy exploring the country, collecting antiquities, and making detailed drawings of monuments and sites. Because their activities were well known to the army at large, when, during construction work at Rosetta (in the western Delta), an inscription was uncovered featuring three different scripts, the scholars were immediately notified. One of the texts was in Greek, which was easily read; the other two were in ancient Egyptian writing, and it was correctly assumed that all three scripts recorded the same text. The

Rosetta Stone was to become the key to the decipherment of ancient Egyptian. When the French forces were obliged to evacuate Egypt in 1801, their antiquities, including the Rosetta Stone, were surrendered to the British and then deposited in the British Museum. Copies of the Rosetta Stone were, however, widely circulated. The drawings of the French Scientific Commission were eventually published in a series of volumes entitled *Description de l'Égypte* and served to stimulate public interest in the antiquities of Egypt.

The cessation of hostilities in Europe in 1815 made it easier for intrepid visitors to see the sights of Egypt. The new demand for Egyptian antiquities was recognized by the European consuls in Egypt, who now led the way in forming collections with the bemused permission of the Egyptian authorities. The French consul Bernardino Drovetti (1776–1852) was the first in the field, but he was followed by the British consul Henry Salt (1780–1827). Salt employed the former circus performer Giovanni Battista Belzoni (1778–1827) as his agent. Belzoni was responsible for the discovery of the tomb of King Sethos I at Thebes and the opening up of Abu Simbel in Nubia.

When he and Salt parted company, he returned to London and put on an Egyptian exhibition in Piccadilly that furthered public interest in ancient Egypt, its antiquities, and its history.

Attempts to read ancient Egyptian had been under way since the discovery of the Rosetta Stone. Scholars remained hampered by the pervading belief that the hieroglyphic script was purely symbolic and not alphabetic. Thomas Young (1773–1829) identified the royal names in the hieroglyphic text, but it was left to Jean-François Champollion (1790–1832) to recognize the true nature of the hieroglyphic script. He had been attracted to the study of ancient Egypt since childhood, and his ambition was to decipher the ancient language. In preparation, he had mastered the Coptic language and script that was to be revealed as the last form of ancient Egyptian. His study of the royal names, identified from the surrounding rings known as cartouches, convinced him of the largely alphabetic nature of the hieroglyphic script, and he announced his discovery in 1822 in his *Lettre à M. Dacier*. He was able through the royal names to determine the basic ancient Egyptian alphabet, and then, with the help of the Rosetta Stone and his knowledge of Coptic, to read the texts themselves. His *Précis du système hiéroglyphique des anciens égyptiens*

outlined his discoveries and opened the writings of ancient Egypt to the modern world. His familiarity with Egyptian antiquities was increased by visits to the collections in Italy, and he was instrumental in obtaining Salt's second collection for the Louvre Museum, where he became keeper of Egyptian antiquities in 1827. In 1831 he was appointed professor of Egyptology at the Collège de France, the first academic post in the subject.

The decipherment of the hieroglyphic script opened the way to a more intense

ABOVE: Giovanni Battista Belzoni was employed by the British consul-general, Henry Salt, to undertake several tasks that required extraordinary resourcefulness. One of them was the removal of a fragment of a colossal statue of Ramesses II (1279–1213 BC) from the Ramesseum (the king's mortuary temple at Thebes) in 1816, shown here in Belzoni's own drawing. The sculpture is now in the British Museum, London. E. T. ARCHIVE

LEFT: The first European to see the temples at Abu Simbel was the Swiss explorer John Lewis Burckhardt on 22 March 1813, but it was the Italian excavator Giovanni Battista Belzoni who, in 1817, reached the interior of the large temple, seen here in his own drawing. PETER CLAYTON

AUGUSTE MARIETTE, THE FOUNDER OF EGYPTIAN ARCHAEOLOGY

Auguste Mariette (1821–81), one of the giants of nineteenth-century Egyptology, was a native of Boulogne. He became a teacher of French and drawing in England for a time, but then he returned to France and took up teaching as well as editing the local newspaper in his hometown. His interest in ancient Egypt was aroused in 1842 when he was asked to examine the papers of a deceased relation, Nestor l'Hôte, one of Champollion's artists. Mariette was also inspired to further studies in Egyptology by the collection of Egyptian antiquities in Boulogne originating from the Napoleonic expedition. He obtained a minor position at the Louvre Museum in 1849, enabling him to continue his research, but the post was soon abolished. However, in 1850 he was appointed by the Académie des inscriptions to travel to Egypt to obtain Coptic manuscripts for France's national collection, and, as an afterthought, he was also empowered to carry out excavations for antiquities.

On reaching Egypt, Mariette soon learned that the Coptic manuscripts were unavailable. Instead, he determined to excavate at Saqqara, near Cairo, where the discovery of sphinxes by the dealers in antiquities had suggested to him the possible location of the Serapeum, the burial place of the sacred Apis bulls described by a Roman author. Although his funds ran short and he had to borrow money from the obliging French consul, he persisted, after having discovered Greek statues and Egyptian antiquities. Finally, in November 1851, he located the underground burial chambers that contained the sarcophagi of the bulls as well as numerous stelae (inscriptions on stone) erected by workmen and priests. These stelae permitted the chronological framework of the last phase of Egyptian history to be fixed with some certainty. Mariette's successful excavation led to his permanent appointment to the Louvre, a decoration, and funds to continue his work. Disagreements with the Egyptian authorities were ironed out, and the Louvre received a large part of the discoveries. Mariette returned to France in 1854, but he was anxious to resume his excavations in Egypt. In 1857 he took advantage of a proposed visit to the country by Prince Napoleon to go out in advance to act as his guide. However, he had already discussed the possibility of protecting Egyptian monuments from the ravages of uncontrolled excavation with the former French consul, Ferdinand de Lesseps, who had influence with the Pasha. The result was Mariette's appointment in June 1858 as director of antiquities in Egypt with the authorization to be the sole excavator of ancient sites and to set up a museum of antiquities near Cairo.

Mariette then began an extensive campaign of excavation throughout the country, culminating in work at 35 sites in 1861. He uncovered tombs of the Old Kingdom at Giza and Saqqara, and at the latter site in 1860 discovered the important Saqqara king list. This find was eclipsed by the clearance of the temple of Sethos I at Abydos, where a longer king list was found in 1864. At

ABOVE: *The forecourt of the Ptolemaic (third through first century BC) temple of Horus at Edfu, still encumbered by sand, seen from the top of the pylon in 1839. The second half of the nineteenth century witnessed massive clearances of major Upper Egyptian temples. This was before systematic records of such work started being kept so that casual descriptions, sketches and early photographs often represent invaluable sources of information on the original appearance of these monuments. Watercolor by Hector Horeau. GRIFFITH INSTITUTE, ASHMOLEAN MUSEUM, OXFORD*

Edfu and Dendara he exposed the nearly complete Greco-Roman temples. At Karnak he cleared the great temple of Amun and discovered the annals of Tuthmosis III inscribed on the walls. In the Theban area his workcrew dug out the temples of Medinet Habu and Deir el-Bahri. He pioneered excavation in the difficult Delta region. Unfortunately, he was unable to publish his discoveries as thoroughly as he would have liked.

Mariette opened a temporary museum at Bulaq (a quarter of Cairo) in 1863, although his specially designed building was never constructed. He strongly believed his discoveries should be kept in Egypt, even offending the French government, and turned down opportunities for advancement at home in order to continue his work in Egypt. His monopoly on excavation prevented wholesale looting of the sites and provided important material for the reconstruction of ancient Egyptian history and art.

Mariette pioneered the transformation of the unsystematic digging up of Egyptian monuments to true archaeology, and for this modern Egyptology owes him a great debt.

ABOVE: *Auguste Mariette during his excavations of Old Kingdom (2647–2124 BC) tombs at Saqqara. Even now, some 130 years later, our understanding of these monuments is much colored by knowledge that derives from the early days of Egyptian archaeology. The photograph shows well the methods of excavation employed; the legendary reis Roubi who was in charge of Mariette's workmen is seen on the left. ASHMOLEAN LIBRARY, OXFORD*

study of ancient Egyptian texts. The need for accurate copies of Egyptian monuments was recognized, and a series of epigraphic missions arrived in Egypt to record monuments and also to collect antiquities for their sponsors. Champollion went to Egypt in 1828–29 with the Italian Egyptologist Ippolito Rossellini (1800–43) and the French artist Nestor L'Hôte (1804–42) and many of their drawings were published in the 1830s and 1840s. Robert Hay (1779–1863) formed a team of artists that worked in Egypt in the 1820s, although their work was not published. The French scholar Emile Prisse d'Avennes (1807–79) lived for many years in Egypt and published *Les monuments égyptiens*. Sir John Gardner Wilkinson (1797–1875) was resident in Egypt from 1821 to 1833, during which time he undertook a survey of the main sites and monuments in Egypt and Nubia, drawings of which are now in the Bodleian Library, Oxford. His *Manners and Customs of the Ancient Egyptians* was the most comprehensive view of ancient Egyptian life to date. The work of epigraphy culminated in the Prussian expedition of Richard Lepsius (1810–84) in 1842–45, which resulted in the *Denkmäler aus Aegypten und Aethiopien* in twelve volumes. Lepsius also brought back to Berlin a large number of antiquities. He was appointed professor at Berlin University and director of the Berlin Egyptian Museum. He further

refined and extended the work of Champollion on Egyptian grammar.

The excavation of ancient Egyptian sites in the mid-nineteenth century was haphazard at best and was largely left to the dealers in antiquities and their agents and to the native diggers. From these sources European residents in Egypt formed extensive collections such as that of Henry Abbott (1812–59), now in the Brooklyn Museum, and that of Anthony Harris (1790–1869), now in the British Museum. The arrival of Auguste Mariette was to change the situation dramatically. When he died in 1881, he had established a sound framework for Egyptology in Egypt on which his successors could securely build.

Gaston Maspero (1846–1916), formerly professor of Egyptology at the Collège de France in Paris, was sent to Egypt in 1880 to head the new French Institute in Cairo devoted to the study of epigraphy and archaeology. His tenure there was brief, since he succeeded Mariette as director of the Antiquities Service in 1881. Maspero was less possessive of archaeological sites than Mariette, and he was prepared to allow reputable institutions and private

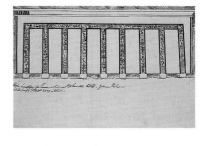

LEFT: Egyptology, or the study of ancient Egypt, started with this inscription. The Rosetta Stone was found by French sappers commanded by P. F. X. Bouchard in July 1799, physically claimed through the force of arms by the British in 1801, but intellectually reclaimed for the French in 1822 by Jean-François Champollion for whom it provided a clue to the decipherment of hieroglyphics. The scripts are, from the top, hieroglyphic, demotic, and Greek. BRITISH MUSEUM, LONDON

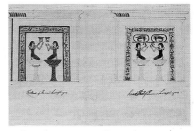

ABOVE: The papers of Sir John Gardner Wilkinson (1797–1875) contain literally thousands of pages with copies and drawings that he made in Egypt between 1821 and 1856. Many of the original monuments have since been damaged, destroyed, or lost, and the copies often represent their only record. Here, Wilkinson recorded the now lost coffin of Queen Mentuhotpe, the wife of King Djehuty (c. 1620 BC). BODLEIAN LIBRARY, OXFORD

LEFT: The pylon (monumental gateway) of Ramesses II (1279–1213 BC) in the temple of Luxor. This view was painted by Hector Horeau in 1839, shortly after the removal of the western obelisk to the Place de la Concorde in Paris. GRIFFITH INSTITUTE, ASHMOLEAN MUSEUM, OXFORD

RIGHT: The hypostyle (columned hall), decorated mostly by Sethos I (1294–1279 BC) and Ramesses II (1279–1213 BC), between the second and third pylons (monumental gateways) in the temple of Amun at Karnak. This watercolor was painted by Hector Horeau in 1839, before any of the major clearances and restorations. GRIFFITH INSTITUTE, ASHMOLEAN MUSEUM, OXFORD

BELOW: The Great Sphinx at Giza, dating to c. 2500 BC, had to be freed from the wind-blown sand engulfing it already in c. 1400 BC by King Tuthmosis IV. In the nineteenth century, there were renewed attempts to improve the situation (this photograph was taken around 1880), but it was not until the late 1930s that the whole statue was exposed. GRIFFITH INSTITUTE, ASHMOLEAN MUSEUM, OXFORD

individuals to undertake work. The French Institute at first concentrated on epigraphy and did not excavate until 1898.

In Great Britain, owing to the enthusiasm of the author Amelia Edwards (1831–92), the Egypt Exploration Fund (later the Egypt Exploration Society) was established in 1882 specifically to excavate in Egypt. In 1883 Édouard Naville (1844–1926), a Swiss, was sent out to work in the Delta. The Fund sponsored epigraphic work by Francis Llewellyn Griffith (1862–1934) and Percy Newberry (1869–1949), who recorded tombs in Middle Egypt, and a Greco-Roman branch that excavated for papyri.

The Fund also engaged the young Flinders Petrie (1853–1942), whose work was to revolutionize Egyptian archaeology. Unlike previous excavators who were only interested in large, preferably inscribed, stone objects, Petrie believed that all artifacts, however small, were intrinsically important in illuminating ancient Egyptian society. His study of pottery was the basis for a chronological system for Predynastic and Early Dynastic Egypt. Petrie eventually fell out with the Fund and set up his own British School of Archaeology in Egypt. He became the first to occupy the chair of Egyptian archaeology at University College, London, established by Amelia Edwards.

The Egyptian Antiquities Service continued to be responsible for major

archaeological discoveries under Maspero and his successors. The inscribed pyramids of the Old Kingdom were explored. In 1881 the cache of royal mummies at Deir el-Bahri in Thebes, which had been known to illicit diggers for at least a decade, was uncovered. A second cache of priestly mummies was found there in 1891, and in 1898 more royal mummies were found in the tomb of Amenophis II in the Valley of the Kings. The Egyptian Museum was moved from Bulaq to Giza in 1890, and finally in 1902 a new museum was opened in central Cairo. The Egypt Exploration Fund was excavating at Deir el-Bahri under Naville and at Abydos under Petrie, who uncovered the most important Early Dynastic royal cemetery and revealed Egypt's early history. An Italian expedition under Ernesto Schiaparelli (1856–1928) was at work near Thebes at the Ramessid workmen's village at Deir el-Medina and in the tomb of Queen Nefertari in the Valley of the Queens. American expeditions were now in the field. One from the Boston Museum of Fine Arts was directed by George Reisner (1867–1942), who concentrated on the site of Giza, uncovering the history and art of the Old Kingdom. Another, from the Metropolitan Museum of Art, in New

York, was led first by Albert Lythgoe (1868–1934) and later by Herbert Winlock (1884–1950) at the Middle Kingdom sites of el-Lisht and Deir el-Bahri. A German Institute was founded in Cairo in 1907 by Ludwig Borchardt (1863–1938) to carry out archaeological work. Excavations were also funded by wealthy patrons such as Theodore Davis (1837–1915), whose excavations in the Valley of the Kings resulted in the clearance of royal tombs and the discovery of the nearly intact tomb of Yuya and Tuya, and the Earl of Carnarvon (1866–1923), who was later to take up Davis's concession.

Work in Egypt was halted by the First World War but resumed shortly thereafter. The Egypt Exploration Society undertook a major campaign at the site of el-Amarna, the capital of King Akhenaten, while the French Institute excavated the site of Deir el-Medina, which yielded a vast amount of information on the lives of ordinary Egyptian workmen. Howard Carter (1874–1939) resumed work in the Valley of the Kings under the patronage of the Earl of Carnarvon, and in 1922 he uncovered the virtually intact tomb of Tutankhamun. The publicity over the find generated increased public awareness and an appreciation of Egyptology that has not abated. The finds from the Valley of the Kings were

paralleled by the burial of Queen Hetepheres (the mother of King Khufu) found by Reisner at Giza, and the royal burials at Tanis unearthed by Pierre Montet (1885–1966).

Posts in Egyptology were now established in almost all major universities and museums throughout Europe and America. In Berlin Adolf Erman (1854–1937) contributed to the study of ancient Egyptian by recognizing the division of the language into phases — Old, Middle, and Late Egyptian. His most lasting achievement was the *Wörterbuch der aegyptischen Sprache*, the

THE OBELISKS AT ALEXANDRIA

RIGHT: The standing obelisk at Alexandria in 1850, seen here in a watercolor painting by E. Hawker. Both Alexandrian obelisks were made for the temple of the sun-god Re at Heliopolis (now a Cairo suburb) in the reign of Tuthmosis III (1479–1425 BC). Later, Ramesses II (1279–1213 BC) added his names and titles to their inscriptions. The obelisks were brought to Alexandria and reerected there by the Emperor Augustus in his eighteenth year (c. 10 BC). One of them came crashing down in 1301, the other remained upright until its removal to New York in 1879–81. GRIFFITH INSTITUTE, ASHMOLEAN MUSEUM, OXFORD

LEFT: Egyptian monuments taken abroad are excellent ambassadors for the country of their origin. The reasons for the removal of obelisks to Rome and Istanbul in antiquity, and to Paris, London, and New York in modern times were, however, little more than attempts to embellish the cities for which they were destined. Britain could, at least, claim some sentimental attachment to "Cleopatra's Needles" at Alexandria: a bloody battle between the British (their commander, General Sir Ralph Abercromby, was mortally wounded in the fighting) and the defending French expeditionary forces, was fought in their vicinity on 21 March 1801. In January 1877, John Dixon, a successful engineer, was contracted to bring the fallen obelisk to London, and the work started only a few months later. GRIFFITH INSTITUTE, ASHMOLEAN MUSEUM, OXFORD

RIGHT: The ingenious plan devised by John Dixon for the removal of the obelisk from Alexandria was to build a metal cylinder round the obelisk, roll it into the sea, and then transform it into a barge (named the Cleopatra) that was then towed to Britain. Here, the encased obelisk is being moved to the waterfront (the other "Needle" is seen in the background). The obelisk was reerected on the Thames Embankment in London in 1878. GRIFFITH INSTITUTE, ASHMOLEAN MUSEUM, OXFORD/BORGIOTTI PHOTOGRAPH

documents from this phase of Egyptian culture more accessible to interested scholars. In Oxford Bertha Porter (1852–1941) and Rosalind Moss (1890–1990) established the *Topographical Bibliography* to document all hieroglyphic texts, reliefs, and paintings.

The period after the Second World War saw increased archaeological work in Egypt — despite the instability in the region — both by the Egyptian Antiquities Service and by numerous foreign missions. Egyptian Egyptologists such as Labib Habachi (1906–84) at Elephantine, Karnak, and el-Qantir; Ahmad Fakhry (1905–73) at Dahshur; and Zakaria Goneim (1911–59) at Saqqara made significant discoveries and contributions to the subject. The construction of the new Aswan Dam generated a rescue campaign in Nubia in the 1960s, resulting in a major advance in knowledge of all phases of the history and culture of that region and in the removal of many temples, notably Abu Simbel, that would otherwise have been lost. Recent archaeological work in Egypt has tended to concentrate on town sites, especially in the area of the Delta, that had been neglected by earlier excavators. Much has been accomplished in bringing about an understanding of the political and social history, art, and literature of the ancient Egyptians. Problems remain, but these continue to be solved by ongoing work in the field and in museums and universities.

most authoritative dictionary of the ancient Egyptian language. The British Egyptologist Sir Alan Gardiner (1879–1963) published many hieroglyphic and hieratic texts bearing on Egyptian administration. Jaroslav Černý (1898–1970), professor at Oxford, made available the documentary texts discovered at Deir el-Medina, while his French colleague Georges Posener (1906–88), a specialist in Egyptian literature, advanced the knowledge of many literary pieces. The linguist Hans Jacob Polotsky (1905–91) brought new understanding to the study of Coptic and Egyptian grammar. Demotic specialists such as Stephen Glanville (1900–56) made

LEFT: The Egyptian archaeologist Zakaria Goneim discovered and excavated the unfinished step pyramid of King Sekhemkhet (2609–2603 BC) at Saqqara in 1952–56. Archaeology can, however, be a cruel mistress: the sealed sarcophagus in the pyramid's burial chamber was found to be mysteriously empty. ASHMOLEAN LIBRARY, OXFORD

ABOVE: Threatened by drowning in the waters of Lake Nasser, the rock temples at Abu Simbel were cut into large blocks and carefully reassembled at a safer place nearby. MACQUITTY INTERNATIONAL COLLECTION

LEFT: The First Nile Cataract was the southern limit of Egypt for most nineteenth-century travelers, but some ventured into Nubia, as far south as the Second Nile Cataract. The painting, by Hector Horeau in 1839, shows the approach to the temple at el-Sebua, built by Ramesses II (1279–1213 BC), and its outer court. GRIFFITH INSTITUTE, ASHMOLEAN MUSEUM, OXFORD

LIFE ALONG THE NILE

Janine Bourriau

THE ANCIENT EGYPTIANS appear familiar not only because, on countless tomb and temple walls, they have left us images of their everyday lives, but also because those images have inspired a hundred advertising slogans, interior designs, and jokes. If we dismiss such confusing associations and look at the scenes alone, without other evidence, we still see Egypt through a distorting mirror — like observing Britain for the first time through photographs in *Country Life*. Tomb scenes presented an idealized view of life to be projected into eternity for the benefit of the tomb owner and his family. Hence the emphasis on his status and career. Most so-called scenes of daily life show episodes in the cycle of food production and its climax, the procession of offering bearers approaching the tomb owner. Missing is any hint of suffering, sickness, or old age; among subordinate figures a deformed body may appear or lazy fieldworkers may be beaten, but the central characters are untouched by time or adversity. Some activities are rarely, if ever, depicted: intimate family life, nonfunerary religious practices, warfare (besides formal battle scenes on royal reliefs), expeditions beyond the Nile Valley. Some places rarely or never appear — harbors, royal palaces, streets of houses, marketplaces, public wells.

Since the purpose of tomb scenes is magical, they must conform to rules of ritual decorum but need not be true to life. Thus the tomb owner, whatever his true stature, is always larger than anyone except the king. The repertoire includes anachronistic scenes, such as a scene of hunting hippopotami in the papyrus swamps — wild hippopotami being extinct in Egypt by the New Kingdom (1540–1069 BC). Because the Egyptians show us how they wished to live in the next world, we can deduce their priorities in this one: continuity of society's institutions, comfortable living and physical well-being and acceptance of the obligations as well as the benefits of rank and family. It is above all owners of fine tombs — society's elite office holders and their families — whom we observe. For artisans and peasants buried without tombs, laid in the sand with only a drinking cup at their mouths, we must look elsewhere: to minor figures in the tomb scenes, records kept by an army of officials, and excavations in the towns and villages where they lived. What we know best, from a variety of sources, is life on the country estates of wealthy officials during the New Kingdom; the supplementary picture of town life comes mainly from archaeology.

The family house at the center of the

The garden, in addition to providing fish, fowl, wine, fruit, and vegetables for the table, was enjoyed for its own sake. Water, shady trees, and bright flowers were essential. Egyptians made gardens not only around their houses but also around tombs and temples, planting them even in the inhospitable desert. Among plants identified from desiccated garlands and bouquets are blue and white lotus, poppy, mandrake, cornflower, daisy, larkspur, ivy, vine, tamarisk, willow, acacia, fig, sycamore fig, persea, carob, pomegranate, olive, moringa, date palm, and dom palm. A vine arbor was a favorite garden structure, and another was a shrine dedicated to one of many local snake goddesses.

At the head of the community was the estate owner. The estate may have come as an adjunct to an office possibly

ABOVE: Wall-painting showing a pool with geese, ducks, and fish in the middle of a garden. The various species of fruit trees include the date palm and sycamore fig. From a tomb at Thebes, c. 1375 BC. BRITISH MUSEUM, LONDON

RIGHT: Large wooden figure, some 4 feet (123 cm) tall, of a woman bringing provisions for the tomb of Meketre, c. 1990 BC. The objects in the basket on the woman's head are wine jars with conical mud seals, while in her right hand she carries a duck. THE EGYPTIAN MUSEUM, CAIRO/JÜRGEN LIEPE

estate was built of sun-dried mud brick, painted white and set in a garden surrounded by high walls. Like houses in Egypt today, it aimed to provide relief from a fierce sun rather than protection against cold or wind. Two or three stories high, it boasted a terrace opening into the garden and an exterior staircase leading to the roof. Nakht, a vizier whose villa at el-Amarna has been excavated, had the benefit of 28 rooms. Public rooms were located near the entrance, clustered around a large columned hall where guests were received and official and estate business transacted. Family living rooms were found in the center with private apartments at the back, including bedrooms and bathrooms, reached only by passing through from the front. Above and below there were workrooms, offices, storerooms, and servants' quarters. The interior would have presented an atmosphere of dim coolness with flashes of jewel-bright colors from painted wooden columns, ceilings and doorways, mats rolled down over small high windows or open doors, and garlands of flowers painted against white-washed walls. Outside were stables, granaries, kitchens, bakery, brewery, slaughterhouse, and workshops for the dirtier crafts such as pottery making and carpentry.

LEFT: Large ivory "magic knife" (also "magic wand") c.1850 BC with a series of engraved protective beings, animals, and symbols. These include Taweret (a complex animal deity with the head and body of a female hippopotamus) wielding a knife and leaning on a sa-symbol ("protection"), and a demon figure resembling the god Bes. BRITISH MUSEUM, LONDON

inherited from his father. It was not private property as we understand the term. The status of the owner's wife was lower. She could not hold office, but she could buy and sell her own property and expect to share equally in the life-style of her husband and his provision for the afterlife. Generally speaking, a man had only one wife at a time, though concubines existed in wealthy households.

The quality of a woman's life was inevitably determined by her ability to bear and raise healthy children. As in more modern times, fertility was seen primarily as her responsibility, and common fertility charms depict naked women, sometimes with grotesquely enlarged genitalia. Raising children was a hazardous experience in which both natural and supernatural powers were invoked. Medical papyri show by the number of remedies for infertility, problems of pregnancy and childbirth, and the illnesses of childhood how these anxieties dominated life. The number of baby burials, so many that babies were rarely given elaborate burial but interred under floors in boxes or jars, is a poignant testimony to the difficulty women had raising children.

The most common amulets depict deities whose special concern was protection of women and children: Hathor, goddess of sexual love (and so fertility, since there was no separation between the two); Bes, the lion-man, biter of snakes and fighter of demons; and

Taweret, the "Great One," a monstrous combination of the fiercest animals the Egyptians knew: hippopotamus, lion, and crocodile. Images of Hathor, Bes, and Taweret were all over the house, but especially in the private apartments, on furniture (particularly beds), wall-paintings, storage jars, cosmetic jars,

LEFT: Small crude figurines representing bound captives, sometimes reduced to mere plaques, and inscribed with "execration texts" containing names of foreign localities and their chieftains, first appeared around 2200 BC. Their purpose was magical, to bring disaster on Egypt's enemies. Similar statuettes with purely Egyptian names, such as this one, are also known, and show that the same procedure was used against Egyptian "undesirables" or those whom one might fear. LOUVRE MUSEUM, PARIS

ADORNMENTS

As in most hierarchical societies, costume was a precise indicator of rank. Pure white linen elaborately pleated, heavy wigs of human hair ornamented with coronet of flowers or jewels, earrings, multistringed bead collars, bracelets, armlets, anklets, and sandals of leather or woven reed: this was the "festival" costume of the wealthy of both sexes. The garments were less close-fitting than they appear — artistic convention demanded display of the body's contours through the fine material. For the upper classes, cleansing and painting the face and body was a priority in life as after death, when mummification intervened to arrest the physical process of decay. To be sweet-smelling was an essential attribute of beauty, and without soap this was achieved by the application of scented oils and creams.

ABOVE: *Necklaces of beads and pendants of gold, carnelian, jasper, and faience. From Thebes, c. 1300–700 BC. ASHMOLEAN MUSEUM, OXFORD*

LEFT: *"Broad collar" (wesekh) consisting of cylinder and barrel beads, rhomboid pendants and clasps, all of faience. From Beni Hasan in Middle Egypt, c. 2050 BC. ASHMOLEAN MUSEUM, OXFORD*

ABOVE: *A string of spheroid beads capped with gold, and a gold shen-sign (round "cartouche," related to the oval surrounding royal names) amulet inlaid with faience and carnelian. From Abydos, c. 1850 BC. ASHMOLEAN MUSEUM, OXFORD*

Cones of scented wax were also placed on the head to melt and exude a sweet cooling liquid over head and shoulders. All body hair was removed by both sexes, and the hair of the head was cut very short, wigs being worn for special occasions. A fashion for carefully trimmed moustaches with or without short chin-beards existed during the Old (2647–2124 BC) and Middle (2040–1648 BC) kingdoms. At all periods unkempt hair or chin stubble was a sign of either mourning or low breeding. To emphasize their purity, priests shaved their heads completely.

Both sexes painted their faces, particularly the eyes. The popular substances were malachite, a copper ore yielding a green pigment, and galena, a lead ore providing gray or black. There is some evidence for the use of rouge, and women painted their toe- and finger-nails and hennaed the soles of their feet and their hair.

LEFT: A luxurious cosmetic set of one of the daughters of Senwosret II (1886–1878 BC), Sit-hathor-yunet, from her tomb at el-Lahun in the Faiyum. THE METROPOLITAN MUSEUM OF ART, NEW YORK

spoons, boxes, and mirrors — creating a wall of magical protection against the demons of the night, the desert, and the unquiet dead. We find the same constellation of deities on amulets in tombs, a striking confirmation of belief in the parallel worlds of the living and the dead, and the vulnerability of the newly dead to the same malevolent powers as the newly born.

None of this fearfulness appears in the serene faces of the men and women celebrated in their tombs. They appear eternally youthful, the man perhaps a little plump (rolls of fat were a symbol of wealth and authority), and in their finest apparel.

Living with the estate owner and his wife was their extended family consisting, one might surmise from calculations of life expectancy, of at least three generations. The elderly were highly esteemed, senior officials being supported by a "staff of old age," a younger man, often a son, who carried out duties they could no longer perform. Closest to the family were their personal servants: nurses, barbers, hairdressers, and cupbearers. Next came the estate administrators, stewards, controllers of granaries and store rooms, and supervisors of craftworkers (most craftworkers were male), fieldworkers, and herdsmen. All of them would also be scribes or have scribes working for them,

as we see in the tomb scenes, where every activity has its attendant recorder. The complex bureaucracy of modern states prepares us for the control exercised in Egypt over the use of resources and the extent to which herds were counted, fields measured, lists of commodities and equipment made, and rations issued. In part this strict control arose from a system without money, with labor bartered for commodities measured in units of the basic foods, bread and beer. In part it responded to the need to control food distribution in years of low or dangerously high inundation.

BELOW: Model granary made of baked clay, c. 2000 BC. The painted scenes on the outside are an interesting variation on the figures found in wooden models. The granary consists of ten chambers in two stories; the roofs of upper rooms are domed. CASTLE MUSEUM, NORWICH/ J. BOURRIAU

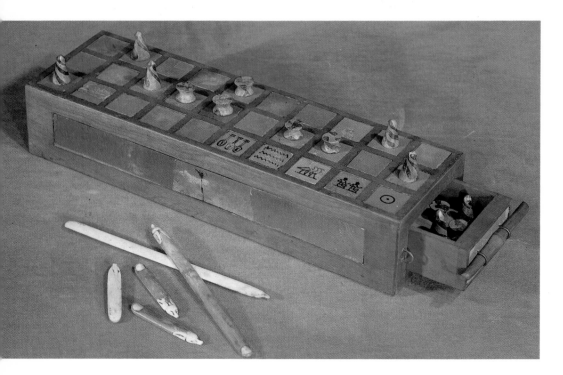

RIGHT: *Wooden model fishing boats with men netting fish, found in the tomb of the chancellor Meketre near Deir el-Bahri, c. 1990 BC. They are of the type traditionally associated with papyrus craft (with a raised prow and stern), although it seems likely that other materials (wood) may also have been used for construction of boats of this size.* THE EGYPTIAN MUSEUM, CAIRO/JÜRGEN LIEPE

BELOW: **Senet**-*game ("draughts") c. 1450 BC, usually played with five or more pieces a side and four casting sticks (used like dice) on a board of 30 squares (3 x 10). This was by far the most popular board game. This is a very smart set made of wood and faience, with a special drawer to hold the pieces.* METROPOLITAN MUSEUM OF ART, NEW YORK

The training of a scribe was long and arduous, but the rewards were substantial. A school text says cynically, "He makes friends with those greater than him." Like the church in medieval Europe, the profession was a passport away from the drudgery of manual labor: "You call for one; a thousand answer you. You stride freely on the road. You will not be like a hired ox." The scribe carried his ink palette and pens and often placed them in his tomb, for the gods of the netherworld must recognize his status. Brushes were of rush, ink of powdered carbon mixed with water. The writing surface may have been an ostracon, a fragment of limestone or pottery picked up from the ground, but plastered wood or papyrus were used for more important documents. It is ironic that ephemeral ostraca discarded after use have survived in comparatively greater numbers than papyri. It has been estimated that a small Old Kingdom temple archive held 10,000 papyrus rolls, yet only thirteen fragments survive. The scribe's or his master's seal, impressed into a lump of wet mud, identified or secured documents and other valuables.

Probably none of the people supervised by scribes could read or write. Their fate in the next world, as in this one, rested with their master. If their names were preserved among his tomb inscriptions, then they could participate in his funerary cult and share eternity with him. On the master's side, it was not unimportant that the whole household be preserved into the next world if all his needs were to be met.

Like a medieval manor, the estate was a self-sufficient community with brewers, bakers, vintners, potters, carpenters, weavers, basket makers, tanners, and butchers, working with raw materials supplied by fieldworkers,

herdsmen, and fishermen. The inundation cycle meant that much of the craftwork was seasonal, all estate workers having to take a turn at farming.

One of the crafts about which we know the most is pottery making, because we can combine evidence from texts, tomb scenes, models, and the pots themselves. The potter was despised by the scribe as "smeared with soil, like one whose relations have died." And "his hands, his feet are full of clay; he is like one who lives in a bog." The range of pottery was widest during the New Kingdom (1540–1069 BC), with styles changing quite rapidly (within about 50 years); most was of alluvial clay from river or canal, or clay mined from soft layers of desert rock. After being prepared by improving plasticity and introducing material to increase or decrease porosity as needed, the clay was shaped on a wheel turned by the potter's apprentice to maintain centrifugal force. Hand-building and shaping in molds were confined to specialized vessels. Before firing, pottery was often slipped or burnished, but complex painted or sculptural decoration was exceptional. Storage jars were closed with mud stamped with the owner's mark or with linen drawn tightly across the mouth, tied with string and stamp-sealed. Ink inscriptions sometimes give quantity, identity, origin, date of filling, and destination of contents.

There is plenty of evidence that all ranks relished leisure, from the simple delight of a seat in the shade to elaborately organized hunting parties in desert or papyrus marsh. Pet dogs, cats, and monkeys were taken along, together with the family and a retinue of servants. Other pleasures were "sitting on the shores of drunkenness" involving both wine and beer, and playing various board games. Music, dancing, and storytelling were professional accomplishments. Musicians, especially harpists, were men of high status, many with decorated tombs of their own. The role of storyteller must have resembled that of the schoolmaster or priest in a rural community before universal education. At least one we know of was also a doctor and a magician.

The division between magic and science in our culture, would have had no meaning for Egyptians. Medical papyri show that the same man would have carried out "scientific" practices, based on observed fact, and practices we would label "magical," based on manipulating supernatural powers. Stories he told, such as the adventures of the noble, Sinuhe, and the quest of the shipwrecked sailor, have survived in many copies. Illustrations of stories of another kind — satirical, ribald fables where animals take the place of humans — have also come down to us. They provide reassurance that this controlled hierarchical society could be turned on its head for everyone's amusement.

ABOVE: Potters in the tomb of Kenamun at Sheikh Abd el-Qurna, c. 1420 BC. From a copy by N. de Garis Davies.

ABOVE: Sketches on ostraca (limestone flakes) often reflect the unreal topsy-turvy world of stories and fables in which the roles of people and animals have undergone strange transformations. Here, a fox acts as a good shepherd guarding a kid. From c. 1300–1100 BC. FITZWILLIAM MUSEUM, UNIVERSITY OF CAMBRIDGE

AN ARTISAN'S HOUSE AT MEMPHIS DURING THE REIGN OF TUTANKHAMUN

Memphis, to the south of modern Cairo, on the west bank of the Nile, was one of the greatest cities of antiquity, comparable with Rome or Nineveh. Athens or Jerusalem would have fitted into one of its smaller suburbs. It was a wonder to Egyptians themselves: "The like of Memphis has never been seen . . . its granaries are full of barley and emmer; its hillocks have herbs, its lakes are full of lotus buds." Visitors are shocked by how little of this grandeur remains, but the city's monuments have been quarried for building stone since Roman times. Archaeologists have dug there for a century, but no systematic study was attempted until 1981, when the London-based Egypt Exploration Society began work. Since then, a corner of the city has been excavated and recorded. New Kingdom mud-brick houses were uncovered, huddled together along narrow alleyways — exactly the type of building the archaeologists wished to find.

A family house in this quarter of Memphis during the reign of Tutankhamun (1336–27 BC) was modest. It consisted of an

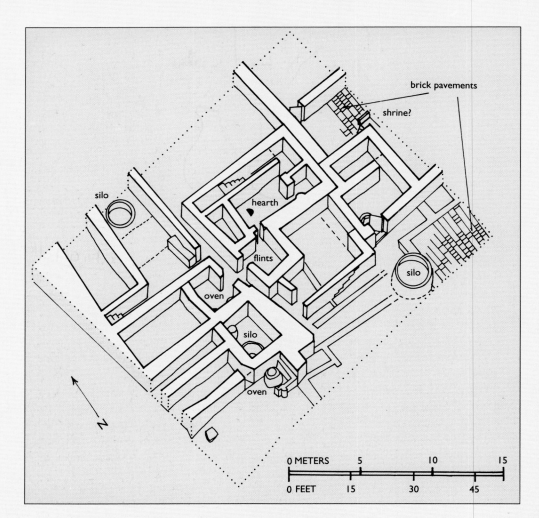

ABOVE: Axonometric view of the remains of mud-brick houses excavated by an expedition of the Egypt Exploration Society, directed by David Jeffreys and Lisa Giddy, at Kom el-Rabia (Mit Rahina, ancient Memphis). Based on a drawing by D. G. Jeffreys. EGYPT EXPLORATION SOCIETY, LONDON

LEFT: Reconstruction of a large pottery Bes jar. EGYPT EXPLORATION SOCIETY, LONDON/W. SCHENCK

outer room to work in, an inner living room with a hearth, two small back rooms for storage or sleeping in, and a stairway to the roof, which provided extra sleeping or storage space and an opportunity to enjoy the "sweet breath of the north wind" in the crowded city. The house's external walls were old, a century or more, but the interior walls showed continuous adaptation in response to the family's changing needs. Rubbish, luckily for the archaeologist, was everywhere. Many objects lay on floors,

dropped and lost in the straw covering them, which subsequently decayed. Every so often, the rubbish was packed down with soil and a clean mud floor was laid. Pits for rubbish were also dug wherever there was room, and piles of it accumulated in the narrow alleys.

The floor of the outer room was covered with a rich scatter of objects: granite hammers, bone awls, flint knives and scrapers, pebbles for polishing, and a basalt quern for grinding grain. A bowl used to anchor thread during spinning was found in the neighboring courtyard. Organic materials — wood, leather, textile, and basketry — had disappeared because the site is damp, its hidden "treasures" subjected for millennia to annual inundations, but what remains points to a pattern of living. The numerous scrapers and knives suggest the family may have been engaged in leather working or basketry. Nearby was evidence of metal working and

TOP LEFT: Jewelry and amulets made of faience, carnelian, glass, and bone. EGYPT EXPLORATION SOCIETY, LONDON/NORBERT BÖER

TOP RIGHT: Bracelet of fine faience disk beads, bone earrings, ring bezel with the name of Tutankhamun, and a scarab-shaped amulet inscribed with the name of Ramesses II. EGYPT EXPLORATION SOCIETY, LONDON/NORBERT BÖER

FAR LEFT: Fertility figurines in the form of women, naked but for their elaborate wigs. EGYPT EXPLORATION SOCIETY, LONDON/NORBERT BÖER

LEFT: Hathor-head plaque made of painted pottery. EGYPT EXPLORATION SOCIETY, LONDON/NORBERT BÖER

bead making for personal ornaments. The family collected grain from an enormous communal silo at the end of the adjacent alley; they ground it themselves but baked their bread in a communal bakery opposite the entrance to their house.

The family was not self-sufficient but bartered goods for food. They fished and perhaps kept pigs, either confined to the roof (goats on roofs are even now a feature of poorer districts of Cairo) or left to scavenge the rubbish. Animal bones, sometimes with butchery cuts, show that cattle were the primary meat source, then pig, birds (possibly duck), sheep, and goat. Fish bones were plentiful, from species living nowadays in the

Nile, the Mediterranean, and the Red Sea. Dog and cat bones occur, along with rats and mice. Botanical remains confirm a varied diet: barley and emmer wheat, lentils, olives, peas, dates, grapes, and persea. Among weed seeds from fuel, stable litter, or floor covering were rye grass, canary grass, daisy, poppy, and gypsophila.

The beliefs of this community are suggested by amulets and votive figurines. Its preoccupations were the universal ones: fertility, seen in charms depicting naked women; protection, in amulets of Taweret, Ptah (the main deity of Memphis), a cobra goddess, and large jars carrying a monstrous Bes image; and death, exemplified by a small bust representing an ancestor. Their recreations were, most conspicuously, drinking (judging by the number of cups and wine jars) and gaming. Great numbers of gaming pieces were found, usually crude disks

cut from broken pottery.

How does this evidence change the picture of their world that the Egyptians themselves represented? It shows us a crowded, noisy, smoky, and dirty city quarter of small houses on narrow alleys with occasional inner courtyards but probably no trees or gardens. The people nevertheless enjoyed a varied diet with access to commodities from other parts of Egypt and abroad (identified by their pottery containers). There is no evidence that they could read or write, and (perhaps most surprising) the technological level of their craftwork, judged by their tools, was simple. Yet these artisans were contemporaries of those who produced the treasures of Tutankhamun at which we marvel.

DEIR EL-MEDINA: A COMMUNITY OF ARTISANS

The community of artisans who built and decorated the royal tombs of the New Kingdom (1540–1069 BC) is a conspicuous exception to the relative paucity of available evidence concerning the Egyptian economy. It settled in the desert, on the west bank of Thebes, and since it was a highly literate group, it has left us thousands of texts, some written on papyrus, but most on ostraca: potsherds and flakes of limestone. These texts together present us with a fairly complete picture of all aspects of daily life, including a wealth of information about the way in which the necropolis workmen earned their living. Yet, we have to keep in mind that it was an exceptional community, the only one of its kind preserved to us in the entire history of ancient Egypt.

The settlement is called Deir el-Medina, the modern Arabic name of the desert valley in which it is situated — the ancient workmen called it simply "the village." The inhabitants were in the service of the state, or, in the Egyptian terminology, of pharaoh. They were neither slaves nor serfs, but free laborers paid by the government. If their wages were in arrears, as happened frequently during the Twentieth Dynasty (1186–1069 BC), they went on strike, leaving the necropolis and sitting down near one of the temples on the Theban west bank. Whether they were indeed hungry, as they angrily protested, is not certain. In general, they were well paid, and they had abundant free time at their disposal — at least regular long weekends — in which they were able to earn a substantial extra income by making and painting coffins and other funerary equipment for the upper classes in Thebes. Through this employment they would have collected enough reserves to bridge a period of disorganization in their provisions, provided it did not last too long.

Since no money existed, they were paid in kind: grain for bread and beer, the staple foods of the Egyptians; vegetables and fruit, fish, oil, salt, and so on, and also manufactured items, mainly garments and sandals. The state gathered the grain in its granaries from taxation levied on the peasants, whereas vegetables and fish were regularly delivered to the community by personnel in its service, appointed and paid by the government. Other products that did not need to be supplied daily were distributed among the households as welcome extras on festival occasions.

ABOVE: One of many Deir el-Medina documents that concern property. Inscribed in the hieratic script, this papyrus concerns the last testament of the lady Naunakhte, and is dated to the third year of Ramesses V (1147–1143 BC). ASHMOLEAN MUSEUM, OXFORD

BELOW LEFT: A hieratic text written in ink on an ostracon (limestone flake) from Deir el-Medina. It records the "money" ("silver") value of various commodities (a bed, two wooden chests, oil, and barley) owed to the workman Penne by the policeman Pasedet. GRIFFITH INSTITUTE, ASHMOLEAN MUSEUM, OXFORD

BELOW RIGHT: The same text transcribed into hieroglyphs by Černý and Gardiner. Some hieratic signs are similar to their hieroglyphic counterparts while others differ quite substantially. GRIFFITH INSTITUTE, ASHMOLEAN MUSEUM, OXFORD

ABOVE: *The kingdom presided over by the god Osiris in which Egyptians hoped to live after death was, in many respects, similar to that ruled by the pharaoh. Here, Sennedjem is represented in his tomb at Deir el-Medina working in the mythical Fields of Ialu. The setting may be fictitious, but the agricultural techniques are confirmed by finds of contemporary implements.* Deir el-Medina (Thebes), c. 1280 BC. MACQUITTY INTERNATIONAL COLLECTION

principle, however, similar. And the diverse sphere of the private business sector, from single-person enterprises to multinational concerns, was completely absent, whereas in our times it constitutes the very core of economic life.

Not a single instance is known of a private firm, in the fields of transport, trade, manufacture, and mining. The larger workshops belonged either to the state or to temples. Expeditions to procure gold, copper, semiprecious stones, or valuable building materials were placed under the supervision of pharaoh's high officials and staffed by personnel recruited solely by the government. If ever there existed minor private entrepreneurs, they have until now escaped our attention. It is conspicuous that no tomb owner ever

stated that he was a merchant or the owner of a workshop. In this respect Egypt differs entirely from medieval Europe, where merchant entrepreneurs formed the nucleus of what became the Third Estate. When in Egyptian texts a person is called a "merchant" or "trader" — this happens only from the New Kingdom onwards — he appears always to be in the service of an institution, usually a temple.

Temple complexes contained workshops of various types, especially textile ateliers. Their products, transported by ships owned by the organizations concerned, were exchanged for goods they needed and could not obtain in any other way, through the medium of traders attached to the temple. These Egyptian temples were in

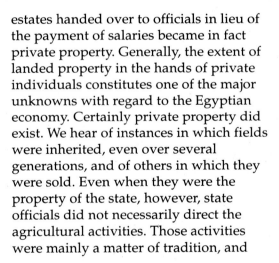

no way churches; an equivalent of the church did not exist. Temples belonged to the state, to pharaoh, who was represented on their walls as the sole offerer to and intermediary with the gods. If he donated part of the war booty or large areas of fields to a particular god — a usual practice — they were not lost to the state. At any moment the government could retrieve them and reallocate them to other institutions, both religious and secular.

The state with all its departments, including the temples, was the largest landowner. It is not clear to what extent estates handed over to officials in lieu of the payment of salaries became in fact private property. Generally, the extent of landed property in the hands of private individuals constitutes one of the major unknowns with regard to the Egyptian economy. Certainly private property did exist. We hear of instances in which fields were inherited, even over several generations, and of others in which they were sold. Even when they were the property of the state, however, state officials did not necessarily direct the agricultural activities. Those activities were mainly a matter of tradition, and

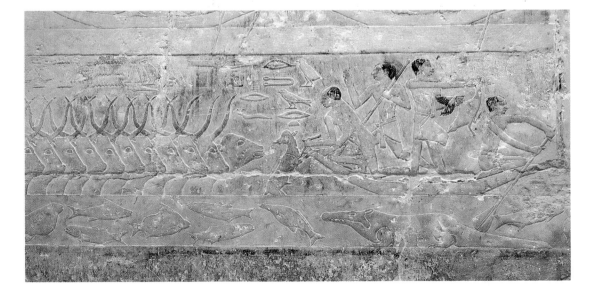

HOUSEHOLD CONSUMPTION

How did a household acquire all that it needed? The answer is: partly by its own production. Most ancient Egyptians were at least part-time peasants tilling small fields. Although the landowners, namely, pharaoh and his officials as well as the temples, claimed part of the yield, in general enough was left to provide a minimal subsistence for the producers themselves.

People also obtained their necessities through the redistribution system. For some, such as the soldiers and the necropolis workmen, this was their main source of income. Others, for example, high officials with their own self-supporting estates, were to a lesser extent dependent upon the state. Most workers needed some copper for their implements— although even during the New Kingdom (1540–1069 BC) flint was still widely used. Copper was either mined in the deserts east of the Nile Valley, always by government expeditions, or imported by the state from abroad. It was distributed among the population via various channels. Tomb representations show that pharaoh ceremonially dispensed gold objects to his faithful followers, throwing the objects down from a balcony. In their turn, the recipients donated some of the items to their retainers, and so small gold objects such as rings reached even the lowest levels of society. Similarly, though less spectacularly, other valuable materials such as precious stones, salt, and also copper were distributed by the authorities.

A third method of obtaining what one needed was simply to ask for it as a gift. In

ABOVE: Wooden model of a carpenter's shop from the tomb of Meketre at Thebes, c. 1990 BC. One man is sawing a piece of wood tied to an upright post, others are dressing a beam with adzes, smoothing planks, and cutting slots for tenons. THE EGYPTIAN MUSEUM, CAIRO/JÜRGEN LIEPE

ABOVE: A rather unflattering portrait of an unshaven, bald stonemason with a chisel in one hand and a wooden mallet in the other. This is a quick sketch made with a brush on a limestone ostracon (flake) that was not hindered by the conventions of Egyptian "official" art. Its author may have been the stonemason's workmate and the sketch may have been intended as a joke. It comes from the Theban west bank, probably Deir el-Medina or the Valley of the Kings, and dates to c. 1300–1100 BC. FITZWILLIAM MUSEUM, UNIVERSITY OF CAMBRIDGE

Egypt, as in other societies at a similar level of development, gift giving was an obligation. In the Western world, giving presents is not considered an economic action — except that they are usually bought in a shop. The custom belongs to the social sphere of life, and the motive for it is supposed to be love or friendship — although we are aware that self-interest may well be involved. In ancient times prestige in the community was a preponderant feature of life, and individuals were obliged to be liberal. Moreover, the very act of giving conferred power over the receiver. In this connection, material objects and services are interchangeable. Whether a person helped a neighbor build a house, or provided him with a needed tool makes no difference.

A special case of gift giving was the custom of bringing food to a party. This happens also in our society, but then it was common, and necessary. Only the very rich could afford to arrange a big feast using just their own stores. Normally, each guest brought a contribution, as still occurs in Egypt. These gifts were carefully noted down, for the host had to bring a present of the same value on a subsequent occasion. Of essential interest here is not the custom itself but the economic necessity.

A similar kind of reciprocity involves what we call buying and selling. Rather than

ABOVE: A relief fragment, thickly coated with plaster and painted, showing two carpenters at work. It was in such less formal subjects, settings, and postures that Egyptian artists/craftworkers were able to display their ability to observe, draw and caricature. Probably c. 1400–1350 BC. EGYPTIAN MUSEUM, BERLIN/WERNER FORMAN ARCHIVE

being construed as a profit-making mechanism, the sole purpose of an exchange was to provide an individual with one or more sought-after objects. Many texts from Deir el-Medina demonstrate this. If a man wanted to buy an ox, he had to collect goods such as garments, pieces of furniture, basketry, or small animals, to the total value of the beast. Moreover, they had each to be acceptable to the seller. A bed, which was a relative luxury since most people slept on mats on the ground, figured in many such transactions. Did the buyer in all these instances possess a spare one, and did the seller want one? That seems unlikely.

Most likely, the purchaser of the ox would have demanded the bed from a relation or a neighbor, referring to a service rendered previously or promising to help on a future occasion. The seller of the ox would have accepted the bed if he knew someone who wanted it; with it he could pay off a debt, or create a credit. It was an "open-credit system" in which everyone in a community was at the same time debtor and creditor to many persons. Debts were never wholly redeemed, for then opportunities to request help or gifts would have been lost. The system was complicated, with numerous credit relations bisecting each other. It lacked the financial precision we value, but it was essential in allowing households to acquire what they needed and could not obtain in any other way.

decisions were the responsibility of the local community. A similar situation existed with respect to irrigation works. The state may have exercised a vague supervision over the maintenance of dikes, dams, and canals, but the actual care rested with the local authorities. A specialized state organization for irrigation works never existed.

Despite the role of the state in ancient Egyptian life, Egyptian society did not resemble a modern dictatorship. There were not sufficient means to control the population. Moreover, distances were large with respect to the speed of transport, the quickest mode of traveling being sailing along the Nile. It took about a fortnight to go upstream from Memphis to Thebes, a distance of some 400 miles (650 km). The government did not possess the means to influence the economy, even though its main representative, the vizier, was supposed to receive reports from all regions of the country regularly. Theoretical insight into economic development was still absent. During the Nineteenth Dynasty (1295–1186 BC), silver appears to have depreciated as compared with copper; the ratio that had formerly been 1:100 became 1:60. It is not clear what caused this change, nor whether it could have represented an appreciation of the value of copper. However, it is highly improbable that government legislation

decided this significant economic event.

If there was hardly any scope for private enterprise, that was not the result of a deliberate policy of the state, but a fundamental characteristic of Egyptian society. The only path to individual prosperity was through the hierarchical system: to become an official in the state administration, a temple, or the army, and to ascend to the highest echelons. This path was only available to those who were literate. An artisan may have worked for himself as a potter, sandal maker, builder, or the like, but for such a person to build up a large firm was

ABOVE: An angler anxiously watching the fishing line, his left hand poised ready to club the fish. This is just a small cameo scene that formed part of a much larger composition showing the tomb owner in a papyrus canoe in a marsh. Saqqara, from the tomb of Princess Seshseshet Idut, c. 2300 BC. JAMES H. MORRIS

LEFT: A wooden model of an inspection of cattle on the estate of the chancellor Meketre, c. 1990 BC. Twenty-four models showing such activities were deposited in Meketre's tomb in a valley close to Deir el-Bahri at Thebes. Their function was similar to wall decoration: to ensure continued well-being of the tomb owner by providing him with images of activities indispensable for the existence of a person of his rank. THE EGYPTIAN MUSEUM, CAIRO/JOHN G. ROSS

RIGHT: *A wooden model found in the tomb of Sebkhotpi at Beni Hasan in Middle Egypt. It shows people making bread and brewing beer, as well as a butchery scene, and dates to c. 2000–1800 BC. BRITISH MUSEUM, LONDON/MACQUITTY INTERNATIONAL COLLECTION*

BELOW: *Men treading grapes in the Theban tomb of Nakht, first half of the fourteenth century BC. They maintain their balance by holding onto ropes suspended from the roof over the crushing vat. The extracted juice is collected into a trough and then poured into pottery jars for fermentation.* PETER CLAYTON

virtually impossible. Most craftworkers (who were mostly male), were actually in the service of institutions or of a local community to whom they delivered their products in exchange for being provided with all they needed for themselves and their families. Production for the market and the maximization of profit, to us so essential and self-evident, were unknown. Both parties in a transaction may have gained, since each acquired what it wanted in exchange for something it valued less, but to make a profit was not the aim. The lack of money also made it difficult to measure exactly who gained in an exchange transaction.

There were indeed means to express the value of a commodity; actually, several were in operation at the same time. During the New Kingdom (1540–1069 BC), three were in common use: a weight of copper called *deben* (c. 3 ounces/90 g), a quantity of grain called *khar*, literally "sack" (c. 16 gallons/76 l), and a silver measure the nature of which is still obscure; perhaps it was some type of ring. There was a preference for a particular measure for a particular kind of commodity. Thus copper objects were always valued in *deben*, but baskets in *khar*, since they could be filled with grain. A typical corn basket even cost as much (in grain) as it could contain, a curious way of defining the value of an object. No allowance was made for the value of the material nor for the time needed to produce the basket.

The ratio between the three measures of value was not rigidly fixed. A tunic cost five *deben* of copper or one silver "ring," which suggests that one ring was equal to five *deben*. In some instances, however, it appears to equal four rather than five *deben*. Such inconsistencies are unthinkable in our economy. They are examples of the different mentality of the ancient Egyptians.

The features and structures here described represent all periods of ancient Egyptian history. Development was minor and slow. There were some

technical discoveries, such as the potter's wheel or the shadoof for artificial irrigation, but mostly such changes as did occur resulted from evolution in the political sphere — for instance, the creation of an empire and a standing army to conquer and occupy territory across the border. The growth of the political and economic power of the temples during the New Kingdom also led to a new division of wealth. Yet the essential traits of the ancient Egyptian economy remained constant during Egypt's entire history.

ABOVE: Wall-painting showing an inspection of cattle. Animals of varying colors of skin and with differently shaped horns are depicted. The scribes carrying out the recording can be seen at the left end of the fragment. From a Theban tomb, c. 1450 BC. BRITISH MUSEUM, LONDON/WERNER FORMAN ARCHIVE

LEFT: Men reaping corn with sickles in the tomb of Menna at Sheikh Abd el-Qurna (Thebes), c. 1390 BC. Only the heads of corn were cut to prevent damage to the valuable straw. MACQUITTY INTERNATIONAL COLLECTION

THE PHARAOHS
AND THEIR COURT

J. D. Ray

MODERN EGYPT LIES at the center of the Islamic world. In geographical terms, this is a statement of the obvious, but it is also true that the country acts as the cultural center of the entire region. This state of affairs held true generally for medieval Egypt, and it also seems to apply to the country's ancient history. In the ancient Near East, Egypt had to compete culturally with Mesopotamia. Unlike the situation in Islamic times, it was linguistically and culturally distinct from its neighbors, but its agricultural wealth, the size of its population, and the excellence of its visual arts allowed it to exercise strong influence throughout the known world.

In some ways, Egypt's position in the Near East can be compared with that of France in the development of Europe. It had relatively secure borders and, in spite of strong regional differences, was able to achieve a truly centralized state; indeed, Egypt's creation of a pharaonic court at the end of the fourth millennium BC is an amazing feat that deserves wider recognition from historians than it has received. The culture of the country was in large part courtly, uniform, and imposed from above; and this culture led rapidly to an aristocratic sense of visual style unparalleled in the ancient world. Egypt, like France, was also a great

attracter of talented immigrants who hastened to become more Egyptian than their hosts. Provided they did this, there seems to have been little prejudice against them. The price that Egypt had to pay for its advantages was an exclusiveness, almost a superiority complex toward the rest of the world, which could sometimes hamper intellectual life; most of the technical discoveries made in the Near East were made elsewhere, but once they were realized, the Egyptians lost little time in adapting and perfecting them. No analogy is complete, but the comparison between Egypt and France at least has the advantage of explaining several features of the world's first centralized state.

From the very beginning of Egyptian history, there was a pharaoh. As a piece of abstraction elegantly applied to a social problem, the pharaoh ranks with the Egyptian creation of a 365-day calendar, probably the best ever devised. One of the most striking features of Egyptian thinking was a preference for dualism and the conciliation of pairs of opposites, and in this respect it is surprising that there was only one pharaoh. Nevertheless, the Egyptian preference for dualism is reflected in the double title given to the kings from the earliest dynasties: *nsw bjtj*. These words

were understood in the historical period to refer to a sedge and a bee, the heraldic emblems of Upper and Lower Egypt, the two provinces into which the country was divided. The Greek translation of this title on the Rosetta Stone bears out this interpretation, and the equivalent "king of Upper and Lower Egypt" is now conventional among Egyptologists. However, it is more than likely that this meaning is secondary. The primary force of *nsw* seems to be the divine, unchanging element that characterized the king of Egypt at all periods, whereas the title *bjtj* refers to the king in his human, or accidental and transitory aspects. In a historical inscription, for example, a pharaoh will boast that his exploits exceeded those of all other kings before him; the word used in such contexts is normally *bjtj*. Here, comparison merely with kings of Lower Egypt would be an anticlimax;

the king is referring to the purely physical or historical aspects of previous rulers. It is no accident that, after death, a divine pharaoh is described as "Osiris *nsw*" followed by the king's throne name. This establishes him securely as an aspect of the god Osiris, who governed the underworld and was the prototype of kingship on earth. (It is significant that the word for kingship in Egyptian is derived from *nsw* and not from *bjtj*.) The association of the title *nsw* with the king's throne name, which was conferred on him at his accession and not at birth, might at first sight suggest that the divinity of pharaoh was something extraneous to him, which devolved upon him only at a certain stage in his career. (In Christological terms, this would be the position taken by the Nestorians, adherents to the doctrine of Nestorius, patriarch of Constantinople in the first half of the fifth century.) However, everything we know of Egyptian religion suggests that this is unlikely. The human aspect of the pharaoh was certainly important (if it were not, there would be little point in mummifying his body and surrounding it with personal objects used in life), and it is more likely that the king's human and divine natures were seen as a merged duality. To return to Christology, this idea of a merged duality in Christ is the position held by the monophysites, and it is notable that Egypt, when it adopted Christianity, did so in a monophysite form.

There is some confirmation of this duality in the title regularly applied to the king in official texts; *ḥm.f*, which is conventionally translated "His Majesty." The word *ḥm* really defies translation, but it is generally agreed that it represents the form in which a particular ruler manifested himself. It may even derive from the root *whm*, which means "repeat;" a similar term is applied to the Apis bull, the king of all sacred animals, in his aspect as a representative or incarnation of a particular god. In this case, the king is seen as the effective embodiment of kingship at a particular time and place. This reconstruction reminds one of the Platonic theory of forms, a system of incorporeal perfections that may well have some

Egyptian influence behind it. This notion seems easier to accept than the theory that the king was divine only when enthroned, which has a suspiciously modern look to it.

The division between the two aspects of the pharaoh was extremely practical. In 3,000 years, Egypt must have produced its share of kings who were incompetent, perverse, immobile, or mad, but the concept of the "ideal king" remained intact. Thus we are able to read that Khufu (2549–2526 BC), builder of the Great Pyramid at Giza, was a tyrant with cynical disregard for human life, or that Pepy II (2236–2143 BC) perverted justice and had an affair with one of his generals. Admittedly, these are posthumous traditions designed to contrast with the perfection of a later regime, but the fact that such frailties could exist in a king was presumably accepted. In a late romance, we find that a ruler is ill, and the same illness is said to have struck King Izezi, who had died almost 2,000 years before. Whether this is historically true we cannot tell — and the tale has many fantastic elements in it — but the important point is that the

audience would have known that it was permissible to record such weaknesses. Similarly, we know of the birthplaces of occasional pharaohs, such as Merneptah (1213–1203 BC) or Amasis (570–526 BC), and we can read about the hobbies of others. The king was not intended to be a featureless and remote embodiment of godhead.

The king of Egypt was the god Horus, son of the divine Osiris, and he was king because his father had been. The notion often stated that the ruler owed his throne to his mother seems to be groundless; rulers whose mothers were not royal by birth, such as Akhenaten (1353–1337 BC), were accepted by contemporaries. The support of a powerful family on the maternal side may well have favored a prince's chances over other claimants, but it does not seem to have been the deciding factor in his succession. Female rulers were possible, though perhaps thought to be a poor substitute, and one such ruler, Hatshepsut (1479–1457 BC), laid heavy emphasis on her father, Tuthmosis I. Physical paternity could coexist in Egyptian thinking with the notion that the king was begotten by a god, normally a solar one, through the agency of a human mother. Again, a Christian parallel suggests itself.

The pharaoh was surrounded by a court, and court titles exist in bewildering

ABOVE: King Amenophis III (1391–1353 BC) as a conqueror, with bound African and Asiatic foes brought to Egypt in triumph in his chariot or crushed under its wheels. This representation is on a large (more than 7 feet/2 m high, although now fragmentary) stela (stone tablet) found reused in a temple of a later king at Thebes. THE EGYPTIAN MUSEUM, CAIRO/JÜRGEN LIEPE

LEFT: A travertine ("alabaster") slab from a balustrade in the main palace at Akhetaten (el-Amarna). King Akhenaten (1353–1337 BC) and Queen Nefertiti raise libation vases to the god Aten (represented as a shining sun disk with its rays terminating in hands), while Princess Nefer-nefruaten is shaking a sistrum (ceremonial rattle). THE EGYPTIAN MUSEUM, CAIRO/JÜRGEN LIEPE

TUTANKHAMUN'S TOMB

It has often been rather glibly stated that Tutankhamun's sole claim to a place in history is based on the fact that his tomb survived intact until the twentieth century. This view, however, cannot be upheld. Tutankhamun ruled during one of the most unusual historical periods. With the religious revolution of his father, Akhenaten, in ruins, the young king must have been personally involved in the difficult restoration and reconciliation efforts taking place at that time. Tragically, when his short life came to an abrupt end in 1327 BC (he was only about eighteen years old), the Tuthmosid line of kings died with him.

The first of the steps leading to Tutankhamun's tomb in the Valley of the Kings was discovered by Howard Carter on 4 November 1922, and the intact seals on the entrance on the following day. Carter's work was financed by the Earl of Carnarvon.

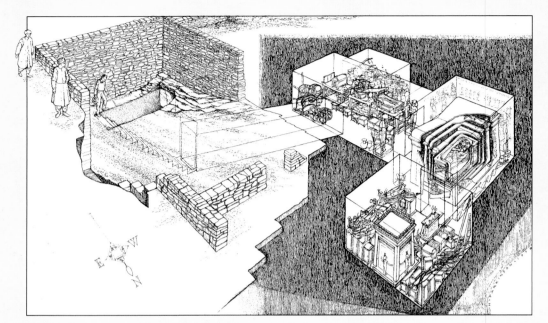

ABOVE: An axonometric view of Tutankhamun's tomb. The king's death must have been so unexpected that his own tomb was far from ready, perhaps hardly begun, and so another, nonroyal, tomb was quickly modified and used. Sixteen steps lead down to a descending corridor that opens into a series of rooms: an antechamber with an annex, the burial chamber, and a storeroom ("treasury"). H. PARKINSON

LEFT: A view of the antechamber that confronted visitors when they emerged from the corridor and looked to their left. Parts of chariots, couches, stools, chests, and food boxes were piled up in a fairly disordered manner. All rooms of Tutankhamun's tomb were filled with the king's funerary equipment; the only exception was the burial chamber, which was almost entirely taken up by shrines containing the sarcophagus and coffins. GRIFFITH INSTITUTE, ASHMOLEAN MUSEUM, OXFORD

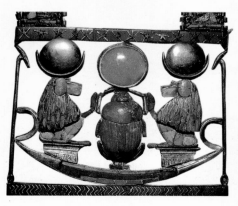

LEFT: Among the many items of jewelry found in the tomb was this open-work pectoral, made of gold inlaid with lapis lazuli, turquoise, carnelian, and travertine. The scene in the solar barque refers to the birth of the sun-god, and shows a scarab (dung beetle) holding the emerging sun disk. The event is greeted by two baboons (these animals are known to shriek at sunrise). THE EGYPTIAN MUSEUM, CAIRO/ AUSTRAL/CAMERA PRESS

ABOVE: This painting on the northern wall of the burial chamber shows Tutankhamun's successor, King Ay (1327–1323 BC), as a setem-priest wearing a panther skin and performing the "Opening-the-Mouth" ceremony. The deceased Tutankhamun is represented as the mummiform god Osiris. The ritual implement that Ay holds in his hands is a miniature adze. AUSTRAL/CAMERA PRESS

ABOVE: *Four shrines contained Tutankhamun's quartzite sarcophagus. The goddesses Isis, Nephthys, Neith, and Selkis are represented on its four corners and with their outstretched wings protect the body of the deceased king. The sarcophagus and the first (outermost) anthropoid (human-shaped) coffin are still in the tomb in the Valley of the Kings.* ANCIENT ART AND ARCHITECTURE COLLECTION/RONALD SHERIDAN

ABOVE: *Three anthropoid coffins were placed inside Tutankhamun's sarcophagus. The third (innermost) was entirely made of beaten gold up to about a tenth of an inch (3 mm) thick. The whole coffin weighs 243 pounds (110.4 kg). The king is wearing the royal nemes (headdress) and the two goddesses Wadjit (cobra) and Nekhbet (vulture) rest watchfully on his brow.* THE EGYPTIAN MUSEUM, CAIRO/JÜRGEN LIEPE

ABOVE: *A gold mask covered the head and shoulders of Tutankhamun's mummified body. The headdress is inlaid with blue lapis lazuli, and this is also used to outline the eyebrows. In addition, aragonite, quartz, carnelian, green feldspar, obsidian, and faience can be found on the eyes, cobra, uraeus, beard, and collar.* THE EGYPTIAN MUSEUM, CAIRO/THE IMAGE BANK/DEREK BERWIN

LEFT: *The head of a lioness from one of the three couches found in the antechamber. These were made of wood covered with gesso and gold. The nose, tear drops, and eye frames were inlaid with blue glass and the eyes were made of crystal over painted details.* THE EGYPTIAN MUSEUM, CAIRO/ AUSTRAL/CAMERA PRESS

RIGHT: A small (9 inches/23 cm high) statuette of Akhenaten (1353–1337 BC) and Queen Nefertiti. The king is wearing the so-called Blue Crown, Nefertiti a headdress that was her special characteristic, both with uraei (cobra serpents) at the front. The provenance of this piece is not known. LOUVRE MUSEUM, PARIS/JOHN G. ROSS

BELOW: A bronze figure of King Taharqa (690–664 BC) offering two vases to the rather obscure Upper Egyptian god Hemen. The god is represented as a hawk with a serpent between his talons, and the statuette is made of schist covered with gold foil. This may be a votive object commemorating a "miraculous" inundation which averted a famine. LOUVRE MUSEUM, PARIS

RIGHT: King Ramesses III (1184–1153 BC) as a hunter, on the outer face of the first pylon (monumental gateway) of his mortuary temple at Medinet Habu. Profound symbolism is concealed behind the apparent realism; the king asserts his right and duty to safeguard the world's order (maet). JOHN G. ROSS

number, especially in the earlier periods. Most such organizations have the leisure to devote themselves to protocol, ritual, and intrigue. The Egyptian court must have shared these responsibilities, and officials rose, intermarried, and fell in ways that are probably not recoverable to us. Political power resided in the court, although in practice almost all regimes reduce to a small committee; some such body must have governed Egypt at most periods, determining its own internal balance of interests. Economic power, however, need not always have coincided with the royal court, and dynasties of provincial landowners existed alongside this institution, enjoying a shifting relationship with it. Greco-Roman writers present a picture of the pharaoh dominated by ritual, and to an extent this picture is borne out by native records. However, in practice rule solely by ritual would have been unworkable. The reality must have been a combination of ritual and practical administration, elaborated over centuries and capable of subtle changes. A king could choose to operate without the traditional squirarchy, appointing officials who were dependent solely on him for patronage. Hatshepsut

and Akhenaten did this, and it is significant that both these rulers challenged tradition in other respects. Their appointees knew the risks: if the ruler fell, they would fall also.

Anyone who follows the tranquil procession of dynasties in a history book can be forgiven for thinking that the system was unchanging. The rate of change was certainly slow, as in all preindustrial societies, and there were many features that made for stability, but there are also signs that the government was more precarious than we imagine. True continuity can sometimes be seen when royal names alternate within a dynasty according to the pattern ABAB; Egyptians frequently named sons after their grandfathers. Parts of the Twelfth and Eighteenth dynasties illustrate this feature well. However, the latter dynasty consists of a central family, that of the Tuthmosids, which ended with the heirless Tutankhamun. It then terminates in a series of unrelated monarchs who were presumably adopted into the family to secure legitimacy. Even the concept of a dynasty is a shifting one; recent work has shown that the so-called Twenty-ninth Dynasty was essentially a conflicting series of warlords maintaining a struggle against the Persians, whereas the following dynasty was closer in modern terms to a military junta.

Although the outward forms remain the same, the reality of government may have varied greatly from one period to another, even in those periods thought to have been prosperous and stable. Ancient Egypt may well have had more history than we credit.

The system of government was certainly authoritarian, and Egyptian society had high expectations of conformity, but the regime was often redeemed by a concept of shared humanity and common values. Safety valves were necessary in such a closed society, and some of these were provided by the concept of *maet*. This is another untranslatable word, but it includes the notions of truth, harmony, social responsibility, and appreciation of reality. Under this concept, a peasant can tell the builder of the Great Pyramid that his proposal to experiment on a prisoner for amusement is immoral and contrary to the gods' will. Another pharaoh can write in a testimony to his son that the same gods weigh men's actions in judgment, and they apply this judgment also to kings. Remorse and conscience come to rulers as well as to subjects in such literary episodes; presumably in reality Khufu could have tortured prisoners if he had a mind to do so. The point is that a moral consensus did exist in matters of this sort, and this consensus was reinforced at least by religious sentiment, if not by sanction.

Another safety valve is more surprising. Like their modern counterparts, the ancient Egyptians had a marked satirical streak, and this could extend as far as the crown. The ribald stories told about King Amasis, which are preserved in Herodotus, are in an honored tradition, and it is probable that wise rulers tolerated such excesses and even encouraged them; it is difficult to fear and resent a king whose honeymoon with a foreigner was ruined by drink, or who went for boat trips rowed by girls dressed only in nets. A further palliative to the system seems to have been that everyone, at least in theory, had the right to appeal to pharaoh. A slightly cynical maxim advises the vizier, who was effectively the king's deputy, never to reject a petitioner, on the grounds that he

would rather be heard attentively than have his complaint put right. Accounts of the assemblies (*majlis*) of modern Middle Eastern rulers often show a remarkable degree of blunt speech from humble complainants. A similar latitude may well have been allowed in ancient Egypt.

Egypt saw some pharaohs deposed, and at least one attempted assassination is known, but the system lasted, in all its grandeur and humanity, for nearly three millennia. The France of the ancient Near East never met its 1789.

ABOVE: King Ramesses II (1279–1213 BC) receives the royal insignia heket *("crook" or sceptre) and* nekhakha *("flail," flagellum, or lash) and a scimitar (sword) from the enthroned god Amun-Re who also holds a wand with symbols indicating "a million of royal jubilees." The goddess Mut stands behind Amun-Re. Such highly symbolic scenes are typical of Egyptian temple decoration. In the Ramesseum (the king's mortuary temple) at Thebes. C. M. DIXON*

PHARAOH: THE "GREAT HOUSE"

The basis of wealth in ancient Egypt was land, and in theory all land belonged to the king. This principle is suggested in non-Egyptian sources, and it is consistent with what we know from pharaonic and Ptolemaic texts. (The same principle, strictly speaking, holds true in modern England.) Land was considered to be either crown land or land relinquished to other institutions, notably temples and other foundations. Reclaimed, confiscated, or conquered land automatically devolved to the crown. Private persons held land under these terms and in practice could buy, sell, or dispose of land as if it were their own. However, this was not legal ownership, but usufruct (the right to enjoy the yield). Persons and perhaps institutions owed work to the state under the forced-labor system known as corvée, and it is possible that corvée was the legal payment in return for usufruct on the land. Ancient Egypt was far from being a democracy, but most regimes feel the need for a legal basis for their exactions, so that the system can be seen as fair. Corvée could be exempted, substituted, or replaced by other dues, and a category of funerary servant-figures known as *shabtis* was created to avoid this obligation in the next world. In addition, almost all land paid tax on its produce. This tax was payable to the crown, and fields were assessed by size, type of crop, and the height of the Nile inundation in a particular province and a particular year. A whole bureaucracy was brought into being in order to effect the collection of this tax. The land-owning sections of Egypt were known as "houses" (*prw*, singular *pr*). A *pr* could be an individual estate, a temple, or even a town, although royal foundations were normally designated by another term. Superior to all such "houses" was *pr ʿ3*, "the great (or greatest) house," which alone could levy the land tax. This institution was the royal court itself, and the term is commonly applied to the palace and its administration. From the time of Akhenaten (1353–1337 BC) the phrase is increasingly applied to the king, passing through Hebrew and Greek to become modern "pharaoh." Control of agriculture and the capacity to levy taxes was the main source of royal power, which owed some of its acceptability to the fact that the king was normally above local or sectional interests. The divine associations of the royal office were doubtless important in this respect. The force of the word "pharaoh" can be measured from the fact that in some contexts it is best translated "state" or even "public." (The main street of even a small town, for example, could be referred to as the road of pharaoh.)

LEFT: *A fragment of a tomb wall from Saqqara dated to the reign of Tutankhamun (1336–1327 BC). Haremhab (future king) is shown being decorated with gold collars as a reward for his military achievements. He wears a formal long wig with a cone of scented fatty substance on top and raises his arms in a triumphant gesture.* LEIDEN MUSEUM OF ANTIQUITIES/PETER CLAYTON

ABOVE: *A black granite statue of King Ramesses II (1279–1213 BC) with small figures of Queen Nefertari and Prince Amen-hirkhopshef next to the king's legs. From the temple of Amun at Karnak.* EGYPTIAN MUSEUM, TURIN/JOHN G. ROSS

LEFT: *A group of dandies of the reign of Tutankhamun (1336–1327 BC) whose refined facial features, delicate hands, and well-fed bodies wrapped in fine linen owe much to the lingering effects of the style of the Amarna period. Nevertheless, the artist could hardly have made a more explicit comment on the sharp social stratification of the Egyptian society. The tomb of Haremhab at Saqqara.* EGYPT EXPLORATION SOCIETY, LONDON

crown, but in reality they were more like government departments than independent units. The pharaohs made regular inventories of temple property, since it was in theory theirs to command. The king, apparently, had the power to confiscate temple wealth, but this was a risky policy, as shown by King Teos, who in 362 BC tried diverting temple property to finance a campaign. The result was a mutiny by the army, the deposition of the king, and the permanent damnation of his memory by the priestly intelligentsia. He might have done better to donate the land to the temples and recover the land tax. The government of ancient Egypt was a balancing act; the good pharaoh was the one who knew how to maintain the proper balance.

The reality was, of course, complicated, but landholding was the basis of the system. Ancient Egypt has sometimes been described as a feudal state, but similarities with medieval Europe are too few to make this comparison comfortable. The phrase "state capitalism" has also been used to characterize the regime, and it is true that the crown regularly donated spare land to institutions such as temples that were in a position to develop it and pay taxes back to the king. The notion of surplus, if not profit, was certainly recognized and approved. Nevertheless, the system was not capitalist in the sense that grew up in modern Europe. Much royal influence took the form of patronage: appointments to offices, confirmation or extension of privileges (on at least one occasion, an official was permitted to kiss the royal foot rather than the ground in front of it), and above all distribution of wealth in the form of largesse or exemptions. Redistribution played a major role in the economy, and it must have reinforced a feeling of joint dependence on the divine monarch, which made for stability and shared values. The king doubtless had the power to remove privileges once granted, but the degree of firmness that he applied to such cases would certainly be noted. The force of a ruler's personality must have been a factor, as must the extent to which he was seen to right abuses by officials. In practice, it was in the king's interest to be thought of as the protector of his people.

Temples were major foundations (that at Karnak is the greatest religious building ever constructed). It has been fashionable to see the temples as a threat to the authority of the

SHABTIS

Jaromir Malek

The themes of persons of a higher social status interceding for humbler people, or delegating their own social duties and obligations to others of a lower rank, were very common in ancient Egyptian culture. *Shabtis* (also *shawabtis* or *ushabtis*) appeared during the first half of the second millennium BC and became an essential tomb equipment for even very ordinary people, so much so that they persisted for nearly 2,000 years. Most of these small funerary statuettes (usually not more than 4 inches/10 cm tall) represented the deceased person wrapped up in mummy bandages, and often holding agricultural implements (hoes and baskets). The texts inscribed on many of them show that their function was to perform forced labor on behalf of the person for whom they had been manufactured, and so act as their owner's substitutes in the next life. Several hundred such figures may have been deposited in a single tomb.

LEFT: *Limestone shabti of a lady called Djymyro c. 1300 BC, probably from Thebes.* ASHMOLEAN MUSEUM, OXFORD

A Beato

THE RISE AND FALL OF EMPIRES

K. A. Kitchen

I TURN TOWARD THE south *and work
a wonder for you,
I make the grandees of Kush serve you,
bringing all their tribute . . .
I turn toward the* north *and work a
wonder for you,
I bring Farthest Asia to you, tribute on
their backs . . . and children . . .
I turn toward the* west *and work a
wonder for you,
I cause you to seize the Libyans . . . they
build in this fortress . . .
I turn toward the* orient *and work a
wonder for you,
I bring Punt to you, with all manner of
sweet spices . . . to beg peace . . .*

So spoke Egypt's "imperial" god Amun of Thebes to King Amenophis III (*c.* 1380 BC) at the pinnacle of Egypt's splendor. The deity directs the enthroned king to each point of the compass and delivers the peoples there and their possessions to him. Within the sinuous Nile Valley and broad Delta, bounded by deserts and the Mediterranean, ancient Egypt is often described as isolated. This statement is but a half-truth: from earliest times, Egypt had contacts on all sides as varied as the peoples themselves. We follow Amun's pointing finger in each direction in turn.

TOWARD THE SOUTH: NUBIA

The relations of Egypt and its southern neighbor Nubia fall into two great epochs: from about 3000 BC to about 1070 BC and from about 650 BC to Roman times. In the intervening four centuries (1070–650 BC), first there were no relations at all, then came a brief period of Nubian rule over Egypt. In the first of the two great epochs, whenever Egypt was weak or not aggressive, Nubia flourished in its own right. But Egypt repeatedly penetrated, then dominated Nubia, increasingly submerging its local culture, though never completely. Raids into Nubia are known from the reign of King Djer (*c.* 2900 BC), and King Snofru (*c.* 2550 BC) boasted of deporting 7,000 Nubians. Later kings established a copper-smelting outpost at Buhen, near the Second Cataract. Under such pressures, Nubia's flourishing culture withered into decline. But by the Sixth Dynasty, Egypt merely sent long-range trading expeditions, reaching the princedom of Yam (well south of the Second Cataract), focus of a renascent Nubia. Later, the powerful Twelfth Dynasty pharaohs imposed their rule to the Second Cataract with a chain of key fortresses, in order to trade in exotic products from farther south in Africa, by

ABOVE: A detail of a large scene showing Nubians bringing tribute to Ramesses II (1279–1213 BC) in the rock-cut temple at Beit el-Wali in Nubia. The structure was removed to the vicinity of the High Dam at Aswan in the early 1960s. Exotic and luxury products for which Nubia was so famous are shown. AUSTRAL/CAMERA PRESS

ABOVE: African prisoners represented in the tomb of General Haremhab (future king), c. 1330 BC. This is one of the reliefs in his tomb at Saqqara that was rediscovered in 1975. EGYPT EXPLORATION SOCIETY, LONDON

RIGHT: A chain of massive fortifications was built at Egypt's southern (Nubian) border, in the area of the Second Nile Cataract, between c. 1980 and 1860 BC. In fact, huge forts such as this one at Buhen were never used for their intended purpose, and may have been primarily power symbols. PETER CLAYTON

now via Kush, successor to Yam. By the sixteenth century BC, lesser Theban kings shared power on the Nile with an expanded Kush in the south and the Hyksos from the Near East in the north.

During the New Kingdom (1540–1069 BC), "imperial" kings overran all of Nubia up to the Fourth Cataract, imposing Egyptian temples, personnel, and culture. Desert gold mining was now the priority. But as pharaoh's agents steadily exhausted most accessible sources of gold, and over-taxed Nubians quietly moved out south beyond Egyptian jurisdiction, the expense of running the Nubian dominion became a liability; and Egyptian rule ceased by 1070 BC, culminating in the last viceroy's revolt. For 300 years, Lower Nubia's narrow line of green along the Nile saw little life. From the eighth century BC onward, Egypto-Nubian relations were radically different. Outwardly adopting Egyptian cultural style, a new Kushite kingdom expanded north, and during the period 715–664 BC it ruled over Egypt (Twenty-fifth Dynasty), only retreating under the hammer blows of Assyria. Rarely in conflict thereafter, the parallel states of Egypt and Nubia (under its capital Napata, then Meroe) went their own ways, bound only by limited trade, until their absorption into new constellations of powers and cultures. Thus the second great epoch, from c. 650 BC onward, stands in great contrast to the ever-changing interrelations of the earlier great period, c. 3000–1070 BC.

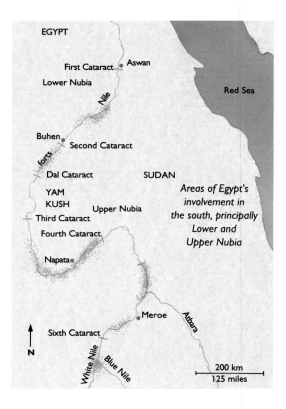

TOWARD THE NORTH: LEVANT AND WESTERN ASIA

From c. 3100 to 1070 BC, trade was Egypt's main bond with the Levant, punctuated by occasional military adventures there. From about 3000 BC until the mid-First Dynasty, Egyptian traders imported themselves and their life style into south Canaanite settlements, building houses with Egyptian-style bricks, and having home-style pottery made locally as well as imported. The name of King Narmer (Menes or his predecessor) has been

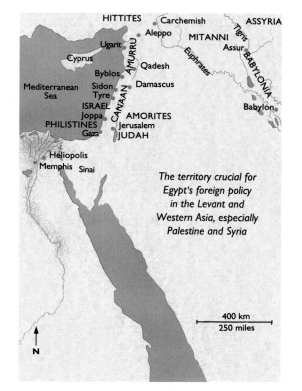

The territory crucial for Egypt's foreign policy in the Levant and Western Asia, especially Palestine and Syria

400 km
250 miles

N

found on jars in such settlements. Later on, Old Kingdom pharaohs shifted their trading north to Syria for Lebanese timber but sometimes still raided Canaan, one official reaching as far as Mount Carmel. Trade and diplomacy dominated Middle Kingdom relations with the Levant, along with occasional raids. Relations with the port of Byblos were especially close; its rulers even adopted the practice of having jewelry and monuments inscribed in Egyptian hieroglyphs with their names and deeds. The Execration Texts (so called because they threatened curses upon all and any hostile folk) show a close knowledge of the principal city-states and tribal groups of Palestine and south Syria. But the Thirteenth Dynasty succumbed to a Levantine takeover by the famous Hyksos kings, who took over the lucrative trade also, with Palestine as well as down into Nubia. Then, on the rebound, fresh warrior pharaohs from Thebes swept the Hyksos out, their armies reaching all the way to the Euphrates, imposing Egyptian rule over Palestine and parts of Syria during c. 1540–1160 BC. That rule was not one of occupation in depth as in Nubia, but of overlordship, with only a few key garrisons at selected points.

The New Kingdom's imperial expansion brought immediate loot from its campaigns. But more economically attractive was the receipt of a regular annual income of tribute from a series of vassal states to pharaoh's coffers. Vassals, of course, needed persuasion — such as regular visits by the pharaoh and his army — to enforce loyalty and payment and to replace would-be rebels. Sons of local rulers were taken to Egypt as

ABOVE: A "geographical list" of localities in the Syro-Palestinian region, personified as crenellated enclosures, with their names written inside, and surmounted by the torsos of bound Asiatic captives, on the sixth pylon (monumental gateway), built by Tuthmosis III (1479–1425 BC) in the temple of Amun at Karnak.
H. CHAMPOLLION

LEFT: A hoard of gold, silver, and lapis lazuli jewelry, dating to the reign of Amenemhet II (1918–1884 BC), was found in the temple at Tod in 1936. At least some of the items may have reached Egypt as foreign tribute or war booty, possibly from Western Asia or the Aegean. A fascinating possibility of interpretation of this discovery has now presented itself because the recently (1991) recorded "annals" of Amenemhet II at Memphis may mention events connected with this treasure.
LOUVRE MUSEUM, PARIS/PHOTO R.M.N.

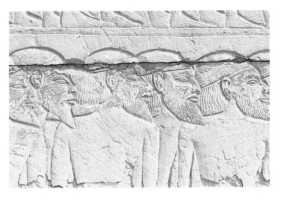

ABOVE: *A tremendous increase in Egyptian military activities in the second half of the second millennium BC was accompanied by improvements in weaponry and military organization. A new bronze battle-axe with a much increased penetrative power was introduced around 1600 BC. The illustrated example is inscribed with the name of King Amosis (1550–1525 BC) and comes from Dra Abu 'l-Naga.* ASHMOLEAN MUSEUM, OXFORD

RIGHT: *Naval battle between the Egyptians under Ramesses III (1184–1153 BC) and the "Sea Peoples," represented on the exterior wall of the king's mortuary temple at Medinet Habu.* H. CHAMPOLLION

hostages, to be sent home to rule at their fathers' deaths. Such men sometimes became imbued with a taste for Egyptian culture and rule and instinctively turned to Egypt when difficulties beset them. Under Akhenaten (obsessed with his exclusivist sun-worship and intolerance of traditional gods), some vassals "opted out," and most of Syria was lost to the Hittites of Anatolia. The Ramessid kings (*c.* 1295–1069 BC, of the Nineteenth and Twentieth Dynasties, so called because the majority of them bore the name Ramesses) sought to regain northern Syria, but after the battle of Qadesh, even Ramesses II had (eventually) to concede its permanent loss to the Hittites.

During the fourteenth and thirteenth centuries BC, the ancient Near East was made up of lesser nations and "superpowers," the rulers of the latter being entitled to the epithet "Great King." Equals addressed each other as "Brother;" inferiors were addressed as "Son," superiors as "Father." Regular diplomatic contacts were maintained through national representatives at foreign courts linked by traveling envoys. Such messengers also linked vassals and overlords. The brotherhood of "Great Kings" required its own "philosophical" framework, inevitably a religious one in the ancient Near East. Thus, each chief god of the pantheons of the superpowers was termed "father of the forefathers" of the respective reigning ruler: Amun for the pharaoh of Egypt, the storm-god of Hatti for the Hittite king, Ashur for the kings of Assyria, Marduk for the kings of Babylon, and Teshub for the ruler of the Syro-Mesopotamian kingdom of Mitanni. The East Mediterranean upheavals of *c.* 1220–1180 BC ended this concert of powers. Egyptian rule in Palestine ended after Ramesses IV or Ramesses VI, leaving Palestine to local rivalries among Philistines (largely on the southern coast; the designation Palestine derives from their name), Israel, Canaanites, and Arameans (mainly in northern and northeastern Palestine and southwestern Syria).

During the early first millennium BC, a more introverted Egypt rarely intervened

in the Levant. Siamun may have acted against the Philistines, Shoshenq I certainly intervened against Israel and Judah in the tenth century BC, and Necho II clashed with Babylon in the Levant in the seventh century BC. But otherwise Egypt was content only to trade in the Near East and to use its petty states as buffers between itself and Assyria — until in due time all alike were swallowed up by imperial Persia.

TOWARD THE WEST:
LIBYA AND THE AEGEAN

Along the North African coast, west of the Egyptian Delta, there extended a limited coastal zone between the Mediterranean and the desert: ancient Libya. In earliest times its people had close links with the western Delta, but pharaonic civilization forged ahead of Libya (as it did with Nubia). During the Old and Middle kingdoms (third to early second millennia BC), a generally peaceful coexistence was punctuated by occasional wars: the pharaohs would march against Libya's inhabitants, the Temehu or Tehenu people, perhaps to dissuade them from trying to settle in the richer lands of the Delta. Such a clash perhaps occurred at the start of the New Kingdom, but relations during the first 250 years remain unknown to us and hence probably

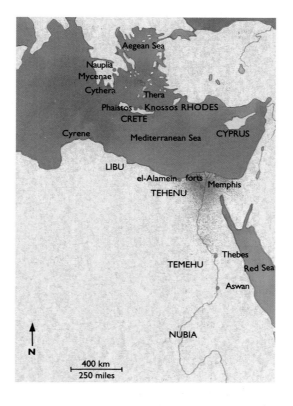

LEFT: *Map of the areas of Egypt's interest in Libya and in the Aegean.*

peaceful. Under Sethos I (1294–1279 BC), things changed dramatically; he launched a full-scale campaign against the land of Tehenu where the names of new tribes were recorded for the first time (including the tribe of Libu, ancestor of our term Libya). Peoples from across the Mediterranean had added to Libya's population, and land hunger probably had driven them to the Egyptian Delta, so

LEFT: *Faience tiles with foreign captives (from the left, a Libyan, a Nubian, a Syrian, a Shasu-bedouin of the Syro-Palestinian region, and a Hittite), from the temple–palace of Ramesses III (1183–1153 BC) at Medinet Habu. Representations of foreigners were placed on the steps leading up to the royal throne so that they would be trodden on, symbolically reinforcing the theme of the all-conquering king. THE EGYPTIAN MUSEUM, CAIRO/JÜRGEN LIEPE*

EGYPTIAN "WAR AND PEACE"

At young Tutankhamun's death (without heir) in 1327 BC, his widow sent to the Hittite emperor asking that a son of the Anatolian king marry her and be next pharaoh. The son was murdered on arrival in Egypt. The outraged Hittite ruler then declared war on Egypt. Hostility smoldered for decades, bursting again into flame when Sethos I flung himself and his troops into Syria, capturing the long-lost land of Amurru (modern Lebanon and environs) and even the key city-state of Qadesh from Hittite control. But under Hittite pressure Egypt had to compromise, leaving Amurru and Qadesh in Hittite hands but retaining rule in central Phoenicia.

This situation much displeased Sethos's ambitious son and successor, Ramesses II (1279–1213 BC). In the fourth year of his reign, he quickly recovered Amurru; he then set out for Qadesh the following year to repeat his father's exploits. That was not to be. In the interim, the Hittite king Muwatallis had prepared a trap as Ramesses neared Qadesh. Two false Hittite "spies" allowed themselves to be captured, telling Ramesses that the Hittite king was skulking in fear many leagues to the north. Ramesses raced recklessly ahead with household retainers and one division, the other divisions straggling along at intervals behind him. But, of course, the wily Hittite was hard by Qadesh itself — and now threw his crack chariotry across the Orontes River to attack

ABOVE: *The fortified city of Qadesh, with the massed Hittite infantry of some 8,000 men, not taking part in the battle, in the foreground. On the pylon (monumental gateway) of the temple at Luxor.* H. CHAMPOLLION

Ramesses and his camp at this vulnerable moment. Even as they were on the way, Egyptian guards caught two real Hittite spies and beat the unwelcome truth out of them: the Hittites were upon them! As the Hittites plowed through one Egyptian division and approached his camp (panicking another division), Ramesses rallied his immediate supporters to push the enemy back with desperate gallantry. At that moment, an auxiliary force arrived in good order "from the shore of Amurru," to the west. Their timely help turned the tide. With their aid, Ramesses stopped the Hittite force and then routed them back to the river in an undignified scramble for the opposite bank. The next day, it was the turn of Ramesses to mount a "set piece" attack on the Hittites, but to no avail — they stood their ground. Muwatallis proposed peace, probably on the same terms as his father had to Sethos I. This Ramesses would have none of, and he marched back to Egypt with no Qadesh. The Hittite triumph, too, was hollow, as Assyria took over one of their protectorates. In the years that followed, Ramesses regained control of his south Syrian possessions, but repeated campaigns in north Syria (outflanking Qadesh) gained him nothing.

The next Hittite ruler, Hattusil III, found himself at war on two fronts: Egypt and Assyria. To bow to Assyria was unthinkable, but peace with Egypt was not inconceivable.

LEFT: *Ramesses II countercharging the Hittite chariotry in an attempt to break out of the encirclement and join the Egyptian forces still en route to Qadesh. On the pylon (monumental gateway) of the temple at Luxor.* H. CHAMPOLLION

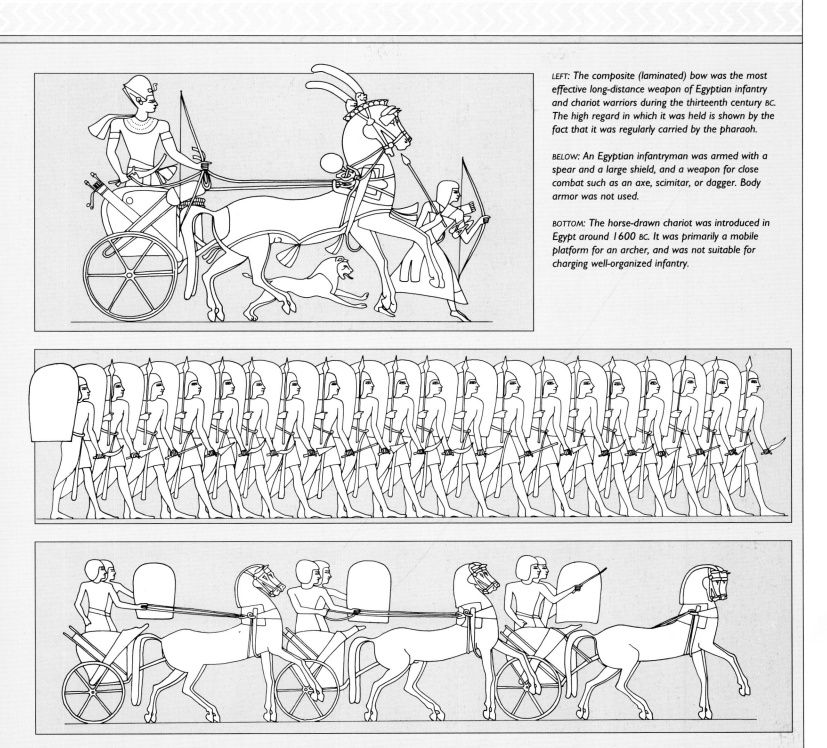

LEFT: The composite (laminated) bow was the most effective long-distance weapon of Egyptian infantry and chariot warriors during the thirteenth century BC. The high regard in which it was held is shown by the fact that it was regularly carried by the pharaoh.

BELOW: An Egyptian infantryman was armed with a spear and a large shield, and a weapon for close combat such as an axe, scimitar, or dagger. Body armor was not used.

BOTTOM: The horse-drawn chariot was introduced in Egypt around 1600 BC. It was primarily a mobile platform for an archer, and was not suitable for charging well-organized infantry.

So came the historic treaty of peace and alliance between Hatti and Egypt in the twenty-first year of Ramesses II, attended by much official rejoicing and messages of congratulation between the two royal courts. After 75 years of conflict, this was a momentous event.

A dozen years later, relations were so good that Hattusil III offered his eldest daughter's hand in marriage to Ramesses II. Negotiations again took time; at one point,

the ebullient Ramesses scandalized the Hittite queen by saying (in effect) "if you can't send the girl, at least send the dowry!" However, in the year 34, the princess finally arrived, and "she was beautiful in His Majesty's opinion, and he loved her to distraction." Still later, Ramesses married a second Hittite princess, accompanied by a fabulous dowry, as highly poetic inscriptions tell us with gusto. The fame of these marriages lasted a thousand years — in the

fourth century BC, in Thebes, the priests of the god Khons wove a tale about the healing abilities of their god around Ramesses and the princesses of "Bakhtan." The tale reflected one gain the Hittites made from the peace — they could draw upon the medical skills of Egyptian physicians, the high technology of that age. For its part, Egypt doubtless gained from trade with the entire Levant, Egyptian and Hittite, in this sunset age of peace.

ABOVE: A group of Amu-nomads represented in the tomb of Khnemhotpe at Beni Hasan, 1880 BC. The inscription accompanying the scene refers to an expedition organized in order to procure material for the preparation of dark eye-paint, perhaps galena from the Gebel el-Zeit area on the coast of the Red Sea. The Bedouin would have been encountered during such expeditions.
H. CHAMPOLLION

RIGHT: A pictorial record of the land of Punt is found in the mortuary temple of Queen Hatshepsut (1479–1457 BC) at Deir el-Bahri. Some of the remarkable details of its fauna and flora provide clues to its location. Among the represent-ations of its inhabitants is Ity, the wife of the "Chief of Punt." The original relief has been removed and is now in the Egyptian Museum in Cairo.
WERNER FORMAN ARCHIVE.

once more the pharaohs sought to defend their land from encroachment. Ramesses II (1279–1213 BC) established a line of "foreign legionary" forts all the way out west to el-Alamein, to keep vigil over Libyan movements. Merneptah (1213–1203 BC) and Ramesses III (1184–1153 BC) had to engage in wars there to ward off the threat of invasion. But military victory did not relieve the pressure in Libya, and infiltration replaced invasion. Libyan prisoners and settlers became important in postimperial Egypt, providing it with the Twenty-second to Twenty-fourth dynasties of kings. Thereafter, but for a clash under Psammetichus I (664–610 BC), relations relaxed, as the Libyan element was gradually absorbed into the Egyptian populace and culture.

Across the blue Mediterranean, there developed the Minoan and Mycenaean civilizations of the Aegean isles and mainland Greece. Minoan traders reached Egypt in the Middle Kingdom, and interchange continued in the New Kingdom. There was some indirect mutual impact in art; Aegean ships in the paintings on the island of Thera (or Santorini, in the Cyclades, destroyed by a volcanic eruption) show some influence of Egyptian and Near Eastern nautical tradition, while Aegean artistic features (such as outlined rocks and the flying gallop) occasionally enlivened Egyptian art. Cretan envoys were even shown in

Egyptian tombs. Egyptian place-name lists include Knossos, Lyktos, and perhaps Phaistos in Crete, plus Cythera, Nauplia, and Mycenae itself. Although never conquerors in the Aegean, the Egyptians did build up a knowledge of its towns and ports. The eclipse of the Aegean cultures from 1200 BC led to a long gap in relations until the period from the seventh century BC onward, when classical Greece became Egypt's trading partner and sometimes ally against Persia — until Alexander took all, and the Ptolemies (305–30 BC) inherited Egypt down to the conquest by Rome.

TOWARD THE ORIENT: PUNT AND THE RED SEA

In all periods, Egyptians exploited the arid deserts that lay between their fertile Nile Valley and the enervating heat of the Red Sea. Farthest north, just east of the Delta, the rocky peninsula of Sinai was exploited for almost 2,000 years, from the First Dynasty to the Twentieth, for its deposits of brilliant bluish tur-quoise. Much farther south, the valley of Wadi Hammamat linked both river valley and seacoast at their nearest point and provided schistlike stone for statuary and buildings. Desert exploration here and southward led to gold mining and the search for a variety of semiprecious stones — besides Sinai turquoise, there were carnelian, amethyst, and others.

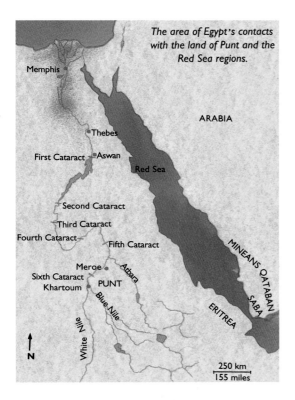

The area of Egypt's contacts with the land of Punt and the Red Sea regions.

The Nubian eastern deserts yielded still more gold.

But southeastern connections reached much farther. Already in late prehistory, glittering black obsidian stone was traded up from the south end of the Red Sea, from Ethiopia and (indirectly) from southern Arabia. This trade did not last, but the Egyptians retained the memory of exotica. So, from the Old Kingdom onward, the pharaohs sent expeditions down the Red Sea to Punt, mainly to bring back aromatics (myrrh, incense) as well as gold, leopard skins, and exotic creatures. The Middle Kingdom pharaohs established a seaport on the Red Sea coast for the dispatch of expeditions to Punt. But where was Punt? In the light of current knowledge, Punt seems clearly to be located along the Red Sea coast of Sudan and Eritrea, and inland, westward from that coast, embracing the northwest part of the Ethiopian highlands and the Sudan plains to the Nile south of Khartoum. Rain that fell on the "Mountains of Punt" drained into the Nile — which definitively excludes the old theories that located Punt in Arabia or Somaliland. As early as the New Kingdom, the only possible tenuous link with ancient Arabia may have been the fleeting visit by the Genebtyu people, bringing aromatics to Egypt in the time

of Tuthmosis III (1479–1425 BC), if they were distant ancestors of the later Gebbanitae of southern Arabia, mentioned by Pliny, the Roman statesman and scholar (AD 23–79). The newly emerging evidence for a Bronze Age western Arabia in the second millennium BC makes this now conceivable.

Punt's great distance from Egypt precluded military conquest — relations seem always to have been mercantile and peaceful. And relations were not all one-way: Puntites came north to trade in their simple sailing vessels, as Theban tomb paintings make clear. The most evocative record of Punt is the great set of sculptured scenes in Queen Hatshepsut's temple at Deir el-Bahri in western Thebes, showing the local huts on stilts, the Red Sea fish, the aromatic trees, the exotic fauna (giraffes, rhinos, baboons), as well as the Puntites themselves, who appear to be of African stock. Ramesses III (c. 1180 BC) records the last known link with Punt. Thereafter, Egypt ceased sending state expeditions so far away; and conditions in East Africa also changed. Not till the time of the Ptolemies did sailing enterprises again brave the Red Sea, linking up with the old South Arabian incense trade of the South Arabian kingdoms of Saba, Qataban, and the Mineans; then, in Roman times, the monsoon trade route to the wealth of India opened up a vastly wider world.

Their dealings with their neighbors during all periods show the ancient Egyptians to have been by no means the starry-eyed, colorless idealists obsessed with death and religion that some moderns imagine. Rather, they were hard-headed realists, and economic gain was often their main motivation in relationships abroad, whether (as most of the time) through regular trade or (at certain times) by imperial conquest, ideologically formulated as "widening the frontiers of Egypt" at the behest of the god Amun by the valor of his son, the victorious pharaoh. The surviving records of those relationships, both texts and pictures (supplemented by discovery of imported artifacts), offer a treasury of information on Egypt's neighbors in antiquity as well as about Egypt itself.

ABOVE: *A colossal statue of the Persian king Darius I (521–486 BC) during whose reign Egypt was part of the Persian empire. The statue was found at Susa in western Iran, and is inscribed in Egyptian hieroglyphs and the cuneiform script (Old Persian, Elamite, and Akkadian). The statue's Egyptian style is unmistakable, although the garment and the boots are Persian.*
MUSEUM IRAN BASTAN, TEHERAN/MICHAEL ROAF

THE WORLD OF THE GODS

Waltraud Guglielmi

EGYPTIAN RELIGION CAN be followed across a longer period than any other religion — its deities were revered for well over 3,000 years. Throughout this period, names and iconography remained largely constant, and the external appearance of temples also changed little; thus a text in the temple of Edfu, built by kings of the Ptolemaic Dynasty (third to first centuries BC) and almost perfectly preserved, asserts that it was erected according to a design of the architect Imhotep from the time of King Djoser (2628–2609 BC), almost 2,500 years earlier. This immutability and constancy, the expression of an unbroken cultural identity, made an impact even on classical travelers. Herodotus was overwhelmed by the piety of the Egyptians and fascinated by the embrace of the religion that permeated virtually every sphere of the culture. The Egyptian sense of the religious has also found its way into Judeo-Christian tradition; it is highly probable that the sun hymn of Akhenaten is echoed in Psalm 104 and the *Instruction of Amenemope* in Proverbs 22:17–23:11.

But the myriad guises and especially the animal forms of Egyptian deities also elicited a response of disgust. In the second century AD Lucian, a much traveled Greek writer (born at Samosata in Syria) mocked the dog- and cat-headed deities and made fun of the dog-headed Anubis, the "howler." Whereas Lucian took the manifestation in animal form for the divinity itself, other authors display a different evaluation of the phenomenon. Plutarch construed the animal form as a symbol for particular superhuman qualities ascribed to deities. Beside deities with animal heads such as the crocodile-headed Sobek, snake-headed Renenutet, and ibis-headed Thoth, there are also deities in purely human form, such as Isis and Osiris, as well as deities in purely animal form, such as the Apis bull or the scarab beetle, an incarnation of the sun-god Kheper. Cosmic phenomena and heavenly bodies could also be forms of deities, for example, the sun-god or Sothis, the star Sirius that heralds the Nile flood. The number of deities is infinite; the Egyptians spoke of "millions" and never attempted to compile a catalog of them all. Although innumerable religious texts are attested, the Egyptian religion was a religion not of the book but of the cult — the gods were worshiped in their images. Egypt was the classic land of the Golden Calf.

Deities cannot be explained merely in terms of their form or cult place; Amun, principal deity of the New Kingdom and "king of the gods" of Karnak, is usually

TOP: The god Bes in the **mammisi** *("birth-house") of the temple of Hathor at Dendara, second century BC. THE IMAGE BANK/ALAIN CHOISNET*

ABOVE: The head of a gold temple image of the god Horus represented as a hawk, probably c. 2250 BC, with later modifications. THE EGYPTIAN MUSEUM, CAIRO/JOHN G. ROSS

OPPOSITE: Statue of the god Ptah, made of gilt wood, blue faience, and bronze. Found in the tomb of Tutankhamun (1336–1327 BC) in the Valley of the Kings. THE EGYPTIAN MUSEUM, CAIRO/THE IMAGE BANK/CO RENTMEESTER

represented as a man wearing a tall plumed crown but can also be shown as a ram or a goose. Hathor, goddess of the sky and of love, appears usually in the guise of a cow but can also be worshiped as a snake or in her cult object, the sistrum (ceremonial rattle). The cow form can then also be assumed by other sky goddesses such as Nut, Methyer, and Neith.

Egyptian deities lack the fixed character that the Greek deities tend to have. The gods can intertwine and meld together like fields of energy. For example, Isis tends to be identified with Hathor in the later periods. Names and epithets also fuse in the case of the so-called syncretistic deities, where one deity becomes the aspect of another. Thus in the combination Ptah–Sokar–Osiris the Memphite funerary god Sokar becomes an aspect of Ptah, the city-god of Memphis, and simultaneously the Memphite aspect of Osiris, universal god of the dead.

In contrast to our concept of god as utterly otherworldly, Egyptian deities are conceived as present within the world, in cosmic manifestations, in animals and plants, in cult objects and their statues, and indeed in the king who was taken to be the earthly incarnation of the god Horus. The king is divine as bearer of the office, because in him a god is made manifest, but he is not himself a god other than in exceptional circumstances.

THE DIMENSIONS OF KNOWING GOD

In a model developed by the German Egyptologist Jan Assmann, the divine has four dimensions.

The Cultic or Local Dimension

Each main deity plays the role of landlord and owner of a temple, which it inhabits in the form of its cult image, shielded in the sanctuary from all that is profane and serviced by priests bound to strict regulations for purity. A ritual comprising 66 sections and attested in several manuscripts and temple reliefs shows that the daily service for the cult image was conducted the same way in all temples from the New Kingdom (1540–1069 BC) and that the service was performed as a means of communication among gods, not between humans and

god. According to this idea, the king constantly plays the role of a god, a part then taken in practice by a priest as his substitute.

The cult image was borne into the outside world only on festival days, on a portable shrine but still concealed by a curtain. Each temple presents two architectural ideas: it is the hidden dwelling-place of god, and it is a processional way for the sacred barque. At the same time, in mythological terms, it embodies the "primeval mound," the place upon which the divine came to rest at the beginning of the world when it arose out of Nun, the primeval waters. In the cultic dimension the gods are local lords, gods of cities and nomes (districts), and together they constitute the symbolic representation of the land. The symbolic presence of the gods occurs in their cult images and reliefs and is understood as a temporary habitation.

The Cosmic Dimension

The cult performed in the temple also has a bearing on cosmic events. It is intended to keep the course of the world in motion, as in the rising and setting of the sun or the flooding of the Nile at the right time and to the right height. Therefore, each temple is also made to appear as an image of the cosmos, and each main deity has a connection with a cosmic phenomenon. Included are not only cosmic deities proper, such as Nut the sky-goddess, Geb the earth-god, Shu the air-god, Re the sun-god, or the moon-gods Khons and Thoth, but also gods at work in nature such as Hapy, the god of the Nile flood, or the god Ptah, who incorporates the creativity of the earth and is patron of artists and craftworkers. To the Egyptians, cosmos and nature appear as a web of actions of miscellaneous powers, the benevolent and the harmful, in which gods operate. Nature and distant transcendental heaven are thus understood not as a single "world" or "cosmos" but as a plurality, the action of many deities. The goddess Nut is not just the sky but what the sky does; she gives birth to the sun and the stars and holds them within her, thus being also a mother and funerary goddess. The work of the sun-god receives expression not only in the daily cycle of the sun, but also in the nurturing of food on earth.

LEFT: Marble statue of the god Anubis, recognizable by the jackal ("dog") head and a moon disk, in a Roman reinterpretation of ancient Egyptian iconography of the deity. Second century AD. EGYPTIAN MUSEUM, VATICAN/C. M. DIXON

BELOW: The temple of the goddess Satis at Elephantine in the First Nile Cataract area. The veneration of the goddess and the development of the sanctuary can be followed from a simple rock niche, perhaps as early as c. 2900 BC through the rest of ancient Egyptian history. H. CHAMPOLLION

FUNERARY BELIEFS

In the Egyptian conception, death was not the end of life but the threshold to a new otherwordly existence. Extensive funerary practices and rituals surrounded this threshold. Since bodily integrity was part of the otherwordly form of existence, the body was conserved, that is to say, mummified. The dead hoped to be able to rise as a "transfigured" body from the preserved mummy that was prepared for the dangerous journey into the other world. A central role was played by the construction of the tomb, the "house of eternity" to which the embalmed body was conveyed after 70 days.

BELOW: Spell 15 (a hymn to the sun-god Re) and a vignette (illustration) from a papyrus with the text of the Book of the Dead, c. 1300 BC. The "Overseer of the army of the Lord of the Two Lands (Upper and Lower Egypt)," Nakht, and his wife, the "Songstress of the god Amun," Tuiu, before the seated god Osiris and the goddess Maet. Behind them, the Goddess of the West is shown receiving the setting sun into her outstretched arms. BRITISH MUSEUM, LONDON

The tomb meant more than a place of burial; it was a visible sign of social status and contained the autobiography summarizing the earthly life of the deceased, to enable the person to proceed before posterity and in the other world. At the same time, it immortalized the individuality of the deceased not only in the form of the mummy in the sarcophagus chamber, but also in the inscriptions, representations, and statues that amounted to substitutes for the body of the deceased.

Whereas in the Old Kingdom (2647–2124 BC) an afterlife was guaranteed by the king who therefore arranged for an elaborate burial, in the Middle Kingdom (2040–1648 BC) the special immortality of the king gave way to a form in which the ordinary dead could share through the democratization of the Osiris religion. Each person became an Osiris through death and the completion of the necessary rites. Survival was determined by sharing in the fate of Osiris, and the idea of immortality became accessible to everyone.

Just as in the mythical trial Osiris received justice against his murderer, Seth, and gained dominion over the underworld, so too the deceased received status in the other world. The tribunal in the other world with its principle of justification was extended and made more overtly ethical in the New Kingdom to become a general tribunal of the dead to which everyone, including the king, had to answer. The deceased had to justify themselves before a divine accuser by setting out a denial of sins, including sins against the community, temple, and cult as well as sexual deviations. In this process the heart of the deceased, considered the seat of consciousness, was weighed against *maet*, "truth," symbolized by a feather. If the deceased had committed sins, the heart sank under the weight and the light feather rose. In the instance of conviction by 42 judges of the other world, the deceased suffered damnation, a second death, and was devoured by a monster called the "Gobbler."

The other world was now a combination

of the celestial afterlife of the king and the underworld of Osiris. Before the longed-for approach to Osiris or Re in the solar barque, there was featured the journey through the other world, which the deceased could only overcome through knowledge. The purpose of the spells on Middle Kingdom coffins and New Kingdom papyri lay above all in equipping the deceased with the knowledge and spells to protect them from the dangers of the other world and to allow them to pass trials. The Osirian underworld was guarded by demons and monsters. The idea of the underworld was bound to that of regeneration from the time of the Middle Kingdom. The central image of the solar cycle in which the sun-god dies and is reborn anew each day was expanded around the motif of the midnight reunion of Osiris and Re.

In the Old Kingdom the bearer of otherworldly existence of the person was the *ka*, a type of life energy dependent on material provisioning of the deceased. The *ka* inhabited a statue, received food and drink,

ABOVE: *Judgment scene c. 1050–950 BC from a papyrus with the text of the* Book of the Dead *of the "Songstress of Amun," Anhay. The deceased is brought before Ptah–Sokar–Osiris by the god Horus–Thoth. Her heart is being weighed against* maet *(represented by a small figure of the goddess) by the jackal-headed Anubis. The female monster Ammit ("Gobbler") waits hopefully for the result that will be recorded by the ibis-headed god, Thoth. On the right, Anhay raises her arms in jubilation at the successful outcome of the judgment (indicated by the ostrich* maet *feathers in her hands and suspended from her elbow), "protected" by the Goddess of the West.* BRITISH MUSEUM, LONDON

and communicated with the living. Beyond this the otherwordly form of existence was above all the *ba*, a type of external soul. The *ba* manifested itself most often as a bird or a human-headed bird and stood for the longed-for freedom of movement. The deceased undertook the underworld journey as *ba* in the retinue of Osiris and the sun-god and joined the world of the gods. For material nourishment the *ba* needed only water and was enticed by water emplacements in the necropolis to reunite with the mummy that it had left at death.

Although the existence of the gods seems never to have been doubted, the Middle Kingdom witnessed the awakening of skeptical voices over the material measures taken against death and the concept of a real presence in the other world.

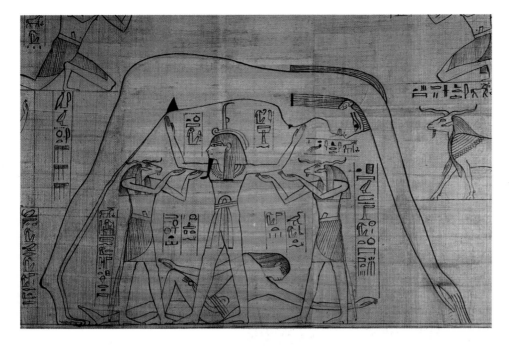

ABOVE: *The air-god Shu separating the sky-goddess Nut and the earth-god Geb, in a vignette (illustration) on the funerary papyrus of the "First chief of the female personnel of the god Amun-Re," Nesi-tanebt-ashru, c. 950 BC. Her papyrus contains spells from the* Book of the Dead *and the* Pyramid Texts. BRITISH MUSEUM, LONDON

ABOVE: *The god Harsiesi with Nefertari, in her tomb in the Valley of the Queens.* AUSTRAL/SIPA

RIGHT: *The goddess Isis with Nefertari, one of the wives of Ramesses II (1279– 1213 BC), in her tomb in the Valley of the Queens at Thebes.* AUSTRAL/SIPA

In this dimension, the role of the king consists of helping to bring to fruition the cosmic order, which like the social order is encapsulated in the word *maet*; he acts not only in the cosmos but also in history. Thus the political enemies of Egypt and the enemies of the sun-god are identified with one another; a victory of pharaoh over the Libyans is therefore celebrated as restoration of the cosmic order.

The Mythical Dimension

In the mythical dimension the personal aspect of the gods takes the foreground. Texts on deities rarely assume the form of a continuous narrative; the sole connected related myth is the Osiris myth, preserved for us in the Greek language by Plutarch. Egyptian texts concerning deities present something more general, a forerunner of myth. They include everything that can be stated about a deity: its name, its stock epithets, its status and role within the world of the gods, and its "constellation," i.e., activity and life history in the community of the gods. Thus the god Osiris is unthinkable without his brother Seth, who murdered him, or his sister and wife Isis, who buried and transfigured him (performed the rites) and conceived from his corpse their son, Horus. Osiris is, indeed, unthinkable without Horus himself, who avenged him and triumphed over Seth. These constellations are immediately related to the arrangements of the human world, prototypes of human patterns of behavior. Thus every dead person becomes Osiris through the conduct of funeral and transfiguration rites, and every son takes up the role of Horus in this context. The king is called Horus and is the son of the gods; therefore all cult, and not just funerary cult, is built on the father–son "constellation." The triumph of Horus carries within it the end of conflict and the inauguration of a new age of well-being and peace; it represents the model for the accession of the new king. In healing magic the patient takes the part of the helpless child Horus, Isis taking the role of the doctor. This Horus–Isis "constellation" is often reproduced in images and provides a direct antecedent to the representation of the Madonna with the child Jesus.

Myths are intended to make clear the meaningful structure of the world; they are set in a timeless past but refer to the present. Of the versions of the creation, that of Heliopolis is the oldest; it casts the world as an emanation of the primeval god Atum, who produces out of himself the first pair of deities, the air-god Shu and moisture Tefnut, who then produce the earth Geb and the sky Nut; their children in turn are Osiris, Isis, Seth, and Nephthys. The names Shu and Tefnut are later replaced by the concepts "life" and "order" (maet), and so express the notion that life and order operate in the cosmic process. The *Book of the Heavenly Cow* describes how the separation of humans and gods came about, producing the human condition characterized by suffering and conflict. Together with the biblical tale of the flood, it belongs to primeval guilt myths, and in it humankind is saved only by a ruse.

Personal Piety

After a number of antecedents in the early Eighteenth Dynasty, there arose in the New Kingdom a new religious movement supplementary to the official temple cult; the term "personal piety" has become entrenched as the label for it, the fourth way of knowing god. It is based on the perception of a personal god in life, a god who intervenes to determine destiny in the life of the individual and who is close in his workings to the person who prays to him; thus it is based on a new image of humanity as dependent on god for its actions. This reciprocity in the relation of god to human beings, the personal approach of humans to god, and the merciful grace of god to humans, represents a new departure in Egyptian religion, reaching full breakthrough in the Ramessid period (1295–1069 BC). It goes hand in hand with a new perception of the world and a feeling of insecurity in life. Instead of being locked into the all-embracing order of *maet*, human life is now directly dependent upon god. The future is unknowable and thus placed in the hand of god; the world no longer earns any trust because the immanent order no longer holds any value.

Two phenomena are characteristic of personal piety: the oracle from the deity and the prayer of the person with a confession, generally inscribed upon a stela (inscription on stone). Both are products of a need for immediate access to god. The stelae often present particular emblems, such as ears that symbolize the plea for the hearing of the prayer or its

fulfillment, or again the divine eyes in human form that symbolize omniscience.

In essence, personal piety was not tied to any particular place and was practiced in the private domain, as demonstrated by small items such as scarabs worn in daily life as rings with inscribed maxims (for example, "Amun is the strength of the lonely," "There is no refuge for my

MUMMIFICATION

Jaromir Malek

The preservation of the body was essential for the survival of the *ka*, *ba*, (see page 93) and other "modes of human existence," and mummification (embalming) of the more privileged dead was practiced throughout Egyptian history. The forms and methods varied widely according to the period and the person's means. Traditionally, 70 days passed between the death and funeral. The most important part of the complicated embalming process was dehydration of the body, which was probably effected by dry natron (a naturally occurring dehydrating agent, a compound of sodium carbonate and sodium bicarbonate). The application of various exotic embalming materials such as resins, oils, myrrh, and incense was, contrary to popular belief, less essential for the desired practical result. Finally, the body was wrapped up in elaborate bandages (in later periods some of these were inscribed with texts from the *Book of the Dead*). Amulets were added between the bandages for the body's protection.

The earliest attempts at the preservation of bodies, after c. 2900 BC, consisted of wrapping them in many layers of linen. Around 2500 BC the internal organs began to be removed and placed in four containers ("canopic jars"). The evisceration was accomplished through an incision in the left flank. The peak of the embalmer's art was reached around 1000 BC when the brain was also removed and a more lifelike appearance was achieved by means of subcutaneous packing of the body and limbs. A tendency towards formality, as if in recognition of the ultimate futility of the task, became more noticeable from c. the seventh century BC. More and more care was lavished on elaborate bandaging and on sarcophagi and coffins rather than on body preservation.

The largest collection of Egyptian mummies is in the Egyptian Museum in Cairo. The most famous among them are those of the pharaohs and their royal ladies of c. 1550–1000 BC, discovered in their secret hiding places at Deir el-Bahri in 1881 and in the Valley of the Kings in 1898. Exhibiting mummies poses ethical problems. On the one hand, it presents an unparalleled opportunity to be face to face with some of the most famous figures of Egyptian history. On the other hand, it is argued that publicly showing their mummified bodies deprives them of dignity to which they are, just like all other human beings, entitled. Modern Egyptian authorities have vacillated in their views. The

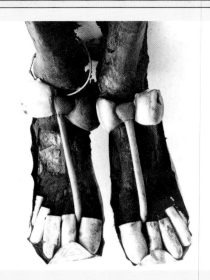

ABOVE: Tutankhamun's feet, with gold sandals decorated by chasing to imitate the rushwork of real sandals, and gold toe-stalls with incised toenails. GRIFFITH INSTITUTE, ASHMOLEAN MUSEUM, OXFORD

royal mummies in the Egyptian Museum in Cairo have not been on show for more than a decade, but the need to encourage tourism and to make visitors happy is a very strong incentive and seems to be winning at present, because there are plans to reopen the display in the near future.

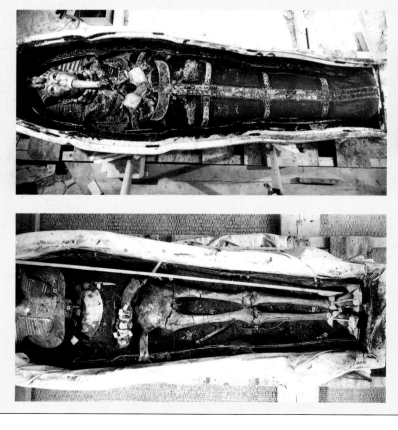

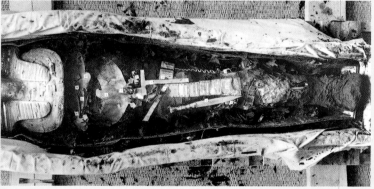

ABOVE LEFT: The mummified body of King Tutankhamun (1336–1327 BC) as it appeared to archaeologists when the lid of the third gold coffin was raised on 28 October 1925. Mummies provide information that cannot be gathered from other sources; for instance, we learn that Tutankhamun was only 5 feet 5 inches tall (168 cm). The gold mask and hands are still in place, as is a gold ba-bird pectoral. Inscribed bands, also made of gold, can be seen placed over the blackened and carbonized wrappings. GRIFFITH INSTITUTE, ASHMOLEAN MUSEUM, OXFORD

ABOVE: Amulets and other items, such as a pectoral ornament in the shape of a hawk, and a dagger, were revealed when the outer layers of the mummy wrappings started being removed. GRIFFITH INSTITUTE, ASHMOLEAN MUSEUM, OXFORD

LEFT: The last stage of the unwrapping of the mummy, with the lower part of the body completely exposed. GRIFFITH INSTITUTE, ASHMOLEAN MUSEUM, OXFORD

heart beside Amun," "God loves him who loves him," or "Every good deed Ptah repays manifold"). Their monuments include not only stelae but also more modest dedications such as ostraca (smooth limestone flakes suitable for writing), graffiti, small figures and hand-made votive offerings, especially in the vicinity of temples, in private chapels, and in the reuse and fresh interpretation of older sanctuaries. For example, the Great Sphinx at Giza, a representation of the Old Kingdom pharaoh Khephren (2518–2439 BC), was revered in the New Kingdom as an image of the sun-god Harmakhis. The desire for access to god, "to behold god," was fulfilled both by processions, in which movements of the sacred barque were interpreted as oracles, and within the sectors of the temple that were accessible to laity. These were the forecourts with their colossal statues, their sphinx- and ram-alleys leading to the pylons, the entrance gateways and enclosure walls with reliefs of deities, ceremonial courts with their shrines, and especially the so-called contratemples constructed for the laity at the back of sanctuaries. There was one at Karnak called the abode of the "hearing ear." The laity was excluded from the sanctuary itself and for its own prayers preferred tangible images of deities, such as prominent reliefs and statues, which then acquired, like Christian miraculous images, their own names ("Amun-Re amidst the thickness of the walls," "Amun-Re who hears prayers," "Ptah of the Great Gateway," "Ptah of the Column," or "Ptah who answers prayers").

Feeling dependent on the deity, human beings seek grace and see themselves as weak and needy. Regardless of actual social status they name themselves "poor," "servant," "refugee," "aggrieved," or "silent." Such forms of humility of the pious are compounded with assertions of obedience and loyalty: human beings act, or are, "on the water" of god, "walk upon his way," "place him in their hearts," or "abandon themselves to him." Beside the master–servant relationship stands the love that praying people bring before god. They dedicate themselves to the

deity and donate to it all their property.

The deity for its part answers the prayers and forgives the guilty, appears as protector, incorruptible judge, and rescuer in the hour of need, and frees humanity from the darkness of godlessness or actual blindness. The might of god that ensures that crime does not go unpunished is proclaimed in a confession upon a stela, a document that binds the person to god. If the text speaks of "god" in the singular, it does not imply monotheistic belief. The pious can attach themselves to any deity. The choice falls not only on principal city-gods such as Amun of Thebes or Ptah of Memphis, but also on less important or locally revered deities such as the "mountaintop" in western Thebes, Near Eastern deities such as Reshep and Qadesh, deities connected with one's profession such as the deified Amenophis I, patron of the artists and craftworkers of the royal tombs, or the animal forms of deities. The plurality of spheres of life corresponds to the plurality of deities of Egyptian polytheism.

THE VISUAL ARTS

Arielle P. Kozloff

EGYPTIAN ART IS perhaps the only national art in human history that, having developed and consolidated a unique style, practiced it for 3,000 years with only the most subtle changes. There were many reasons for this constancy.

First, the complexity and difficulty of the Egyptian script meant that literacy became the accomplishment of only an educated few. Art, therefore, was the great communicator. Both gods and pharaohs could express their might, their principles, and their accomplishments for all to see in a manner easily understood by the largely illiterate agricultural community through images carved on temple walls or in sculpture-in-the-round. The various art forms were actually almost like characters of script since the Egyptian written language was pictographic, with its hieroglyphs representing not only sounds but also ideas. For example, the hieroglyphic word for "cat" included sound-signs followed by another sign in the form of a cat sitting on its haunches, with its tail wrapped around them and curling up at the tip. This latter sign was also the standard form for representations of sculpted and painted cats. Thus, it might be said that the visual arts provided another medium for communication through the most essential symbols.

Second, since the basic elements of kingship and religion were so deeply intertwined and changed little over the millennia, the methods used to express the primary messages also remained the same. For example, the sphinx combined pharaoh's head and lion's body into an amalgamation that represented a special aspect of the sun-god. It made its early colossal appearance as guardian of Khephren's pyramid in the Fourth Dynasty, and since the king's intimate relationship with the sun-god remained constant throughout the millennia, the sphinx also continued to be used throughout the history of Egyptian art in sculpture, decorative arts, and painting.

People today often think of Egyptian art as being morose, because so much of what remains has been found in tombs. The opposite is really true. Rather than a depressing preoccupation with death, the Egyptians had an optimistic and lively vision of the afterlife. The passage to a happy and secure afterlife was not problem-free, but there were ways to deal with the problems, and one of these ways was to furnish one's tomb with the necessary equipment and symbols. Therefore, many works of art were found in tombs, but some are from temples where they were given as gifts to one of the many Egyptian deities either in

TOP: *Limestone bust of Nefertiti, the "great royal wife" of King Akhenaten (1353–1337 BC), from el-Amarna.* EGYPTIAN MUSEUM, BERLIN/C. M. DIXON

ABOVE: *Bronze statuette of a cat, the animal associated with the goddess Bastet, seventh century BC or later.* THE TOLEDO MUSEUM OF ART, OHIO

OPPOSITE: *Diorite statue of King Khephren (2518–2493 BC), found in his valley temple at Giza.* THE EGYPTIAN MUSEUM, CAIRO/WERNER FORMAN ARCHIVE

RIGHT: *The remarkably well preserved statues of seated Rahotpe and his wife Nofret date to c. 2550 BC. Although made as two separate sculptures, they were probably intended to be placed side by side. They are 4 feet/120 cm tall, but this is still considerably larger than most contemporary tomb statues.* THE EGYPTIAN MUSEUM, CAIRO/JÜRGEN LIEPE

gratitude for past favors or in the hope of future ones. Often such gifts are inscribed as offerings that the king, as intercessor between humans and divinity, has given on the behalf of the individual named.

Egyptian art expressed itself in an amazing variety of materials, both natural and fabricated. There is perhaps no area in the world as rich as Egypt in stones, both hard and soft, in a rainbow of colors, from glinty brown quartzite to black granodiorite to smooth yellow jasper to red cornelian and blue-green turquoise to buttery, banded travertine ("Egyptian alabaster"). And in antiquity, a large variety of trees native to Egypt such as boxwood, yew, acacia, and sycamore were used to create furniture, ritual objects, and sculpture. These materials could be made into objects as small as tiny amulets or into colossal sculptures more than 40 feet (12 m) tall. In addition to using natural materials to their fullest, ancient craftworkers invented new ones including "faience" — a glazed powdered quartz — and glass.

Despite the immutability of Egyptian art when compared, for example, to 3,000 years of Near Eastern art or even 2,000 years of Christian art, it does not all look alike to specialists. Egyptologists quickly spot differences in figural proportions (the legginess of Middle Kingdom women in contrast to the low-slung hips of the Late period), clothes (the tight-fitting sheaths of the Old Kingdom in contrast to the lavishly pleated gowns of the late Eighteenth Dynasty), and tonsorial effects (the short-cropped hair and moustaches of the Fourth Dynasty dandies in contrast to the tiered toupées and clean-shaven faces of New Kingdom swells). And despite the persistent use of a few standard poses for royal portraiture, the faces of the kings are so individualized that in time they come to be recognized as old friends.

The monumental throne portrait of Khephren (2518–2493 BC) is carved in diorite, one of the hardest nonprecious stones known, and set a standard for royal representations in the round that was to be repeated by successive pharaohs for centuries to come. It is appropriate that this standard should have been set by the king who

commissioned Giza's Great Sphinx, which set a standard of its own. Although an idealized muscular body was the archetype for every pharaonic portrait, Khephren's realistically rendered open face, with its small eyes and broad, flat planes is a true portrait. He wears the striped *nemes*-headdress and the royal (divine) beard. The sun-god Horus perches in falcon form atop the throne's back, spreading his wings protectively around the head of his earthly counterpart, the king. The lattice work between the chair legs is a design entwining the lily of Upper Egypt with the papyrus of Lower Egypt, a motif referring to the unification of the "Two Lands" that remained in use for the rest of ancient Egyptian history.

Another favorite royal composition placed the king side by side with one or two important personages or deities in a "dyad" or "triad." The most famous of these are the statues found at Menkaure's valley temple below his pyramid at Giza. Several of these half-life-size triads, carved in a dark compact stone, have a striding Menkaure (2488–2460 BC) in Upper Egyptian crown, flanked by the goddess Hathor and the god of a nome or district. Khephren's successor also had a distinctive look, with bulging eyes, low

THE NARMER PALETTE

The fundamentals of Egyptian art were established early. Dating to about 3000 BC, a large ceremonial slate palette (originally intended for the grinding of eye-paint) may celebrate conquests made by the late Predynastic king Narmer, depicted on one side of the palette wearing the conical Upper Egyptian crown with the spiked pillbox of Lower Egypt on the other. This early masterpiece demonstrates the hallmarks of what was to become the traditional Egyptian aesthetic in two-dimensional relief sculpture in terms of composition, figure drawing, and the unification of inscription and picture in the same composition. Both of the palette's surfaces are divided into registers, each marked by a baseline on which the main figures stand. This invention of organizing large flat surfaces — eventually tomb and temple walls — into separate zones provided the possibility of presenting several different aspects or parts of the same theme or event in such a way that all facets of the whole could be easily grasped at one glance.

The Narmer palette also provides one of the earliest examples of what was to become the standardized Egyptian two-dimensional human figure, with each of its various parts represented in its most characteristic, easily

recognized form: the face in profile, the eye frontal; the arms, legs, and feet in profile; the chest — male pectorals and female breasts — in profile, but the shoulders frontal.

LEFT: Narmer's palette (sometime after 3000 BC), reverse. The name of the king is written inside a serekh that imitates a building, perhaps the royal palace, flanked by two cow-headed goddesses. The main scene below shows the king smashing the head of a foreign captive with a mace. The picture in front of the king may be a complex pictogram that contains elements of the later hieroglyphic script: "the king (= hawk) has captured (= rope) 6,000 (six papyrus stalks, by analogy with lotus plant = 1,000) foreign prisoners (= foreign bearded head)." This is not how the developed hieroglyphic script worked but may represent the "prehieroglyphic" phase of Egyptian writing. THE EGYPTIAN MUSEUM, CAIRO/WERNER FORMAN ARCHIVE

Finally, Narmer's palette illustrates how effortlessly writing and representation — each being simultaneously picture and symbol — combine to form an integrated pictorial whole in Egyptian art. So gracefully do they coexist in this composition that it takes some concentration to single out the signs for the king's name — the *nar*-fish and the *mer*-adze — from the larger pictorial composition.

The ancient Egyptians did not argue with success: these became the standard Egyptian formulae for representations in drawing and relief sculpture for the next 3,000 years.

CONVENTIONS OF EGYPTIAN TWO-DIMENSIONAL ART ALREADY PRESENT ON NARMER'S PALETTE

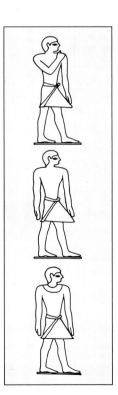

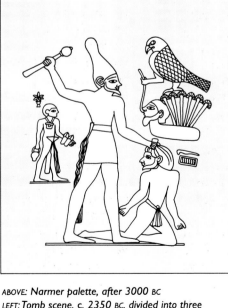

ABOVE: Tomb scene, c. 2400 BC, showing the principles of figure drawing

ABOVE: Narmer palette, after 3000 BC
LEFT: Tomb scene, c. 2350 BC, divided into three registers
RIGHT: Tomb scene, c. 2350 BC, demonstrating the integration of representations and hieroglyphs

COMPOSITION: The space is organized into registers, with figures placed on baselines. Figures placed higher in the space were understood to be farther away, or chronologically earlier.

FIGURE DRAWING: A figure is an assembly of various parts of the human body shown in their most characteristic forms (the face, chest, arms, and legs in profile; the eyes, eyebrows, and shoulders in frontal view); the front foot of a man is planted well forward, as if striding, while the feet of a woman are shown closely together.

INTEGRATION OF REPRESENTATIONS AND INSCRIPTIONS: The hieroglyphs fill empty spaces and the representations often function as enlarged hieroglyphs. The hieroglyphs next to the heads of the captive and the man behind Narmer convey their names or functions, while those above the animal in the tomb scene read "a young ox."

RIGHT: *Although this black granite statue is not identified by an inscription, comparison with other such pieces leaves little doubt that it represents Amenemhet III (1859–1814 BC) A short kilt with a triangular front panel, on which the king's hands rest palms down, is an innovation that was introduced into Egyptian royal sculpture only during the preceding reign.* CLEVELAND MUSEUM OF ART, OHIO

BELOW: *A small (4.5 inches/11.5 cm long) blue faience statuette of a standing hippopotamus, dated* c. *2000–1650 BC, found at Dra Abu 'l-Naga (on the west bank at Thebes). The beast's natural habitat is indicated in a surprisingly modern way by plants, flowers and birds painted on the animal itself.* THE EGYPTIAN MUSEUM, CAIRO/MAXIMILIEN BRUGGMANN

cheekbones, and a bulbous nose, and the deities by his side are given the same features.

Courtiers close to the king benefited from his largesse by being allocated materials and workers to create tombs, and spirit (*ka*—see page 93) images for themselves. Portraits of private individuals, as opposed to royalty, are usually restricted to limestone or wood. The most spectacular of these is a pair of life-size seated figures — Rahotpe and his wife Nofret — found in their tomb at Maidum, south of Giza, and now in the Egyptian Museum in Cairo. Their surfaces pristinely preserve their original paint, which not only colors their bodies with the standard Egyptian sexual stereotype — brown for him and yellow for her — but also carefully delineates her period-piece diadem and necklace and his Fourth Dynasty style moustache. Their eyes — painted rock crystal within copper sockets — have an amazingly lifelike appearance, thanks to the sculptor's skill in their manufacture and the uncanny ability, true of the best Egyptian artists, to set the eyes so accurately that they seem to return a piercing gaze to their viewer.

The pharaohs of the Middle Kingdom — particularly those of the Twelfth Dynasty (1980–1801 BC) — had a distinctive long, bony face, with a protruding jaw, sunken eyes, drooping upper lids, and large, stuck-out ears. They were not a particularly handsome lot, and their

sculptors captured their appearance with care, except that one cannot help but wonder if these same artists did not cheat somewhat on the bodies, where in good pharaonic tradition the king is depicted in full youthful muscularity. Granodiorite from Aswan became a favorite stone for royal portraits of this period, and many extraordinary sculptures survive both in Egypt and in museum collections around the world. Still more Middle Kingdom royal statues were usurped by later kings, especially Ramesses II (1279–1213 BC), their faces, and often their bodies, too, recut to resemble his, and the cartouches (oval frames surrounding the names of kings in hieroglyphic writing) with their names erased and filled with his own.

A type of animal statuette peculiar to the Middle Kingdom and well known today, thanks to a few beautifully preserved examples, is the faience hippo. Hippopotami were both feared and revered as spirits of the underworld,

which was conceived as a watery place, a perfect abode for this species. While hippopotami no longer inhabit the Nile in Egypt, in antiquity they were ubiquitous nocturnal marauders of the grain fields and, vicious when disturbed under water, posed a constant threat to river traffic. They would have been just as disturbing in the afterlife if the ancient Egyptians had not made small images of them and broken their legs — it is thought — to render the beasts harmless. The most common color for faience, and these hippos are no exception, was a brilliant copper-induced turquoise blue. In addition, drawn on their backs and heads in manganese paint beneath the glaze, are lotus flowers, papyrus umbels, birds, and insects, the whole effect meant to suggest that the hippos are safely contained under water in their swampy abode.

One of the most complex and beautiful examples of Middle Kingdom painting is preserved on the sides of the outer coffin of Djehutinakht, found in his collapsed tomb at Deir el-Bersha in Middle Egypt and now in the Museum of Fine Arts, Boston. Its main scene, usually the primary representation on tomb walls, shows the deceased comfortably seated and waited on by a priest amid the heaps and lists of offerings that he takes with him to the afterworld. These offerings are not piled up but are drawn one above the other, each one being a clearly and immediately recognizable symbol of the real offerings. Looking back at Narmer's palette, one sees that the bodies of the conquered foe were also arranged in this way, as though laid out on the ground with space between each and the next, a method of composition that had already lasted a thousand years.

Although an occasional arsenic copper statue is known from the Old and Middle Kingdoms, true bronze, an alloy of copper and tin, did not become common until the New Kingdom, beginning with the Eighteenth Dynasty. Its most effective use, of course, was in weaponry, but it was also fashioned into vessels, statuettes, and other decorative objects, such as mirrors. The reflective properties of the mirror disks are now dulled by the patina developed over centuries of

contact with the elements in the soil where they were buried. However, their surfaces were once quite shiny and provided the owner with high-quality reflections — one side was slightly convex for a wide-angle view and the other side concave for a close-up look.

Besides being decorative and utilitarian, mirrors were rich in symbolism, being sacred to the goddess Hathor, who was both a sky goddess and a mother goddess with a special relationship to the sun, perhaps represented by the gleaming disks. We now believe that Hathor was one of the goddesses identified with the Milky Way, into which the sun disappeared at night and from which it seemed to be born each morning. However, Hathor had a number of other characteristics as well. She was the goddess of love and of music and drunkenness. According to mythology, Bes, the dancing lion-headed dwarf represented on mirror handles, accompanied Hathor on a voyage she was thought to have made to Western Asia, where a similar goddess named Ishtar was worshiped.

ABOVE: A nude servant girl attending to three female guests, perhaps rearranging their earrings, at a banquet depicted in Theban tomb number 52 at Sheikh Abd el-Qurna. The colors of the tomb's decoration, painted on walls covered with a thin layer of mud and plaster, are remarkably well preserved. Its owner, Nakht, lived in the first half of the fourteenth century BC. AUSTRAL/CAMERA PRESS

ABOVE: Three female musicians from a mural painting showing a banquet, in the tomb of Nakht at Sheikh Abd el-Qurna (Thebes). They are playing, from the right, the boat-shaped harp, lute, and double oboe. Nakht was probably a contemporary of Tuthmosis IV and Amenophis III (between 1401 and 1353 BC). AUSTRAL/CAMERA PRESS

LEFT: Egyptian hand-held mirrors were often very decorative. Here, on an object dating to c. 1450 BC the handle is in the form of the "family god" Bes, a bearded, bow-legged, long-tailed, dwarf who lifts the bronze mirror's shiny disk in his outstretched arms. CLEVELAND MUSEUM OF ART, OHIO

THE ART OF THE GOLDEN AGE

Amenophis III (1391–1353 BC) ruled Egypt at the height of what is often called the Golden Age, the Eighteenth Dynasty, when Egypt's influence and power reached far south into the Sudan and east into Western Asia. Unlike some of his predecessors who focused their efforts on expanding the realm militarily, Amenophis III, during his 38-year reign, undertook a campaign of splendor. He enhanced the empire with his building projects — always in the name of divinities — and cultivated the artistic workshops both for his own and his court's satisfaction, and for the diplomatic and economic value of trade abroad.

The beneficent face of Amenophis III, with its slanted, almond-shaped eyes and its wide, slightly upturned mouth is familiar to many museum-goers, who may encounter it in almost any major collection. The Cleveland Museum's slightly smaller than life-size portrait shows the king wearing one of many styles of Egyptian wig, and over it the carved representation of a diadem with streamers terminating in protective cobras.

Amenophis III would be encountered even more frequently if Ramesses II (1279–1213 BC), the great usurper, had not — during his own 66-year reign — had his sculptors recarve much of Amenophis III's statuary in his own likeness. Egyptologists and art historians are beginning to recognize the clues that identify recut sculptures and to extrapolate the previous shape of faces, bodies, and limbs, thus identifying the original subject of the portrait. For example, close examination has shown that one monumental granodiorite statue, originally part of a series made for Amenophis III, was altered by Ramesses II's sculptors to favor their own king. Because they could not add stone to the cheeks to make the face look fatter, they lowered the headband onto the forehead and

ABOVE: A small (less than 4 inches/9.5 cm high) female head, probably representing Tiy, the queen of Amenophis III (1391–1353 BC) and mother of Amenophis IV (Akhenaten). It is made of a combination of materials, principally yew wood, and the appearance of the sculpture, particularly the wig, was considerably altered in antiquity. EGYPTIAN MUSEUM, BERLIN/WERNER FORMAN ARCHIVE

raised the beard higher onto the chin, thus shortening the face top to bottom and giving the illusion of greater width.

The most famous portrait of Amenophis III's queen, Tiy, was probably made after her husband's death. Carved in yew wood and inlaid with silver, gold, glass, and stone, this fist-size masterpiece is an amazingly realistic depiction of an elderly woman, carved

within only a very few years of the much more famous and often illustrated painted limestone bust of the elegant Nefertiti, her eyes — like Rahotpe's and Nofret's — inlaid with painted stone and metal. Both portraits are in the Egyptian Museum in Charlottenburg, Berlin.

Another small "gem" from this same reign is the charming glass vessel in the form of a fish now in the British Museum. Fragments of similar fish were found in the remains of a glass-makers' workshop at Amenophis III's Malqata palace, near Thebes, but this lively bottle was found at el-Amarna, the city founded by Amenophis III's son and successor, Akhenaten.

Some of the largest free-standing sculptures from all of Egypt's history were made during the reign of Amenophis III. Those 30 feet (9 m) tall and taller are still for the most part in Egypt, either at their original sites or in the Egyptian Museum in Cairo. However, some monumental works made their way into European and American collections already in the early nineteenth century. Two of the most magnificent but least well known are the grand red granite sphinxes carried back from Amenophis III's mortuary temple on the west bank of Thebes to Czar Alexander I's St Petersburg, where today they still flank the quay opposite the imperial palace on the Neva River.

Amenophis III's courtiers also benefited from his patronage of the arts; large numbers of portraits of members of the court survive not only in the traditional painted limestone, but also in expensive hard stones such as granodiorite and brown quartzite. Most important of these

ABOVE: One of the two red granite sphinxes of Amenophis III (1391–1353 BC), originally from the king's mortuary temple at Thebes, now in St Petersburg. The sphinxes were excavated by the famous Greek excavator and supplier of antiquities, Ioannes Athanasios (known to his contemporaries as Giovanni d'Athanasi, or Yanni), and were brought to St Petersburg in 1832. LEONARD HEIFITZ

LEFT: A gray granite scribe-statue of Amenhotpe, son of Hapu, found near the tenth pylon (monumental gateway) of the temple of Amun at Karnak. Amenhotpe's name was the same as one of those of his royal master, Amenophis III (1391–1353 BC). "Amenophis" is a Graecised version of the Egyptian "Amenhotpe" which means "The god Amun is satisfied." THE EGYPTIAN MUSEUM, CAIRO/JÜRGEN LIEPE

officials was Amenhotpe, son of Hapu, who as overseer of the king's building projects was essential to the success of Amenophis III's campaign of splendor. He was so successful that the king built him a mortuary temple of royal proportions on the west bank of Thebes not far from his own, and he was revered enough to be eventually deified — one of the very few nonroyalty in Egyptian history to be so honored. His best-known portraits were found at the feet of a colossal statue of Amenophis III at Karnak temple. He is shown sitting on the ground in the traditional position of a humble scribe, hunched over a papyrus rolled out across his folded legs.

The Eighteenth Dynasty (1540–1295 BC) was a period of famous kings and queens: the conqueror Tuthmosis III; Hatshepsut, the queen who ruled as king; Amenophis III, the great builder; the rebellious Akhenaten; and most renowned of all because of the discovery of his nearly intact tomb, Tutankhamun. The traditional styles that developed in the Old and Middle Kingdoms continued to form the basis for New Kingdom art. Theban tomb paintings depict scenes that are quite similar to those in Old Kingdom tombs up north. In the tomb of an official of the reign of Amenophis III, the deceased Menna is shown in mirror images spearing fish and lofting throwsticks at birds, representing spirits of the water and the air that had to be brought under control on one's journey to the afterlife. The same method of portraying the human figure — profile face, chest, and limbs; frontal eye and shoulders — is used here as it was on Narmer's palette nearly 2,000 years earlier. A comparison of the wigs and clothing with those worn by Rahotpe and Nofret in their Fourth Dynasty sculpted portraits shows how much — or how little — styles had changed. Menna is clean-shaven but wears a much more elaborate wig, and he has a T-shirt rather than going bare-chested. Menna's wife wears the elaborately pleated dress and shawl typical of her day and a long wig, plaited in infinitesimal braids in contrast to Nofret's tight sheath and short, blunt haircut.

When the son of Amenophis III, Amenophis IV (1353–1337 BC), changed his name to Akhenaten, diverted the focus of Egyptian religion from the god Amun to the sun disk, the Aten, and sailed the court up north to el-Amarna, artistic traditions were thrown overboard. If Middle Kingdom portraits made their pharaohs look ungainly, Akhenaten's made him bizarre. He was given a long, inverted face with rubbery lips and a cantilevered jaw. His chest was sunken, his abdomen enlarged, and his hips low-slung. Not only the king but also his family members were depicted this way. Whether some disease actually deformed him or whether these features were the result of artistic experimentation is not known. It is interesting, however, that also during the Amarna period a portrait of such classic elegance and supreme beauty as the bust of Nefertiti now in the Egyptian Museum in Berlin was made.

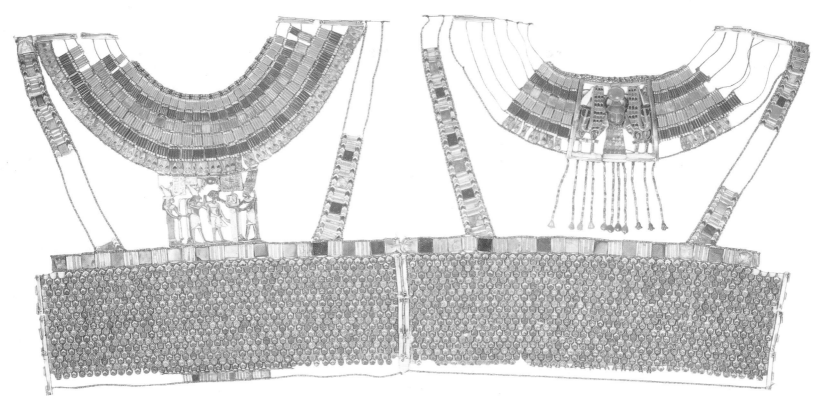

The Amarna period is usually noted for its "naturalism," but actually the hallmark of this period that remained consistent despite swings from the weird to the classic in terms of the human figure was a love for a curvilinear, almost serpentine outline. In two-dimensional art this preference was eloquently expressed in the exaggerated elongation of certain elements, such as the fingers of a hand dropping fat onto a fire depicted on the fragment of a wall relief from one of Akhenaten's temples that was destroyed after his reign and reused as rubble fill in the interior of a subsequent one.

The dazzling discovery of Tutankhamun's tomb provided us with more than a king's ransom. It informed us that, if such an unimportant king could have been buried so lavishly, then the ancient stories of imperial treasures were true. It was the largest single find of royal jewelry from any period, and a tremendous amount is to be learned from studying the techniques of goldsmithing and of inlaying glass and semiprecious stone in the objects from Tutankhamun's tomb.

Ramesses II (1279–1213 BC) was the greatest king of the Nineteenth Dynasty and some might say of all Egyptian history. His own true portrait with its large, heavy-lidded eyes, aquiline nose, and pursed mouth is unmistakable. Whereas Amenophis III had himself portrayed in his later years as somewhat corpulent, sometimes obese, and Akhenaten went to strange extremes, statues of Ramesses II always show him perfectly fit and trim in good pharaonic tradition although his physique must have deteriorated a bit during his unusually long reign.

Despite Egypt's political decline after the reign of Ramesses II, it held fast to its artistic traditions. The carved relief wall images of Twenty-sixth Dynasty officials, such as one of Montuemhet wearing the leopard skin of a priest, show exactly the same conventions for depicting the figure as on Narmer's palette.

Bronze casters developed new levels of technical skill and proficiency from the Twenty-sixth Dynasty on, making votive statuettes and other items more accessible to a wider range of customer and therefore increasing greatly the numbers of such objects. Statuettes of animals sacred to various deities abounded over the next few centuries as did bronze coffins for such animals. Usually these statuettes and coffins were fashioned in the animal's most characteristic, easily recognizable — "hieroglyphic" — form, for the object was, after all these centuries, both an image and a symbol.

ABOVE: A "corslet" of Tutankhamun (1336–1327 BC) that was worn on ceremonial occasions. This is a complex item of the royal attire made of gold, faience, glass, and semiprecious stones (agate, carnelian) and consists of a broad collar with a pectoral underneath, shoulder straps, and a corslet proper. THE EGYPTIAN MUSEUM, CAIRO/JÜRGEN LIEPE

ABOVE: Relief showing "the fourth prophet of the god Amun" Montuemhet (attested 667–648 BC) wearing the ceremonial garment of a priest, from his tomb at Asasif (Thebes). THE CLEVELAND MUSEUM OF ART, OHIO

MONUMENTS OF THE MIGHTY

Cathleen A. Keller

IF THERE IS ONE ancient culture renowned for the monumentality of its physical remains, that culture is ancient Egypt. Its tumbled-down temples, shattered statuary, and ruined palaces are images that virtually exemplify the word "monument." However, vastness of size was by no means a universal characteristic of ancient Egyptian monuments. Those (usually kings) who were capable of organizing large numbers of people and massive amounts of material to honor the most powerful beings in the universe (the gods and deceased ancestors) appear to have had aspirations toward the immense. However, the urge to commemorate or memorialize one's existence was not limited to kings; private individuals of all stations in life could and did erect their own monuments, whose form and scale often differed markedly from those undertaken by the pharaohs.

The all-inclusive category of ancient Egyptian "monuments" (*mnw* in Egyptian, from the verb meaning "to endure," unconnected with the modern English word "monument") includes such diverse items as: the "colossi of Memnon," dedicated to his "father," Amun, by Amenophis III (1391–1353 BC); the Gebel Barkal stela (inscription on stone) of Tuthmosis III (1479–1425 BC),

inscribed for the god Amun-Re; funerary stelae commissioned by relatives of the deceased; and very modest images of middle-class Egyptians. The "business" of making and dedicating monuments was part of the very fabric of ancient Egyptian society. From the beginning of the pharaonic period, it is clear that artisans were considered essential to the well-being of the state; the subsidiary burials that surrounded the funerary complexes of the rulers of the First Dynasty included those of different craftworkers, each accompanied by the tools of their trade. The preference for permanent materials for monuments (in contrast to the use of more perishable substances for dwellings and objects of daily life) is also characteristic of ancient Egyptian culture. Rare or hard-to-work materials had a higher status, and the elite was prepared to go to extraordinary lengths to obtain them. Quarrying expeditions to obtain granite from Aswan or *bekhen* stone (probably graywacke or a similar rock) from the Wadi Hammamat were large-scale undertakings, headed in the New Kingdom by such illustrious personages as Amun's high priests.

The building of temples of the great gods and tombs of the kings were large-scale projects taking a considerable

TOP: *Painting of the Memnon Colossi made by the Scottish artist David Roberts during his visit to Egypt in 1838–39.* A. K. BOWMAN

ABOVE: *Early in the reign of Amenophis IV (Akhenaten), after 1353 BC several temples dedicated to the new state god, the Aten, were built at Karnak. After the Amarna period these structures were systematically dismantled and the stone reused in the temples of later kings. Some of the original wall-scenes have now been reconstructed.* LUXOR MUSEUM OF ANCIENT EGYPTIAN ART, EGYPT/JAMES H. MORRIS

OPPOSITE: *The two large (nearly 54 feet/16 m high) seated statues of Amenophis III (1391–1353 BC), on the west bank of the Nile at Thebes, are known as "the Memnon Colossi" (Memnon was the son of Eos, Dawn, according to the Greeks).* C. M. DIXON

RIGHT: *The largest of the series of rock-cut temples built in Nubia by Ramesses II (1279–1213 BC) is Abu Simbel, adorned with four colossal seated statues of the king. When Nubia was to be flooded with the creation of Lake Nasser, the temple was moved some 230 yards (210 m) farther away from the Nile in an operation completed in 1968.* H. CHAMPOLLION

ABOVE: *Detail of one of the statues of Abu Simbel, showing the face of Ramesses II.* H. CHAMPOLLION

ABOVE: *King Sethos I (1294–1279 BC) offering an image of the goddess Maet in the inner columned hall of the temple that he built at Abydos. Maet has an ostrich feather, which could also be used to write her name, in her hair, and in her hand an ankh or life sign. The photograph was taken c. 1890 by J. P. Sebah.* GRIFFITH INSTITUTE, ASHMOLEAN MUSEUM, OXFORD

amount of time in which a significant percentage of the available wealth of the society was invested. And even the more modest votive dedications of private individuals, such as the statuary and stelae commissioned for the shrine of the deified Old Kingdom official Hekaib on Elephantine Island near the First Cataract, demanded that stone and skilled labor be available for local projects. The production of monuments was an integral part of the ancient Egyptian economy.

On a more theoretical level, commemorative objects constituted both stimulus and response within the intertwined systems of human and divine communication that enabled the cosmos to function. They both made the divine a concrete object of worship (as cult images) and made permanent the human gestures of gratitude for beneficences bestowed. The king and the gods, as sources of "life-oriented goals" (those enjoyed during one's lifetime) such as longevity, economic prosperity, and good health, could expect to receive tangible reminders of their beneficence. These reminders ranged from entire temples (for the deceased or deified kings and the

gods) embellished with depictions of the king rendering appropriate homage to the deities to whom the complex was dedicated, to individual pieces of cult paraphernalia, such as sumptuously decorated barques to hold the divine processional image. Although Egyptian culture is often resistant to modern distinctions, it may be convenient to refer to monuments directed at (or in response to) achieving life-oriented goals as "donations."

Donations concentrate on gifts presented or acts performed on behalf of someone (or something) who is usually *not* the donor. A king may commission a statue of a divinity and have it placed in a temple. The immediate beneficiary is, therefore, the god depicted by the sacred image. However, in exchange for such acts kings and private individuals derive benefits, which may in fact be mentioned (or implied) in some manner in the votive object itself or in an accompanying dedicatory inscription. Thus in temple offering scenes, the king is depicted proffering both tangible substances (wine, beer, bread, cloth, and so forth) for the nourishment and enjoyment of the gods, and symbols of the legitimacy of his rule (such as the figure of Maet, the female personification of cosmic order; or the eye of Horus, which exemplifies the sacrifices made by the living king for his immediate predecessor — of whom he is the legitimate heir). The ability of a king to offer *maet* or the eye of Horus demonstrates that he is entitled to receive in return "all life, stability, and dominion" over Egypt.

In an interesting twist on the "votive" image, the statues of private individuals placed in the open courts of New Kingdom and Late period temples as a gesture of respect (or act of favor) toward the individuals represented (so that they could partake in the divine offerings in perpetuity) could themselves be solicited for further beneficences. The scribal statues of Amenhotpe, son of Hapu, discovered before the tenth pylon at Karnak, became a focus of prayer by later generations as a result of his deification after death.

In contrast to the donations, "memorials" have as their main focus the individual royal or private person (often the donor) as the immediate recipient of the beneficences mentioned or depicted. The most obvious memorials erected by individuals were their tombs. These "afterlife-oriented" monuments seek to obtain a slightly different set of benefits than do donations. The goals appear at

once to conflict and to overlap to an unnecessary extent, largely because of the ancient Egyptian belief that an individual human being consisted of several different elements, only some of which (the body and the shadow) had even partially concrete forms; whereas others (the "spiritual" aspects of personality called *ka*, *ba* [see page 93] and *akh*, and the personal name, *ren*) were essentially incorporeal. Providing for the continuance of each of these aspects within the context of the tomb (subject, of course, to changes that took place in Egyptian religious thought over 3,000

ABOVE: The sanctuary of Hekaib on the island of Elephantine, opposite Aswan, is one of the rare instances of veneration of famous nonroyal persons of the past. Hekaib lived during the reign of Pepy II (2236– 2143 BC). DR KUHLMANN, GERMAN INSTITUTE OF ARCHAEOLOGY, CAIRO

LEFT: The temple at Luxor was built essentially by two kings, Amenophis III (1391–1353 BC) and Ramesses II (1279–1213 BC), although there was an earlier, Tuthmosid shrine in the area. The main deity worshiped in the temple was the god Amun. DEREK BERWIN/THE IMAGE BANK

THE VALLEYS OF THE KINGS AND THE QUEENS

The New Kingdom royal cemeteries on the west bank at Thebes were in use for more than four centuries. During this time, hundreds of subterranean chambers were dug in the limestone strata of the low desert, located away from the public view in the valleys behind the Theban cliffs, in the shadow of the Peak of the West. The most spectacular examples were produced between the reigns of Tuthmosis III and Ramesses XI (c. 1479–1069 BC). Executed in similarly increasing scales of size and complexity as those exhibited by the contemporary mortuary temples, these funerary monuments *par excellence* are situated in the areas known today as the valleys of the Kings (called "the Great Field" by the ancient Egyptians) and the Queens ("the Place of Beauty").

The royal tombs of the New Kingdom are, like their nonroyal counterparts (the burial chambers of private tombs), curious monuments. Their main purpose was to protect their contents from profane contact with the living (through seclusion from public view) and to affirm the prestige of an occupant in the world of the dead. They thus combine external anonymity with internal splendor. The only eyes for which their contents (and decoration) were intended were those of the deceased (and now deified) king and his divine companions: the gods.

By Ramessid times the royal tomb was a large-scale construction project that necessitated the full-time employment of an entire crew of workmen. Completely clothed in brightly painted reliefs right from its imposing entrance portal down through a series of long, narrow, descending corridors (*setjau-netjer*, "god's paths") and one or more

ABOVE: *The intense heat and sheer desolation of the Valley of the Kings make it an awe-inspiring resting place for some 30 pharaohs of the New Kingdom (1540–1069 BC). The rock-cut tombs had no conspicuous superstructure above ground.*
STOCKSHOTS/M. BENDON

intervening chambers (*weskhet*) to the large, vaulted burial chamber (*per-en-nub*, "house of gold"), the tomb was in effect an enormous model of the sun's path around the earth. Each evening the solar disk entered the western mountains at the end of its daily journey, only to rise again on the eastern horizon. So too the king, entombed as the "golden one" in his glittering shrines, entered his tomb, was recharged (as was the sun), and emerged, reborn, at dawn to illumine the

world from Karnak, "the Horizon." The sun barque's journey from west to east beneath the visible world was not without peril. Chief among those opposing its course was the great serpent Apophis, the embodiment of disorder. Should he succeed in arresting the barque on its journey, the sun (and king) would not rise and chaos would achieve domination over *maet* in the cosmos.

On the ceiling of the burial chamber of Ramesses VI (1143–1136 BC) the sun's path through the day and night skies is depicted: the red solar disk is born from the loins of the sky-goddess Nut; the solar barque passes beneath her body; the disk is swallowed up in the evening; and the barque passes along the starry form of her nightly counterpart until once again the disk is reborn at sunrise.

RIGHT: *Scenes from Egyptian "underworld books" depicted on the walls of the tombs in the Valley of the Kings are full of fantastic creatures and nightmarish beings. Serpents are particularly well represented. Illustration based on a detail from the so-called Book of the Gates in the tomb of Sethos I (1294–1279 BC).*

In the more modest tombs of the king's wives and sons, most of which were located in the Queens' Valley, this overt identification of the deceased with the sun-god is lacking. In both the queens' and princes' tomb chambers, the decoration features the usual divine offering scenes and is otherwise based on representations from the *Book of the Dead*. However, only in the tombs of his sons does the king assume the role of intercessor with the gods on behalf of his deceased offspring; the gods Anubis (god of mummification, protector of tombs usually represented as a jackal or at least jackal-headed) and Thoth (the god of writing and learning, often associated with the ibis-bird or baboon) take on the function in the tombs of his queens and subjects.

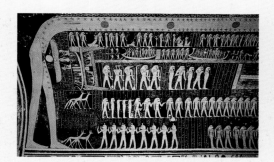

ABOVE AND RIGHT: Details of the "astronomical ceiling" in the tomb of Ramesses VI. JAMES H. MORRIS

The supercharged atmosphere of the royal tomb was also appreciated by the workmen who created them. When opened in modern times, many of the Ramessid tombs contained, in addition to the plundered remains of the burial equipment, a series of votive ostraca (smooth limestone flakes suitable for writing) commissioned and executed by the artists responsible for the decoration of the tomb. These unusually large ostraca bore representations of the artists worshiping the sun-god Re-Harakhti (a combination of the gods Re and Horus-of-the-Horizon), the gods of the Theban necropolis, and divinities associated with the Osirian "cycle:" Osiris, Isis, and Nephthys. The dedicators did not desire to partake in some aspect (or status) attached to the king in the afterlife, but rather seem to have believed that the deposition of their votive items in the ritually (and iconographically) potent royal tomb was an effective means of getting their message across to the deity represented. Like their royal masters, these workmen felt a need to communicate with the world beyond.

LEFT: The sarcophagus chamber in the tomb of Ramesses VI (1143–1136 BC) in the Valley of the Kings has a painted "astronomical ceiling." This and similar depictions and lists in other tombs and on coffins represent our main source of information on the astronomical knowledge of the ancient Egyptians. JAMES H. MORRIS

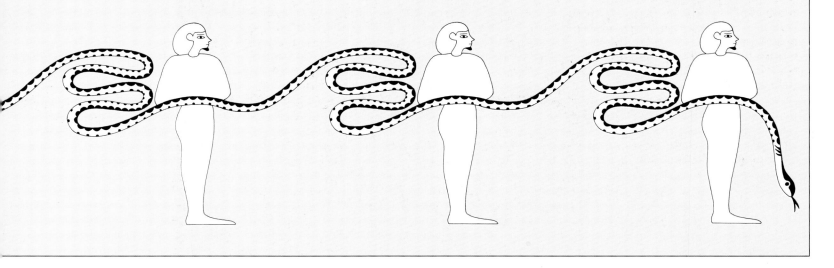

RIGHT: *The Giza tomb of Meresankh III, a queen of Khephren (2518–2493 BC), had a massive, stone-built, free-standing superstructure, but also a less usual rock-cut underground chapel. The chapels of most of the other contemporary tombs formed part of their superstructure.* JAMES H. MORRIS

RIGHT: *The tomb of Sirenput II (also called Nubkaure-nakht) at Aswan is a good example of a rock-cut tomb of a provincial administrator of the Middle Kingdom. Its owner lived during the reign of Amenemhet II (1918–1884 BC).* JAMES H. MORRIS

ABOVE: *Detail of artwork in the tomb of Sirenput II.* JAMES H. MORRIS

years) thus formed the basis for the specific forms of funerary architecture and iconography that were produced during the various periods of Egyptian history. For example, the continued sustenance of the *ka* (through some form of an eternally repeated offering ritual) was ensured by inscribing both the offering prayer and depictions of the offerings themselves in the tomb chapel; and freedom of movement for the *akh* was provided through the presence of written assurances — on papyri, coffins, or tomb walls — of its power to overcome all conceivable obstacles. Of particular importance seems to have been the maintenance of the deceased's status vis-à-vis both the living and the dead through visual display.

Tombs may be seen as directing status-enhancing display toward two distinct audiences: the inhabitants of the readily perceivable world (i.e., the living) and those whose major (but not only) sphere of activity lay beyond the boundaries of the ordinary senses (i.e., the dead and the gods). These two audiences were accommodated by the two major portions of the tomb: the superstructure that housed the cult chapel used by the deceased's relatives and the substructure, the main purpose of which was to protect the corpse and its accompanying burial equipment and to serve as a place of transformation from death to rebirth.

The form and decoration of the cult chapel (whether royal mortuary temple or private offering place) and the superstructure within which it was contained had to accommodate a living audience: the paintings and/or relief decoration and statuary "memorialized" the deceased and provided a visual focus for the cult; and offering paraphernalia (tables, stands, and vessels) provided for the continued sustenance of the *ka* of the tomb owner. Hence the predominance throughout the pharaonic period of the basic offering scene, in which the tomb owner (royal or private) was the recipient of sustenance. Documentation of the sources of this sustenance began with the depiction of rows of offering bearers responsible for the transport of foodstuffs and burial equipment to the tomb. The scene became abstracted with the practice of personifying the estates from whose marshes, fields, and meadows the sustenance was derived. The form reached its fullest extent of graphic elaboration in the so-called genre scenes depicting the means by which the nourishment of the deceased was obtained: through fishing, fowling, hunting, farming, and commodity production.

That the tomb-chapel depictions were intended to be seen and appreciated by the living (as well as benefiting the deceased) is demonstrated in a general way by an increasing emphasis (from the Sixth Dynasty onward) on the individual lifetime attainments of the deceased in the "tomb autobiography." More specifically, a remarkable inscription from the tomb chapel of an official named Shoshenq of the Twenty-sixth Dynasty exhorts the visitor to observe and enjoy the quality of its decoration!

In addition to its interior decoration, the external architectural form of the tomb chapel signaled the presence of a funerary structure and further specified a particular cosmological orientation; thus, the pyramidal superstructures of both royal and private tomb chapels possessed a solar association that connected the afterlife of the deceased with the sun-god.

The royal cult was carried out in a chapel (or temple) located at a site and of a form appropriate to its chronological period and religious milieu. The structure was erected on a scale and of materials commensurate with the king's status as intermediary between the gods and humans, subject to the resources available for its construction. The mortuary temples of the New Kingdom rulers were located on the fringe of the cultivation to the west of Thebes. They were planned as variants of temples with tripartite sanctuaries inspired by the cult temples of Amun, Lord of Thebes and were erected on a grander or lesser scale — and finished or left incomplete — depending on the length of the specific king's reign or the willingness of his successor to complete his monument.

In contrast to the offering place with its necessary accommodation for the living, the subterranean burial apartments were sealed immediately following the burial and opened only thereafter to accommodate additional burials. Their architectural features and decoration did not enhance the status of the tomb owner to the public but rather ensured proper standing in the afterlife and the appropriate respect of the gods and the deceased ancestors.

In the New Kingdom (1540–1069 BC), wall and ceiling decoration of burial chambers was more common in royal

ABOVE: The tomb chapel of Maya, "Overseer of the Treasury" of Tutankhamun (1336–1327 BC), is spectacularly decorated in a style which subtly blends the artistic innovations of the Amarna period with the more classical conventions. Such tombs continued to be built at Saqqara for the next 150 years. EGYPT EXPLORATION SOCIETY, LONDON

LEFT: The career of Montuemhet (attested 667–648 BC), the owner of tomb number 34 at Asasif in Thebes, spanned the end of the Nubian Twenty-fifth and the Saite Twenty-sixth dynasties; Theban tombs of this period were rock-cut but provided with large outer courts and pylons. JOHN G. ROSS

THE PYRAMIDS

Jaromir Malek

In a country of powerful and lasting images, none surpasses the pyramids, and the first encounter with these artificial "mountains of the pharaohs" is unforgettable. Although Egypt is regarded as the land of the pyramids, at least as many pyramids — and possibly more — can be found in the cemeteries of the Kushite kingdom in the Sudan. These are smaller and a thousand or more years later than the last royal pyramid on Egyptian soil, but the inspiration for their construction came from Egypt. In addition to some 50 royal pyramids in Egypt, there are others built for different reasons. Figures quoted vary considerably. Several known pyramids have not yet been located, for example, the pyramid of King Menkauhor (2377–2369 BC), most probably at northwestern Saqqara. The identification of others, such as the "capless" pyramid, probably of Merykare (c. 2060 BC), at northern Saqqara, is still disputed.

ABOVE: While the design and measurements of the pyramids of Khufu, Khephren, and Menkaure (between 2549 and 2460 BC) have been scrutinized (sometimes with some strange conclusions) for centuries, the layout of the site is still difficult to understand. There is, however, no doubt that even here little was left to chance. JÜRGEN LIEPE

LEFT: Sections showing the interior of the pyramids of Khufu (2549–2526 BC), Khephren (2518–2493 BC), and Menkaure (2488–2460 BC) at Giza.

BELOW: The size of the pyramids and the precision of their construction are remarkable feats of engineering. AUSTRALIAN PICTURE LIBRARY/STEVE VIDLER

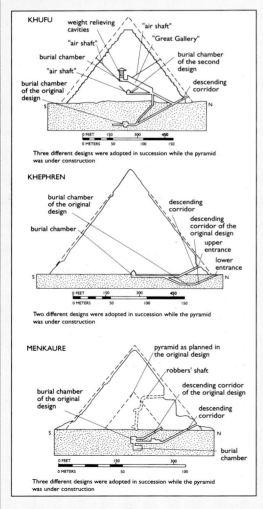

KHUFU

weight relieving cavities

"air shaft"

"air shaft"

"Great Gallery"

burial chamber

"air shaft"

burial chamber of the second design

burial chamber of the original design

descending corridor

0 FEET 150 300 450
0 METERS 50 100 150

Three different designs were adopted in succession while the pyramid was under construction

KHEPHREN

burial chamber of the original design

descending corridor

descending corridor of the original design

burial chamber

upper entrance

lower entrance

0 FEET 150 300 450
0 METERS 50 100 150

Two different designs were adopted in succession while the pyramid was under construction

MENKAURE

pyramid as planned in the original design

robbers' shaft

burial chamber of the original design

descending corridor of the original design

descending corridor

burial chamber

0 FEET 150 300
0 METERS 50 100

Three different designs were adopted in succession while the pyramid was under construction

The pyramid was the simplest three-dimensional form that an architect designing along straight lines and right angles (as ancient Egyptians did) could devise. Nevertheless, it did not evolve immediately. The earliest, built for King Netjerikhet Djoser at Saqqara around 2620 BC, was a step pyramid (153 x 129 yards/ 140 x 118 m plan, height 66 yards/60 m). Its shape was the result of changes in the design of a structure that started as a *mastaba*-tomb (from the Arabic word for "bench," to describe its appearance) of a rectangular plan, probably with a flat roof. The ideas behind the transformation into a step pyramid are not entirely clear. Some brick-built *mastabas* of the preceding period contained a stepped core and, although Djoser's architect need not initially have tried to imitate it, it may have helped to define the final form of the step pyramid and made it acceptable. The first "true" pyramid appeared at Maidum in the reign of Snofru (2573–2549 BC) when casing was applied to a stepped core, and from then on the external form of these monuments remained constant (except for variations in size and the angle of the slope of their sides) for the rest of Egyptian history. The similarity between the shape of the pyramid and the summit of the obelisk of the sun-god of Heliopolis is almost certainly significant.

Egyptologists have no doubt that the largest pyramids were tombs of the kings who ruled in the third and the first half of the second millennia BC. This function is shown by the arrangements inside (the sarcophagus for the body of the king, niches for containers with his internal organs, the *Pyramid Texts* to help him on his journey to join the gods) as well as outside (the presence of a temple for the king's funerary cult). Nevertheless, many questions remain concerning construction and the function of some of the adjoining buildings.

The pyramids at Giza excite the greatest interest because of their size and the perfection of their construction. The pyramid of Khufu (2549–2526 BC) is the largest in Egypt (252 x 252 yards / 230 x 230 m plan, original height 160 yards / 146 m) and constructed with astonishing precision. The mathematical properties of its design have been the subject of esoteric — and mostly scholarly unacceptable — interpretations; one feels, nevertheless, that the "Great Pyramid" still has some surprises in store for us. The other two pyramids at Giza belong to Khephren (2518–2493 BC) and Menkaure (2488–2460 BC).

The pyramid was only one element among the buildings that formed the royal burial complex. The purpose of the complex was to provide the deceased king with all he needed for his continued existence after death. The entrance was through the valley temple, so called because it was situated at the edge of the cultivated area, several hundred yards to the east of the pyramid. From the valley

ABOVE: *The Step Pyramid of Netjerikhet Djoser (2628–2609 BC) is without doubt the most romantic of all ancient Egyptian monuments. It is surrounded by buildings connected with ceremonies which the king would undergo in the next life.* JÜRGEN LIEPE

temple, a rising causeway (ceremonial way) led westward to the cult temple (also called the pyramid temple or mortuary temple by Egyptologists). The king's afterlife was ensured by ceremonies that were performed there and by offerings presented in the temple's chapel. Dismantled boats or their imitations in stone, for the king's use in his celestial journeys, may have been deposited nearby. One or more smaller pyramids in the vicinity of the royal pyramid were either part of the cult arrangements or tombs of royal relatives, particularly queens. The royal pyramid was the tomb proper, sealed after the burial and from then inaccessible. The form of the pyramid complex continued to evolve, and as they were endowed with land, people, and income, such complexes came to play an important part in the economic life of the country.

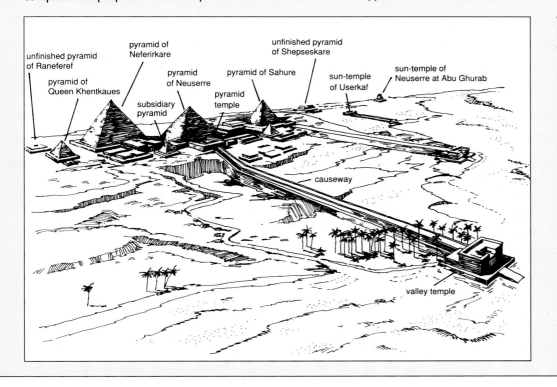

unfinished pyramid of Raneferef

pyramid of Neferirkare

unfinished pyramid of Shepseskare

pyramid of Queen Khentkaues

pyramid of Sahure

sun-temple of Neuserre at Abu Ghurab

pyramid of Neuserre

sun-temple of Userkaf

subsidiary pyramid

pyramid temple

causeway

valley temple

LEFT: *An artist's reconstruction of the appearance of the pyramid field at Abusir around 2350 BC.*

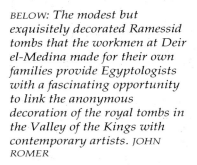

than in private funerary monuments. Texts and representations focused on the deceased monarch's transition from the transitory state of death to his regeneration as a god — usually as Re or Osiris. The *Pyramid Texts* of the Old Kingdom (2647–2124 BC) and the body of New Kingdom royal mortuary literature (e.g. *Amduat, Book of the Gates, Litany of Re*) constituted the primary iconographic sources for the decoration. It was not common to decorate the walls of the contemporary burial chambers of private individuals, except in cases of the official's unusually high status or close proximity (and immediate access) to the royal prototypes.

Tombs were not the only "memorials" commissioned by the Egyptians: family cults focusing on deceased ancestors are known from the New Kingdom sites of Gurob and Deir el-Medina. The forms taken by these smaller-scale monuments (stelae and anthropoid busts) have a distinctly archaic appearance. And the staggering number of Middle Kingdom (2040–1648 BC) cenotaphs set up at Abydos (ranging from entire temples to single stelae) testify to a strong desire to be associated with the Osirian rites. Finally, *shabtis* (funerary figures) belonging to private individuals were apparently secreted in caches in royal cemeteries, such as those at Abydos and el-Lisht, as well as interred with some of the royal burials of the Eighteenth Dynasty. The motive for this practice is nowhere explicitly stated; however, it may have ensured the *shabti* owner a close association in the afterlife with the king in or near whose tomb the object was placed.

"Memorials" thus have as their main focus the individual royal or private person (who is often the donor) as the

immediate *recipient* of the beneficences mentioned or depicted.

Another interesting way of viewing monuments is in terms of their manner and place of deposition. Temple enclosures and cemeteries (the major "sacred" areas) were not the only sites in which cultic and memorial dedication took place. Certain geological formations, such as the Peak of the West, the pyramid-shaped pinnacle of the western cliffs at Thebes, were personified and worshiped in their own right. High up on the side of the Peak was a small group of shrines containing stelae dedicated by local inhabitants. And many of those same individuals were also responsible for the incised graffiti that remain visible on the Theban cliffs. These rock-cut inscriptions frequently provide not only the name and title of individuals, but depict them, occasionally with other family members, in acts of obeisance before the deities associated with the Theban necropolis: Ptah of the Valley of the Queens, the cobra goddess Mertseger,

and the triad Amun-Re, Mut, and Khonsu. Quarrying sites in the Sinai and Eastern Desert, such as the Wadi Maghara and the Wadi Hammamat, have produced similar commemorative depictions.

Although to the modern speaker of English the word "monument" (and particularly its adjectival derivative, "monumental") implies large size and sumptuous decoration, the single factor unifying all of the ancient Egyptian votive and memorial remains (*mnw*) was permanence. Whether providing for the eternal sustenance of the private or royal *ka*, the memorialization of a lifetime of correct conduct, or the perpetuation of cosmic order, an ancient Egyptian monument converted the single act of donation into an infinitely repeatable cycle of offering, commemoration, and maintenance. Should the funerary or cult offerings cease to be placed on the altar and the ritual texts outlast their mortal celebrants, the monument's survival alone ensured that its purpose would endure.

ABOVE: The inhabitants of Deir el-Medina, the village of Ramessid workmen employed in the construction of tombs in the Valley of the Kings, represent the best-documented community in ancient Egypt. Intimate personal histories of its inhabitants can be reconstructed from papyri and ostraca found there. JOHN G. ROSS

CONTINUITY
AND CHANGE

Invaders and Conquerors

A. K. Bowman

WHEN ALEXANDER THE GREAT entered Egypt in 332 BC and released it from the oppressive domination of the Persians, he inaugurated a new era in Egyptian history that was to last for almost a millennium — an era during which Egypt was a vitally important part of the Greco-Roman world. For the first three centuries of this period, Egypt was one of the most powerful of the Hellenistic kingdoms. Thereafter, it became a province first of the Roman and then of the Byzantine empire until AD 642, when, almost three years after the original invasion by the Arabs, Byzantium finally surrendered it by treaty to the Islamic caliphate.

When Alexander left Egypt in 331 BC he entrusted it to the control of a viceroy. In the political convulsions that followed Alexander's death in 323 BC Egypt was seized by the most astute of his successor generals, the Macedonian Ptolemy, son of Lagos. But it was not until 305 BC that Ptolemy was secure enough openly to assume an independent kingship as Ptolemy I Soter ("Savior"). Egypt was ruled by his descendants (Ptolemies II–XIV, at times ruling jointly with their wives/sisters, usually called Cleopatra) until the death of Cleopatra VII in August, 30 BC. It was the wealthiest of the Hellenistic kingdoms and for much of the

period politically the most powerful, controlling an empire that at its greatest extent, around 200 BC, included its western neighbor Cyrene, Cyprus, and much of the Levant. And Egypt was the last of the Hellenistic kingdoms to fall under Roman domination.

Internally and externally, the Ptolemies reinforced the stability of their dynasty by various means, including extravagant parades of regal power in Alexandria, the practice of associating a son and heir in his father's rule, marriages between royal brothers and sisters, as well as dynastic marriage alliances with other Hellenistic ruling families.

The foundations of Ptolemaic power and prosperity were laid under the first three rulers — Ptolemy I Soter, Ptolemy II Philadelphus ("Sister-loving") and Ptolemy III Euergetes ("Benefactor"). After 200 BC the dynasty was weakened by dissension and power struggles within the royal house, increasingly frequent outbreaks of native unrest, and the growing power of Rome. The last century of Ptolemaic rule is predominantly a period of political decline, but Egypt's wealth was still immense. Cleopatra VII, the last of the Ptolemaic monarchs (and the only one who spoke the Egyptian language), had ambitions to revive the

TOP: The cult of the god Sarapis appeared early in the Ptolemaic period. PETER CLAYTON

ABOVE: Portraits painted on wood or canvas and attached to elaborately bandaged but rather poorly mummified bodies were introduced in Egypt in the first century AD. LOUVRE MUSEUM, PARIS/PETER CLAYTON

OPPOSITE: The tomb of Petosiris at Hermopolis West has predominantly Greek-style decoration. PETER CLAYTON

PREVIOUS PAGE: The temple of Isis and associated structures were moved in the 1970s from the island of Philae to the island of Agilkia to save them from periodic submersion in the waters of the Aswan Dam. THE IMAGE BANK/GIULIANO COLLIVA

Egypt thus became a province of the Roman empire and one to which the emperors were particularly sensitive — it was the wealthiest province in the empire, producing a large proportion of the food supply of the city of Rome, and potentially a serious security risk. Risks were to be demonstrated in the succeeding centuries not merely by internal unrest — such as uprisings by the Jewish population in AD 66 and 115–117 — but by threats to Roman imperial power itself. The emperor Vespasian's successful bid for power was first proclaimed at Alexandria on 1 July, AD 69. Domination of Egypt by a hostile foreign power, such as that by the rulers of the Syrian city of Palmyra in AD 270–72, could strike at the very lifeline of the Roman empire.

In the period after AD 300, with the triumph of Christianity, the division of the Roman empire into West and East (the Byzantine empire), and the foundation of Constantinople as an eastern counterpart to Rome, Egypt's role was reoriented toward the eastern Mediterranean. In the fifth and sixth centuries, Byzantine emperors had to struggle to maintain control in the south against the tribes of the Blemmyes and Nubades in Nubia near the Nile Cataracts. The main struggles for power, however, were played out in the world of church politics, where the patriarchs or bishops of Alexandria fought to maintain

prestige of the dynasty by using the power of Roman generals to aggrandize their friends and allies. She became enamored of Julius Caesar when he pursued Pompey to Egypt, and she bore him a son named Caesarion. Her more notorious liaison with Mark Antony might have recreated an empire in the east that would threaten the power of Rome. Instead, it culminated in their defeat at the battle of Actium (September, 31 BC). Eleven months later the victorious Octavian, Caesar's heir, was in Alexandria when Cleopatra and her Roman lover committed suicide.

THE PTOLEMAIC DYNASTY

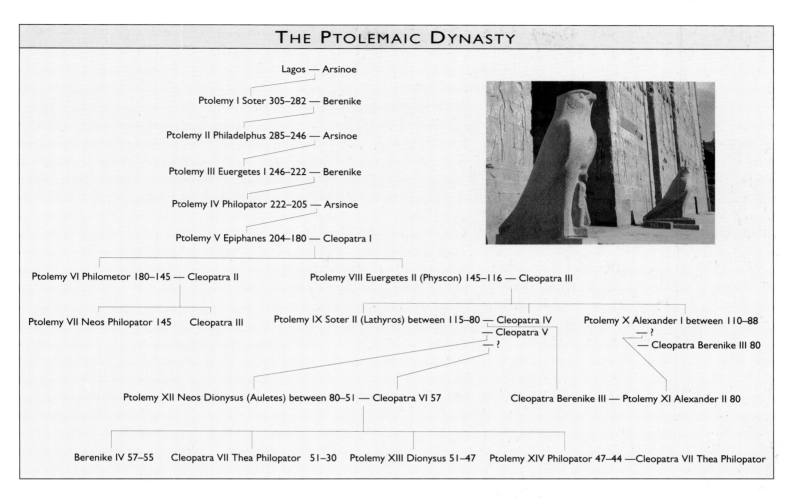

Lagos — Arsinoe

Ptolemy I Soter 305–282 — Berenike

Ptolemy II Philadelphus 285–246 — Arsinoe

Ptolemy III Euergetes I 246–222 — Berenike

Ptolemy IV Philopator 222–205 — Arsinoe

Ptolemy V Epiphanes 204–180 — Cleopatra I

Ptolemy VI Philometor 180–145 — Cleopatra II   Ptolemy VIII Euergetes II (Physcon) 145–116 — Cleopatra III

Ptolemy VII Neos Philopator 145   Cleopatra III   Ptolemy IX Soter II (Lathyros) between 115–80 — Cleopatra IV   Ptolemy X Alexander I between 110–88
— Cleopatra V   — ?
— ?   — Cleopatra Berenike III 80

Ptolemy XII Neos Dionysus (Auletes) between 80–51 — Cleopatra VI 57   Cleopatra Berenike III — Ptolemy XI Alexander II 80

Berenike IV 57–55   Cleopatra VII Thea Philopator 51–30   Ptolemy XIII Dionysus 51–47   Ptolemy XIV Philopator 47–44 —Cleopatra VII Thea Philopator

their ecclesiastical and political supremacy over rivals within Egypt and the power of their see over that of Constantinople in the Eastern Church.

Despite the debilitating effects of such struggles, Egypt's power and wealth were still vital to the emperors of Byzantium. But a Persian invasion and occupation from AD 619–28 was a harbinger of more serious changes, which began elsewhere with the flight of Muhammad from Mecca to Medina in AD 622. Twenty years later the Arab general Amr Ibn al-As marched into Alexandria.

Egypt, during this period, in many ways less isolated than under the pharaohs, offers striking contrasts in continuity and change. The foundation of its prosperity under the Ptolemies, a governmental system designed to exploit its natural wealth, owed something to the organization imposed by the Persians earlier in the fourth century BC. Directly under the control of the king was a group of officials with jurisdiction over the whole land. The group comprised a finance minister, a chief accountant, and a chancery of ministers in charge of records, letters, and decrees. Beneath them, was a pyramid of subordinate officials with authority in limited areas, from each of the 30 or more district divisions (nomes) down to the chief administrator of each individual village. During the first century of Ptolemaic rule, such officials were appointed almost entirely from the elite Greek immigrant population, and the same was true of the soldiers, who formed a favored group of holders of land allotments when not on active service. Such positions gradually became more readily available to those native Egyptians who were willing and able to assimilate the language and culture of the Greek ruling elite.

With the advent of Roman rule, Egypt no longer had a resident monarch but was governed by a viceregal prefect appointed by the Roman emperor (the first was the poet, soldier, and statesman Cornelius Gallus) and garrisoned by Roman legionary and auxiliary soldiers. The upper echelons of the provincial administration were staffed by outsiders

ABOVE: The family tree of the Ptolemaic dynasty (305–30 BC). Only the more important members of the dynasty have been included. The temple of Horas, at Edfu (pictured above) was begun by Ptolemy III and completed by Ptolemy XII. (Photograph: AUSTRALIAN PICTURE LIBRARY/D. & J. HEATON)

ABOVE: A wine factory at Marea on the southern shore of Lake Mareotis, southwest of Alexandria (fifth or sixth century AD), an area famous for its wine. The large square basin received juice pressed on the sloping floor and from an adjacent room through a spout.
A. K. BOWMAN

ABOVE AND RIGHT: Vintage scenes from the tomb of Petosiris at Hermopolis West (Tuna el-Gebel) showing (right) men (one of them nude) picking bunches of grapes from a vine over their heads and (above) the juice from the crushed grapes draining into a vat from which it is taken away in large amphorae for registration. Fourth century BC.
ANCIENT ART AND ARCHITECTURE COLLECTION/MARY JELLIFFE

of high status, whereas the local positions were filled by Greco-Egyptians. The Roman government of Egypt, like the Ptolemaic, aimed at maximizing wealth and extracting revenue. It introduced a minutely detailed census procedure for the recording of all inhabitants and their property; this procedure was to form the basis of a complex system of taxation on property, persons, trades, and commercial transactions of all kinds.

Despite the power of the central bureaucracy, however, the Romans did introduce into the towns of the Nile Valley some of the features of autonomous civic administration that already existed in Alexandria and the other "Greek cities" in Egypt, Naukratis in the western Delta, and Ptolemais in Upper Egypt. An attempt to place some of the burdens of administration on the local elites had only limited success, and a series of administrative reforms in the late third and early fourth centuries again centralized power in the hands of very small groups of powerful officials, often wealthy landholders. At the same time, Egypt was subdivided, for administrative purposes, into a number of smaller provinces with separate military and civil officials. By the mid-sixth century, however, Emperor Justinian had to recognize the failure of this policy, and he combined the powers in the hands of a military officer with a civil deputy as a counterweight to the power of the church authorities. By this time, however, it was for all practical purposes impossible to separate secular and ecclesiastical power effectively.

The underlying realities of Egyptian history are ultimately based in its natural economy. For Greeks, Romans, and Byzantines alike, management of the land and its resources was of paramount importance. Under the Ptolemies the population of Egypt increased considerably; so too did agricultural productivity as large areas of land were newly brought into cultivation, particularly in the Faiyum, where there was a heavy concentration of Greek settlers. Egypt's fertility was legendary, and good management of the irrigation system, through a system of dikes and the traditional water wheels and shadoofs, produced handsome surpluses as long as the annual inundation of the Nile reached the right level. Ownership and management of the land was carefully controlled by the royal bureaucracy in the Ptolemaic period, but under the Romans there was a greater emphasis on private land ownership. This emphasis became even more marked in the Byzantine period. As virtually all state-owned land was sold off to private

LEFT: At the village of Karanis in the northeastern Faiyum there are extensive remains of mud-brick domestic buildings (mainly second and third century AD) and of two temples of which the more southerly is dedicated to the local crocodile gods, Pnepheros and Petesouchos. A. K. BOWMAN

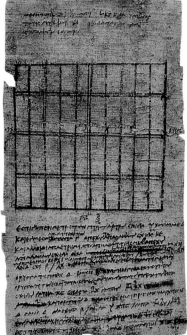

persons, large landowners became very powerful, exploiting their holdings and oppressing their tenants.

Greater integration into the political structures of the Hellenistic and Roman world also created greater opportunities for trade, industry, and commerce. Despite maintaining a closed currency system through the mint at Alexandria, Egypt played an integral role in the Mediterranean economy. Contacts with the East through the ports of the Red Sea coast that opened up under the Ptolemies were further exploited under the Romans as road building in the Eastern Desert and water-transport facilities increased. Although the vast majority of the Egyptian population was engaged in

ABOVE: The irrigation system on the estate of Apollonius, finance minister of Ptolemy II Philadelphus (285–246 BC), at Philadelphia in the Faiyum. The text has an estimate of the cost of digging canals and moving earth. The main irrigation channels are represented by double lines, the dikes by single lines. A. K. BOWMAN

LEFT: The Nilometer built into the quay at Elephantine Island dates to the Roman period and is matched by many other examples up and down the valley. In this area the river began its rise in June and the floodwaters receded in September. ANCIENT ART AND ARCHITECTURE COLLECTION/E. HOBSON

ALEXANDRIA

On 7 April, 331 BC, Alexander the Great founded the city that was to bear his name and was to dominate the eastern Mediterranean world politically, culturally, and economically until the foundation of Constantinople in the fourth century AD. It was also to be Alexander's last resting place, in a tomb that all the efforts of modern archaeologists have so far failed to locate. Alexandria was founded specifically as a Greek city with civic organs of administration, and hence it stood somewhat apart from its Egyptian context. Nevertheless, within a few years of its founder's death, it replaced Memphis as the Egyptian capital, a position it was to retain throughout the Roman and Byzantine periods.

Although few of its ancient buildings can be traced in the modern city, ancient writers (such as the geographer Strabo, who visited Alexandria in the early Roman period) bear abundant witness to the spectacular beauty of its buildings — the palace complex of the Ptolemies called the Brucheion, the amphitheater and stadium, the gymnasia, theaters and baths, the great temple of Sarapis, and the Caesareum begun by Cleopatra for Mark Antony and completed in the reign of Augustus. The latter was described by the Jewish philosopher Philo as "a precinct of enormous breadth, embellished with porticoes, libraries, chambers, groves, gateways, broadwalks, and courts and adorned with all the most extravagant fitments." The obelisks that stood in front of it until the nineteenth century can today be

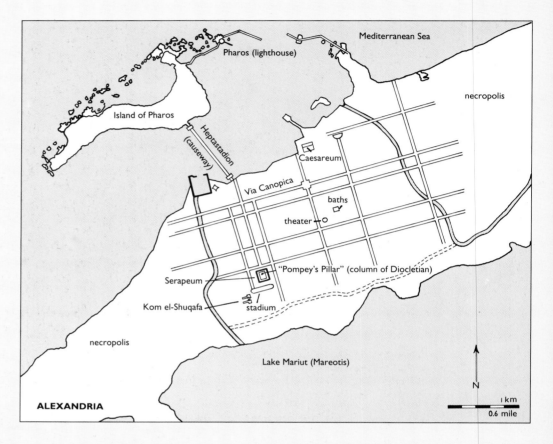

seen, one on London's Embankment and the other in New York's Central Park. An ancient chronicle records that when the Arab invaders entered Alexandria in AD 642, the soldiers gazed in wonder at the width and grandeur of the streets and shielded their eyes from the dazzle of the marble. Equally grand and important were its two great adjoining harbors, marked by the Pharos, the great lighthouse designed in the early Ptolemaic period that is counted as one of the wonders of the ancient world— it was built in three stories, reached a total height of about 400 feet (120 m), and contained a fire that was magnified and projected far out to sea by a reflecting device.

Its position as a natural harbor helped to make Alexandria the most important economic center in the Mediterranean and made the Nile one of the great trading arteries of the classical world. A huge maritime trade made Alexandria a center of the shipbuilding industry, encouraged the manufacture and export of Egypt's special products, notably glass and papyrus, made possible the large-scale transport of grain from the Nile Valley, and opened up a network of trading relations with India and Arabia, bringing drugs, spices, precious metals,

LEFT: The theater at Alexandria was probably first built in the third century AD. The auditorium was adorned at the rear with columns of Italian marble. Graffiti on the seats suggest a later connection with the notorious circus factions, the Blues and the Greens.
PETER CLAYTON

ABOVE: *A decorated tomb of the second century AD from Alexandria, dominated by the traditional motifs of Egyptian funerary art. The corpse on the bier is flanked by figures connected with the goddesses Isis and Nephthys. Above is the winged sun disk.* MACQUITTY INTERNATIONAL COLLECTION

jewelry and other luxury items into the Greco-Roman world. Many of the raw materials came along the trade routes of the East and were manufactured at Alexandria for export.

Some products — notably drugs and works of art such as cameos, mosaics, and sculpture — were intimately connected with Alexandria's importance as an intellectual and cultural center, perhaps its greatest contribution to classical civilization. In an environment divorced from its Egyptian surroundings, the foundation of the museum and library under the early Ptolemies created a focus for royal patronage of the arts and sciences. The major poets of the Hellenistic

ABOVE: *The underground burial chambers at Kom el-Shuqafa (Alexandria) date to the second century AD and show a combination of Greek and Egyptian elements. The decoration in the burial chamber, below the entrance and banqueting hall, shows the traditional Egyptian deities attending the corpse.* ANCIENT ART AND ARCHITECTURE COLLECTION/RONALD SHERIDAN

period — Theocritus, Callimachus, Apollonius of Rhodes — all lived in or visited the city. The librarians and scholars of Alexandria were the first to study and make order out of the manuscript traditions of the great classical writers (particularly Homer). Mathematics and the applied sciences flourished: Euclid wrote mathematical textbooks, Eratosthenes

calculated the earth's circumference, Archimedes studied applied physics and engineering. The school of medicine founded in the Ptolemaic period retained its leading reputation into the Byzantine era, and the greatest physician of classical antiquity, Galen of Pergamum, studied in Alexandria in the second century AD.

During the Roman and Byzantine periods, literary activity and scholarship yielded pride of place to philosophy. The work of the distinguished Alexandrian Jewish philosopher Philo points forward to the second century, when the foundation of the Christian Catechetical School at Alexandria provided the necessary focus for Christian thinkers, such as Clement and Origen, to forge a coherent theology. This theology was formed from the interaction of Christian doctrine with Platonic philosophy and the legacy of traditional Jewish methods of interpreting and commentating upon the scriptures.

It is equally important for the history of ideas that, in the Christian context of the Byzantine empire, the writing and teaching of Platonic and especially Aristotelian philosophy flourished in Alexandria as nowhere else, continuing into the seventh and eighth centuries, when the tradition would be transmitted to the custody of the Islamic world.

LEFT: *The unique, three-roomed schoolhouse at Alexandria belongs to the later Roman period and is part of a complex of public buildings that included the theater and brick-built bathhouse supplied by adjacent water cisterns.* A. K. BOWMAN

RIGHT: *Trajan's kiosk at Philae was built early in the second century* AD. *This was an unroofed temple with fourteen columns linked by screen walls that used to serve as the point of entry into the temple precinct from the river. Painting by David Roberts, 1838–39.* ASHMOLEAN LIBRARY, OXFORD

BELOW: *The temple of Isis at Philae was built in the Ptolemaic and Roman periods and included a chapel of the Nubian god Mandulis. It remained an object of pilgrimage for tribes from the south until the mid-sixth century and there are clear signs of occupation by Coptic Christians. The photograph was taken c. 1870 by A. Beato.* GRIFFITH INSTITUTE, ASHMOLEAN MUSEUM, OXFORD

agriculture, Egypt's economy was by no means a subsistence or barter economy. Even at the village level the degree of monetization and complexity in the economy was marked, goods and artifacts of all sorts being traded on a large scale through the medium of coin. The Ptolemies had exercised careful control over commerce and trade by means of so-called royal monopolies, but the Romans allowed greater freedom for private enterprise and trade. The wealth that could be gained is epitomized by an exaggerated or possibly fictional description of a third-century Alexandrian merchant named Firmus who was so rich that the glass windows of his house were set in pitch, who owned so many books that he could supply an army with paper, and whose ships had brought him two legendary twelve-foot (3.6 m) elephant tusks from India.

In social as in economic affairs, the regime established under the Ptolemies favored the Greek-speaking immigrant elite. The establishment of a social and governmental system in which literacy in Greek was of prime importance perpetuated a hierarchy of status, which was reinforced in various ways, such as by a legal system that recognized distinctions between Greek and Egyptian status. The Egyptian demotic language continued to be spoken and written in to the Roman period, but those Egyptians who wished to better themselves socially and economically needed to learn Greek. After a century or so of Ptolemaic rule, the barriers became easier to cross — a good many mixed marriages took place and, as a consequence many families show a mixture of Greek and Egyptian names.

The advent of Roman rule and Roman law brought refinement to the definition of status, with the creation of a "Greek" urban elite that was privileged socially through membership in exclusive institutions such as gymnasia, economically through lower rates of taxation, and legally through a system of differential penalties. Additional distinctions came as a consequence of Roman citizenship. The "Egyptians" remained at the bottom of the heap, and it was not until the late Roman period, when the Coptic language became a new means of communicating and spreading Christianity among those of lower status, that the Egyptian "national identity" was able to reassert itself in a recognizable form. By far the majority of the many thousands of literary and documentary texts on papyrus from the Ptolemaic and Roman periods are written in Greek — these may not represent the majority of the populace, but they do represent a culturally powerful force.

In the sphere of religion, too, we can observe the coexistence of the different traditions. There are numerous opulent mummies from the Ptolemaic and Roman periods, and the strikingly realistic facial portraits that served as headpieces are a fashion of the same periods. Despite losing much of their influence and economic power under the Ptolemies and even more under the Romans, the Egyptian priests continued to maintain their caste system and to tend the bewilderingly large numbers of cults of sacred animals. Temple building in the Egyptian tradition continued on a lavish scale — at Philae, Edfu, Dendara, and elsewhere. The immigrant Greeks brought their traditional cults, which existed alongside the Egyptian, and there were some hybrid creations. The great cult of Sarapis, a combination of Osiris with the Apis bull, was originally established at Alexandria and probably developed because of the need to put Egyptian religious traditions into a form that was comprehensible to Greeks. The Ptolemies developed their own form of ruler cult, which, as the Rosetta Stone shows, was intended to conciliate the powerful priesthood and establish them in the native religious tradition. In due course, Roman emperor-worship developed alongside and in conjunction

with already existing religious practices. There was also an important Jewish presence at Alexandria and elsewhere in the Ptolemaic and early Roman periods.

Later in the Roman period, change became more marked. In the early third century AD there was a temple of Jupiter in the town of Arsinoe in the Faiyum. In AD 250 Egyptians were required to swear an oath that they were not practicing Christians, and at almost precisely this time the series of hieroglyphic inscriptions by Roman emperors on Egyptian temples comes to an end.

ABOVE: A Ptolemaic queen from the temple at Kom Ombo. The main temple was dedicated to the gods Sobek and Haroeris and its well-preserved wall-reliefs date between the reigns of Ptolemy VI Philometor (180–145 BC) and Macrinus (AD 217–218). THE IMAGE BANK/ALAIN CHOISNET

MONKS, MISSIONARIES, AND MARTYRS

C. C. Walters

AN EGYPTIAN CHRISTIAN is known as a Copt, a word that comes from the Arabic *qibt*. This word in turn derives from the Greek *Aiguptios*, "Egyptian," coined to distinguish the native inhabitants of Egypt from foreign elements. Originally, therefore, the word had no religious connotations at all; the distinction was purely ethnic. Only when the majority of Egyptians was converted to Christianity (probably not before the mid-fourth century) was the link between race and religion coincidentally established.

So, just what is "Coptic" Egypt? Is it, in the wider sense, "Egyptian," or is it Christian? If the latter, does it end with the Arab invasion in AD 639–42, or is it still with us? The term is here taken as referring to Egypt's Christian population, with no chronological cut-off point.

The biblical account of the Holy Family's flight into Egypt establishes an immediate link between that country and the new faith of Christianity. The tradition is recalled at several sites, notably the church of St Sergius in Cairo, which is built over one of the supposed resting places, and Qusqam in Middle Egypt, traditionally the southernmost point reached by the family and today the site of the flourishing monastery of Deir el-Moharrak.

Precisely how and when Christianity was brought to Egypt is uncertain. The church historian Eusebius, writing in the fourth century, repeats the tradition that the evangelist St Mark was the bearer of the word. In any case, there can be little doubt that Christianity was brought first to Alexandria and probably to the Jewish population of that city. How quickly and how far it spread is difficult to gauge, but during the first two centuries converts probably came almost exclusively from the non-Egyptian community. During this period the Catechetical School, one of the great centers of Christian scholarship, was established in Alexandria, and during the first half of the third century it was successively presided over by Clement and Origen, two leading figures of the early church. The character of Egyptian Christianity in these early days was noticeably influenced by Gnostic teachings, a complex philosophy that draws upon pagan, Jewish, and Christian doctrines. The popularity of Gnosticism in Egypt was dramatically demonstrated in 1945–46 by the discovery of more than 40 Christian Gnostic treatises, written in Coptic, at Nag Hammadi in Upper Egypt.

The period from the second half of the third century through the early years of the fourth was a doleful period for Christians in Egypt, many of whom died

ABOVE: *In 1945–46 these papyrus books were found in a sealed pot at Nag Hammadi in Upper Egypt. Dating to the fourth century and translated into Coptic from the Greek, they had belonged to a sect of Gnostic Christians whose teachings were viewed as heretical by the church.* JAMES M. ROBINSON

BELOW: *The fifth-century church of Deir el-Abyad ("the White Monastery") at Sohag is one of the most impressive Christian monuments in Egypt. Built in the time of its famous abbot Shenute, its sanctuary is still used for services by the local Christian population.* C. C. WALTERS

RIGHT: *The central semidome of the sanctuary of the church at Deir el-Abyad is decorated, as is customary, with a painting of Christ in majesty dating to AD 1124. Other figures depicted here include Mary.* JAMES H. MORRIS

during the persecutions of the Roman emperors Decius and, especially, Diocletian. So traumatic was the latter episode that Copts date their era from 284, the year of Diocletian's accession.

The situation was transformed at the beginning of the fourth century. Constantine the Great became emperor (AD 306), adopted Christianity, and founded his new capital at Constantinople (AD 330). Suddenly Christianity, from being a persecuted faith, became the sole official religion of the Roman empire. But with the external threat now removed, the church entered a period of bitter internal strife. The unity that persecution had engendered was shattered by a series of theological disputes, as "orthodoxy" was defined and defended. In particular, the issue of

Christ's human and divine natures was argued over at a succession of councils in which Egypt enthusiastically participated. For much of the fourth century Egypt was represented by the immense figure of Athanasius, Bishop of Alexandria from 328 to 373. His career reflects the uncertainty of the times. Himself a champion of orthodoxy, he spent several periods in exile when his doctrinal position happened to conflict with that of the contemporary emperor. Political as well as personal rivalry played no small part in these contentious times, and the decision of the Council of Constantinople in 381 to elevate Constantinople above Alexandria in church affairs merely heightened the nationalistic tendencies of the Egyptian Church.

If 284 was a year that etched itself in the memories of Egyptian Christians, the year 451 was of far more profound significance for the destiny of their church. In that year the Council of Chalcedon debated for the last time the old Christological question, and pronounced in favor of dyophysitism (two natures of Christ) as opposed to the monophysite (single nature) doctrine espoused by the Egyptian Church. The Egyptian patriarch, Dioscorus, was banished, and an imperial nominee installed in his place was murdered by the mob. Subsequent attempts at conciliation between the two factions failed, and the Egyptian Church passed

LEFT: *St Simeon's monastery at Aswan was founded probably in the seventh century and abandoned in the thirteenth. It was built on two levels, the lower catering for nonmonastic visitors and the upper being reserved for the brethren.* JAMES H. MORRIS

ABOVE: *Dominating the upper terrace at St Simeon's monastery is a massive, three-story complex that seems to have functioned as the principal living quarters of the monks, whose cells opened off vaulted corridors.* JAMES H. MORRIS

into self-imposed exile from which it is only now emerging.

Following an occupation by the Persians which lasted for ten years and ended in their withdrawal in 628, the irresistible Arab tide swept over Egypt and it became part of the Muslim world. The treatment of the Christian population by their new masters varied greatly. Freedom of worship was guaranteed by charter and was generally honored. Active persecution of the kind initiated by al-Hakim (996–1021) was spasmodic. With his exception the Fatimid period (969–1171) was one of notable tolerance, during which Copts played an active part in the life of the country. But at the same time, their subservient status in the new order of things was demonstrated in a number of ways. The tax burden fell heavily on their shoulders. Periodically they were called upon to wear distinctive clothing or to signify in some other way their apartness. Arabic replaced Coptic as the official language. Occasionally churches were closed or even demolished, or permission to rebuild was refused. The slow drip of harassment and humiliation caused many to forsake Christianity, and the revolts that occurred between 725 and 830 were futile gestures. The end of the Ayyubid dynasty in 1250 signaled the beginning of an inexorable decline in Coptic fortunes. Under increasing attack within its own country

and cut off from the rest of Christendom, the Coptic Church steadily lost adherents, influence, and vitality.

In recent times there has been a modest revival. Though the Copts form only a small proportion of the Egyptian population, there has been a noticeable attempt to reassert a Coptic identity and to forge closer links with the main body of the Christian Church. The completion of the modern Cathedral of St Mark in Cairo and the return of the saint's relics were important symbols of this new-found confidence. The Coptic language, which for centuries had been used only for liturgical purposes and then alongside Arabic, is now being taught in Sunday schools.

In the context of Egyptian history, the Coptic period — in other words, the 300 years during which Egypt was a Christian country (c. 350–642) — is but an interlude between the pharaonic and Muslim eras. Dwarfed by one, and submerged by the other, Coptic Egypt struggles to gain our attention. Yet its resilience commands admiration, and in one respect at least Christianity owes Coptic Egypt a great debt.

Christian monasticism was born in the deserts of Egypt in the second half of the third century AD. Just what it was that drove the first hermits to withdraw from human society is difficult to say, but some at least were probably escaping from the persecution of Emperor Decius in 251. One such, according to tradition, was Paul the Theban, the first to whom a name is given, but his existence as a historical figure is open to question. The true founder of monasticism is generally accepted as having been St Antony (*c*. 251–356). Though he was one among many and certainly not the first, his example inspired the multitudes who followed. A *Life* of the saint, ascribed to Athanasius, underlines and in part was responsible for his preeminence. By taking to the desert, men like Antony were, according to their understanding of things, doing battle with the Devil and his legions on their own ground. They lived lives of great privation, spending their days in prayer and meditation and fighting the temptations that constantly

COPTIC TEXTILES

The town of Akhmim, across the river from Sohag and the monasteries of Deir el-Abyad and Deir el-Ahmar, was one of the most important centers of Coptic textile manufacture (particularly woolen and silk fabrics) in Egypt. Akhmim textiles were renowned for their strong colors and characteristic motifs, which continued to be used for several centuries after the Arab conquest.

LEFT: *Part of a band or border of woven wool and linen. It depicts a vintager standing beneath an arcade with the border to the right filled with a vine motif springing from an amphora. From Akhmim, fifth to sixth century. ASHMOLEAN MUSEUM, OXFORD*

ABOVE: *A decorative band in woolen cloth dating to the seventh to eighth century. Within the polychrome borders is a repeated pattern based on stylized floral motifs. ASHMOLEAN MUSEUM, OXFORD*

BELOW: *A decorative roundel—perhaps a shoulder piece—on which are depicted five putti, or youths, each holding an ill-defined object that might be a flower or fruit. From Akhmim, fifth to sixth century. ASHMOLEAN MUSEUM, OXFORD*

BELOW: *Part of a border from a hanging or cover. The entwined motif, usually referred to as a guilloche, is similar to that used as a border on mosaic floors. Akhmim, fourth century. ASHMOLEAN MUSEUM, OXFORD*

assailed them. A collection of their sayings, the *Apophthegmata Patrum*, admirably summarizes the simple philosophy by which they lived.

Gradually, their extreme form of asceticism was modified, and a system developed of loose agglomerations of cells occupied by individual anchorites (hermits) and their disciples. At the more heavily populated sites, such as Cellia, northwest of Cairo (c. fourth through ninth centuries), a nucleus of communal buildings, including a church, was soon added. From an early stage this nucleus was walled and contained a *qasr*, or keep, to serve as a place of refuge if, as seems to have happened regularly, the community was threatened by desert tribespeople. Eventually, though probably not before the ninth century, such communities were turned into fortified enclosures by the construction of high perimeter walls. So far as we can tell their inhabitants never adopted a formal set of rules.

Such rules, however, precisely characterized the *coenobia* whose prototype was established at Tabennisi in Upper Egypt by St Pachome around AD 320. In these the needs of the individual were subordinated to those of the community, and every aspect of the inmates' lives was governed by clearly defined regulations and a code of discipline. This "common life" proved immensely popular, and institutions based on the Tabennisi model, though not

necessarily under its jurisdiction, sprang up in many parts of the country.

These Pachomian monasteries, in particular, played an important role in the economic and social life of the nation. Inmates cultivated their own land, employed hired labor, sold the products of their handiwork, and in return purchased what they themselves could not provide. They protected the local population against the excesses of the authorities and gave succor to the needy and homeless. On a wider stage the monks gave unquestioning support to

ABOVE: The early monasteries, like that of St Paul near the Red Sea, grew up around the dwelling place of their founder, which after his death became the focal point for the community. Unlike the later foundations of St Pachome, they were loosely organized without any formal set of rules, and this tradition is maintained by their inmates today. MAXIMILIEN BRUGGMAN

LEFT: The largest and most prosperous monastery in Egypt today is Deir el-Moharrak. According to tradition, the Holy Family lived at nearby Qusqam for three and a half years, and a week-long festival attracts thousands of pilgrims to the monastery each summer. C. C. WALTERS

NEW FAITH IN AN ANCIENT LAND

Native Egyptians, listening as a missionary recounted the story of Christ's death and resurrection, must have been irresistibly reminded of the myth surrounding their own ancient god Osiris, and this association might well have contributed to the evident readiness with which they embraced the new faith. However, for a while at least the setting sun of paganism existed alongside the rising star of Christianity. Not until the temple of Philae was closed in the mid-sixth century can institutionalized ancient Egyptian religious practices be said to have died.

Those early centuries of the Christian era were indeed a period of transition, and nothing exemplifies this transition better than the attitude of the newly converted to their pagan heritage. Outwardly, at least, they displayed exemplary hostility. The *Life* of Shenute gives us a glimpse of the manner in which pagans were hounded and sometimes killed and their idols rooted out and destroyed, while the walls of tomb and temple bear testimony to the diligence with which the new zealots set about defacing ancient images.

But alongside this rejection of the past was a willingness to use what their ancestors had left behind, an instinctive clinging to ancient customs and a reworking of time-honored conventions in a new context. Many Upper Egyptian temples were occupied during the Christian period, some by monastic communities and others by the lay population. The prefix "Deir" attached to the modern name of any site proclaims its monastic connections, as with Deir el-Bahri and the temple of Deir el-Medina, both at Thebes. At

ABOVE: *The temple of Hathor at Dendara was, like other temples, taken over by the Christians. Here, the remains of a fifth-century church stand alongside a birth-house, or mammisi, built in the reign of Trajan (AD 98–117).* JAMES H. MORRIS

Medinet Habu, mortuary temple of Ramesses III (1184–1153 BC), the Coptic town of Djeme survived until the ninth century. On the east bank at Thebes, the temple of Luxor was used as a Roman military camp during the third century and must also have been the place to which Christians were brought during the Diocletian persecution in 303 and commanded to offer sacrifice to the Roman emperor as a divinity, and from which the more resolute were taken to their martyrdom. In due course a church was built within the temple, as happened at other sites such as Philae, Dendara, and Esna, in what amounted to a rededication of the pagan monuments.

LEFT: *The mortuary temple of Ramesses III at Medinet Habu in Thebes became the site of a small fortified town in Roman and Christian times. The Christians built a church within the temple itself and their houses filled the ancient enclosure. The community survived until the ninth century.* THE IMAGE BANK/GUIDO ALBERTO ROSSI

ABOVE: An ostracon bearing an inscription written in Coptic characters. The Coptic script was based upon the Greek alphabet with the addition of a number of signs borrowed from Egyptian demotic to render sounds not found in Greek. Three of these occur in this short text; the Ϥ in line two, the ϣ in line three, and the Ϫ in lines four and six. The writer, describing himself as "I, this humble sinner" (lines one to two), asks the person addressed to pray for him (shleel edjoi) and beseeches God (pnute, line four) to have mercy upon him. GRIFFITH INSTITUTE, ASHMOLEAN MUSEUM, OXFORD

ABOVE: The Coptic language is still used for liturgical purposes, though service books are usually written in both Coptic and Arabic. On this leaf from a manuscript dating to AD 1173, part of St John's Gospel is written in the Bohairic dialect of Coptic. BODLEIAN LIBRARY, OXFORD

The rock-cut tombs of Middle and Upper Egypt were commonly taken over either by individual hermits or, on occasions, small groups. Until recently it was possible to distinguish the rough stone buildings associated with just such a community clustered around the northern tombs at el-Amarna.

It is scarcely surprising to find that at the level of "popular" religion elements of pre-Christian beliefs and superstitions survive almost unscathed. The ancient custom of consulting a divinity for guidance, help, or comfort is unaffected by allegiance to a different god. Coptic epitaphs speak of death in terms that recall ancient funerary texts, and a primitive form of mummification was practiced well into the Christian period.

ABOVE: The temple of Isis at Philae continued to function until the middle of the sixth century, when it was closed by the Emperor Justinian. Christians established themselves on the site and carved the symbol of their faith on the ancient stonework. JAMES H. MORRIS

Coptic art, in portraying Christian themes, displays many of the characteristics of ancient Egyptian art: *horror vacui* (dislike of empty spaces), symmetry, a use of registers which divide the scene into horizontal strips, disregard of perspective, even an element of narrative. The themes themselves are sometimes a straight adaptation of pre-Christian models. The popular warrior-saint figure, usually depicted spearing the Devil in the form of a serpent or dragon, is anticipated by representations of the mounted god Horus attacking the god Seth, the embodiment of evil. The theme of the Virgin suckling Jesus, common enough in Coptic iconography, invites obvious comparisons with compositions showing Isis with her infant son Horus. And the looped cross or ankh (*crux ansata*), deriving from the ancient Egyptian symbol for life, occurs in many contexts.

But it is the language that provides the strongest thread binding Coptic Egypt to its pagan past. The Coptic script was developed in the early centuries AD as a means of overcoming the increasingly obvious shortcomings of the hieroglyphic script and its derivative, demotic (a late, cursive, handwritten form). It employed the Greek alphabet, with the addition of seven signs taken from demotic to represent sounds not accounted for by Greek. The structure of the Coptic language and its vocabulary display many points of contact with ancient Egyptian. Thus, although it died out as a spoken language in the sixteenth century, Coptic's continued use today for liturgical purposes is a link, however tenuous, with Egypt's remote past.

ABOVE: Fresco from one of the funerary chapels at the Christian necropolis of el-Bagawat, Kharga Oasis. The painting, which probably dates to the fourth century, depicts Noah, his wife, and their six children standing within an ornately fashioned ark.
C. C. WALTERS

BELOW: St Antony's monastery, founded in the fourth century, is situated at the foot of the Red Sea hills, below the cave-dwelling where, according to tradition, the founder of monasticism spent his final years. C. C. WALTERS

their patriarch during the years of theological disputation, either on the streets of Alexandria or in the council chambers. One of their leaders was Shenute (c. 334–452), superior of the so-called White Monastery (Deir el-Abyad) at Sohag in Middle Egypt. Scourge of pagans, harsh disciplinarian, Egyptian patriot, he more than anyone typifies the confident, aggressive posture of the monastic movement at this time.

But, following the Arab conquest, the monasteries, like the Coptic Church as a whole, struggled to survive in an unsympathetic and sometimes hostile world. Though numbers declined and influence waned, they held on until 1350, when there was a sudden, catastrophic collapse, perhaps precipitated by an outbreak of the Black Death and the economic ruin that resulted. Monasteries were abandoned, endowments and other sources of income dried up, and recruits to the monastic ranks became increasingly difficult to find. The centuries that followed are a dark age, illuminated only by the reports of visitors to some of the monasteries. Their accounts confirm the sorry state of what had once been flourishing communities.

The first hints of a revival can be detected in the nineteenth century, and today there are clear signs of a renewal, a rediscovery of the old vigor and the original ideals. Nine monasteries maintain the ancient traditions: four in the Wadi Natrun, between Cairo and Alexandria, two near the Red Sea (St Antony's and St Paul's), one in the Faiyum (St Samuel's), one in Middle Egypt (Deir el-Moharrak), and one to the west of Alexandria (St Menas). The number of monks has increased and building activity has been energetically resumed. There has even been an attempt by young Copts to resurrect the hermit's way of life. The spirit of St Antony is still alive in the Egyptian desert.

Coptic Egypt is represented in most fields of craftwork — painting, sculpture,

textiles, woodwork, ceramics, metalwork, and so forth. Such an output, spread over a considerable period of time, does not lend itself to short summary. Painting and textiles have therefore been selected to illustrate the sources, scope, influences, and evolution of Coptic artistic activity.

The earliest unequivocally Christian paintings that exist are found at the necropolis of el-Bagawat in Kharga Oasis. Two of the tomb chapels are painted with scenes drawn almost exclusively from the Old Testament (such as the Exodus, and Noah's Ark). Their suggested fourth- or perhaps fifth-century date would support the idea of Jewish influence. Dating to the same period or perhaps a little later are paintings in the cave church at Deir Abu Hennes in Middle Egypt, which chronicle episodes from the life of Christ in more-or-less chronological order.

Not far from Deir Abu Hennes lies Bawit, the site of the monastery of Apa Apollo, which yielded a particularly rich collection of paintings. The monastery was occupied from approximately the fourth to ninth centuries, though most of the paintings were probably produced between the sixth and eighth. The repertoire is varied. Purely geometric or floral motifs exist alongside figured scenes drawn from the Old Testament (prophets and, especially, a cycle featuring David), New Testament, and pagan or secular sources (hunting scenes, Eros, and Orpheus). Some niches are decorated with a version of a two-zoned composition featuring, above, the risen and enthroned Christ and, below, the Virgin, with or without the infant Jesus

and accompanied by an assortment of apostles, monks, and saints. Most common of all are warrior-saints and monastic worthies, whose rigid, frontal pose and air of gloomy asceticism is unmistakably Egyptian. A rather less varied though essentially similar selection of themes was found at the roughly contemporary monastery of Apa Jeremias at Saqqara.

The centuries following the Arab conquest are represented sporadically by a number of monastic sites, more particularly churches at Abu Makar and Deir el-Suryani in the Wadi Natrun (paintings of the tenth and eleventh centuries), Tebtunis in the Faiyum (similar), Deir el-Abyad (AD 1124), Deir Fakhoury and Deir el-Shouhada at Esna (twelfth century), St Antony's (c. thirteenth through sixteenth centuries), and St Paul's (eighteenth century).

It is not surprising to find that over a period of some 1,400 years the character and style of Coptic painting show significant changes. The earlier dependence upon Jewish, Hellenistic, and even ancient Egyptian traditions is gradually replaced by borrowings from other sources — Byzantium, Persia, Syria, Armenia, Cappadocia, and the Islamic world. Yet, Egypt being Egypt and Copts being Copts, originality never entirely disappears, and loyalty to church, country, and beliefs continues to find expression in art.

LEFT: Fresco from the old church at St Antony's monastery, c. thirteenth century. The mounted figure is St Theodore the General, one of the "warrior saints" so popular in Coptic art. He is shown impaling the Devil in the form of a dragon.
C. C. WALTERS

ABOVE: Fresco from the monastery of St Paul. According to tradition Paul was the first hermit. His monastery is situated not far from that of St Antony and is still inhabited today. This painting from the church dates to the seventeenth century and depicts the Virgin and Child flanked by angels. C. C. WALTERS

LEFT: Column-capital from one of the churches at the monastery of Apa Apollo at Bawit in Middle Egypt. The capitals from this site were either based on the Corinthian model or, as here, belonged to a type known as basket capitals. LOUVRE MUSEUM, PARIS

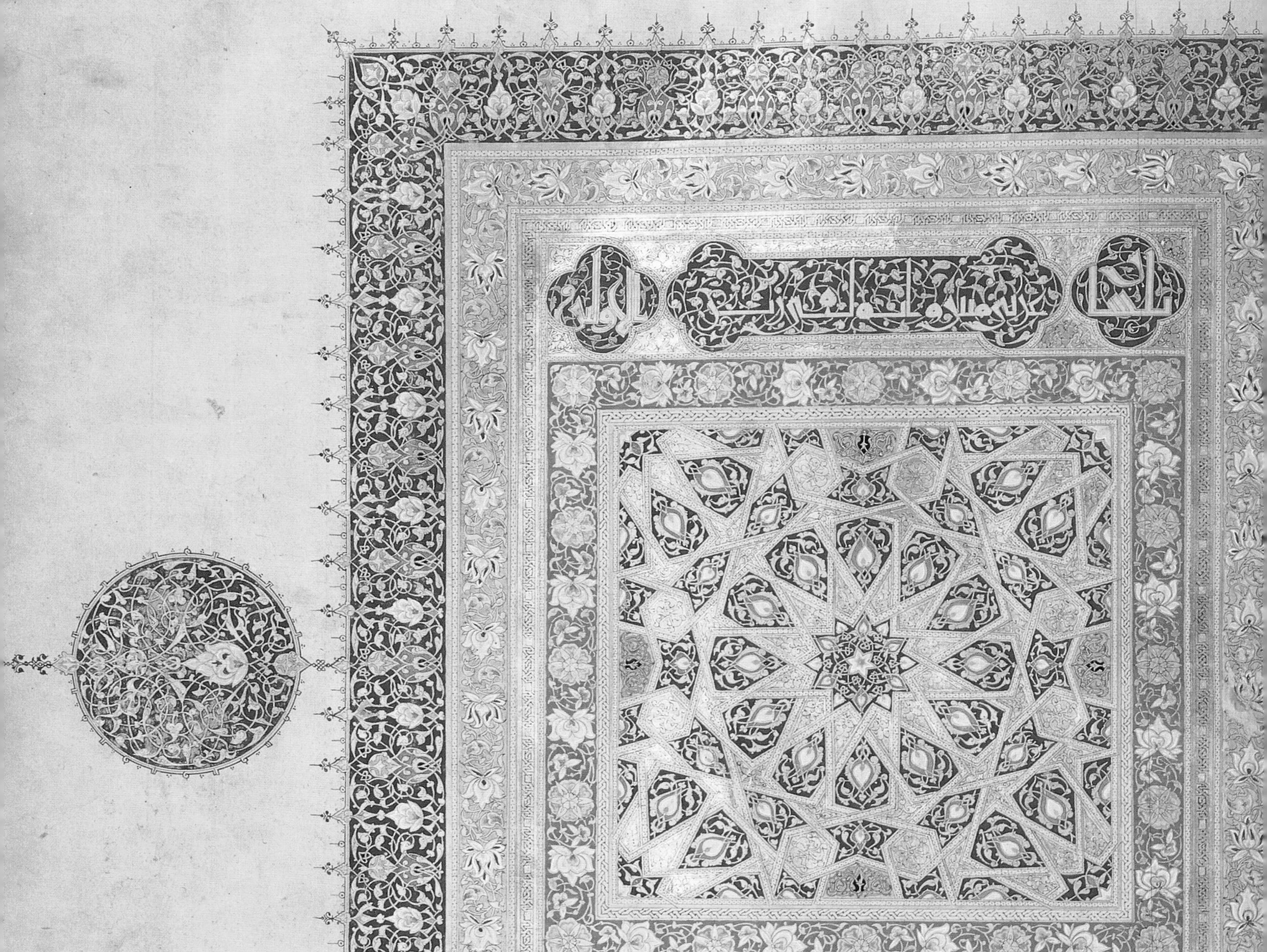

THE SWORD OF ISLAM

D. S. Richards

AS ONE PART OF the great expansion of the new Islamic state, an Arab tribal army invaded Egypt from Palestine in AD 639. The Arabs' siege camp around the Byzantine fortress town of Babylon on the east bank of the Nile became the city of Fustat, settled on tribal lines. This new military and administrative center, strategically placed at the vertex of the Delta but offering escape into Arabia, if needed, was the base for the pacification of the country and further expeditions into North Africa. Throughout the Umayyad period (661–750), new tribes immigrated to swell the Arab Muslim population and to begin the settlement of the Delta, in addition to its scattered garrisoning.

Statistics concerning integration and conversion are lacking, but one may assume that in the Umayyad period the Arab conquerors of Egypt, as those in other parts of the new empire, remained aloof through their strong sense of cultural identity and their new religion, not yet as universalist as it was to become. Conversion of the indigenous people did take place as fiscal advantage or social and career advancement were sought. It has, however, been maintained that large-scale conversion of Copts began only as late as the fourteenth century.

For several generations the Arab warriors, their families, and their dependents, were a parasitical upper layer surviving on the labor of the Coptic peasants and craftworkers, collecting their taxes through a reorganized Byzantine machinery with an almost unchanged personnel. A continuing feature of medieval and premodern history was the prominence of Copts in financial and fiscal administration even after the use of Greek had ceased and Arabic had become the common language for all races and religions. This actual or perceived monopoly caused or exacerbated interfaith tensions.

The Arabs' intellectual and material culture was decidedly inferior to that of the Byzantine and Persian empires they defeated. It could be said that their consciousness of race and their religion prevented the Arabs from being speedily overwhelmed in cultural terms, even though eventually through intermarriage and assimilation (they were always a minority in the conquered territories), their pure bloodlines became diluted.

The mixing of various traditions across the Islamic empire, sieved through the medium of the Arabic language, produced within a century or two a brilliant new civilization in which Egypt

TOP: *A Fatimid rock-crystal jug. Vessels carved from lumps of rock crystal, one source of which was in the area of the Red Sea, were amongst the most prized possessions of Muslim courts.* VICTORIA & ALBERT MUSEUM, LONDON

ABOVE: *General view of excavations at Fustat. Only a small proportion of the pre-Fatimid city has been excavated. The mazy pattern of narrow streets and the evidence for structures of several stories validate literary descriptions.* GEORGE SCANLON

OPPOSITE: *Left-hand frontispiece of the Koran presented by Baraka, the mother of Sultan Shaban, to her madrasa, c. 1366–68.* NATIONAL LIBRARY, CAIRO/ ALEXANDRIA PRESS, LONDON

RIGHT: *Bab al-Nasr ("Victory Gate") and Bab al-Futuh ("Conquest Gate"), both built by Badr al-Jamali in 1087. They replaced earlier northern gates of Fatimid Cairo, and with the associated city walls are impressive examples of pre-Crusader military architecture.* CRESWELL ARCHIVE, ASHMOLEAN MUSEUM, OXFORD

BELOW: *A goblet of luster-painted glass, excavated at Fustat in 1965, one of the earliest pieces of evidence for the technique in Egypt. The inscription states that it was ordered by Abd al-Samad ibn Ali, governor of Egypt for a month in 773.* ISLAMIC MUSEUM, CAIRO/GEORGE SCANLON

BELOW: *A deeply cut Tulunid wood carving typical of the Samarra style. Egypt in the rule of Ahmad ibn Tulun still looked to Samarra, the Abbasid capital in Iraq, for a lead in cultural, and to some extent other, matters.* LOUVRE MUSEUM, PARIS

shared but in no way took the lead. The major intellectual advances were made elsewhere, as indeed were the important political decisions. However, while the caliphate (the succession to the Prophet Muhammad) was still situated in Medina, malcontents from Egypt, dissatisfied with their declining status in the volatile early years after the conquest, had been the most vocal in opposition to the policies of Othman, and had taken the lead in the siege of his house and his murder in 656.

Egypt provided resources, in money and kind, for the central authority of Islam, first for the Umayyad caliphs in Damascus (661–750) and then for the Abbasids in Baghdad (750–1258). The Abbasid revolution, which began in the eastern province of Khurasan, overthrew the former dynasty, when the last of its caliphs, Marwan II, was hunted down and killed in Egypt in 750, but it brought little change to Egypt itself. The Abbasids, now from their new capital in Baghdad, renewed the series of governors sent to rule and make their accommodations with the vested interests of the descendants of the first settlers. During the Umayyad period and almost a century of Abbasid rule, the growing fiscal demands produced a series of Coptic revolts. These revolts were uniformly unsuccessful, but the economic interests of the Copts and the Muslims were converging. As part of an attempt to settle the empire after a damaging civil war, the caliph al-Mamun visited Egypt in 832, the only caliph of Baghdad to do so. In a step that under-lined a growing decentralization of the empire, al-Mamun entrusted Egypt to the control of a leading Khurasanian (a prov-ince now largely in western Afghanistan) general, Abdallah ibn Tahir, who then proceeded to appoint his own deputy.

One such deputy, Ahmad ibn Tulun,

from such a position as indirect representative of the central government, progressed to full personal power. He and his short-lived dynasty (868–905) brought a large measure of independence and self-awareness to Egypt, although the elite and the character of the regime were Turkish and still oriented toward the norms and culture of Baghdad. Ibn Tulun gained control of Syria and thus formed a link that was a recurring feature in this premodern period.

Abbasid authority was restored, but it quickly took on a nominal character as other governors usurped power to varying degrees. Prominent among these were another Turk, Muhammad ibn Tughj (934–946), also known by his Iranian title, the Ikhshid, and the Nubian eunuch, Kafur (966–968), who was both praised and lampooned by the famous poet al-Mutannabi.

After this intermediary period, the Fatimids, supported by their Berber following, conquered Egypt from the west in 969, the sole occasion of any political movement from this direction. The Fatimids (969–1171) were a dynasty that claimed descent from the Prophet through his daughter, Fatima, and presented themselves as infallible religious guides (*imams*). In the ninth century they had carved out a North African state centered on Tunisia. After one or two earlier attempts, a Fatimid invasion force under Jawhar, the general of the caliph al-Muizz, overcame the Ikhshidids. The Fatimids founded a new administrative and cantonment city, which they called "al-Qahira." This city was the capital of a Shiite caliphate with claims to the leadership of the whole community of Islam as comprehensive as those of the Abbasids, their Sunni rivals in Baghdad. The Fatimid state became a Mediterranean power, possessed of a strong navy sufficient to rival that of the Byzantines, but, as far as any plan to topple the Abbasids was concerned, their territorial expansion never went farther than northern Syria.

After a series of strong reigns, the succession of minors and the internecine struggles of the various racial groupings that the state called upon — Berbers, Turks, Armenians, and Sudanese —

caused frequent political turmoil at the center. Yet, Fatimid Egypt remained a significant commercial force, with a firm gold currency (the US dollar of its time), and was the source of artistic production of the highest quality. From the second half of the eleventh century, the Fatimid caliphs were dominated by military men who seized the vizierate (office of the chief minister of state), including a "dynasty" of Armenian origin established by Badr al-Din al-Jamali. Under their influence the caliphs, whose

ABOVE: Bab Zuwaila, the south gate of Fatimid Cairo, in a painting by David Roberts dated 1838–39. It was built in 1092 by Badr al-Jamali. The minarets above are part of the mosque of Sultan al-Muayyad (built 1415). The last Mameluke sultan, Tuman Bey, was hanged from this gate by the Ottoman conquerors in 1517. VICTORIA & ALBERT MUSEUM, LONDON

RIGHT: A basin (c. 1300), inlaid with silver and gold and decorated with scenes of hunting and court life. Louis IX of France reputedly brought it back from a crusade, and it was used to baptise the children of the rulers of France, hence its common name, the baptistère *of St Louis. The mameluke period is noted for its metalwork. LOUVRE MUSEUM, PARIS/PHOTO R. M. N.*

Shiite dogmas had never been adopted by the Egyptian population at large, were shorn of their religious pretensions, and Cairo ceased to be the center of the wide network of Shiite propaganda cells that had spread as far as India.

The weakening of the Fatimids coincided with the Crusades, and they were further marginalized when Egypt became a battleground for the Kingdom of Jerusalem and the Syrian–Mesopotamian forces of the Muslim countercrusade. The latter were victorious and brought Egypt into the orbit of the Turkish Seljuk sultanate and its successor states. Egypt was established once again as a Sunni state owing formal allegiance to the Abbasids. New forms of land tenure were introduced, as were the endowed institutions of higher Islamic learning, most importantly the madrasas (colleges), which had developed earlier in the Islamic East.

It was a Kurd, Saladin, who then emerged as ruler of Egypt (1171–93) to lead the Islamic forces to glory with victories over the Crusaders and the recovery of Jerusalem. Cairo remained the seat of the preeminent branch of Saladin's successors, the Ayyubids, so called after his father, Ayyub. That preeminence passed after Saladin's death to his brother, al-Adil, and the latter's descendants. The huge military efforts of the late twelfth century had exhausted Egypt, so that the stability of the Fatimid

dinar was lost, and a very long period of monetary depreciation commenced, during which the currency of Egypt became increasingly subordinate to the currencies of the Italian mercantile states.

Saladin's successors preferred long truces with the Crusaders on the coast of Syria and Palestine, during which Mediterranean trade could flourish, and commercial and quasi-diplomatic missions could be opened in Egyptian ports, despite the prohibitions of the Pope against European participation. Egypt, as the head of the Ayyubid "confederacy," increasingly relied on Turkish mamelukes to maintain its overlordship. The sultan al-Salih Ayyub (1240–49) built up a powerful mameluke regiment, called the Bahriyya, which helped him to establish his position as overlord, but all the Ayyubid princes cooperated to resist the Crusades that were directed against the coast of Egypt in the first half of the thirteenth century.

After a palace coup, Egypt was taken over by the regime of the mamelukes. They based their claim to be legitimate rulers on their role in the defense of Islam, the major part they had played in the defeat and capture of King Louis IX of France in the Delta in 1250, and their victory in Palestine in 1260 over the Mongols, who had overwhelmed eastern Islam and brought the Baghdad caliphate to an end. A line of Abbasids was set up in Cairo as a puppet caliphate and continued for two and a half centuries to

THE MAMELUKE SYSTEM

The literal meaning of "mameluke" is "owned." It was a common term for a slave, although one of a very special sort. It denoted a male imported into central Islamic lands from the eastern and northern borders, above all from the Turkic peoples, for military purposes. Utilizing the traditional Central Asian skills, mamelukes formed regiments of mounted archers. Individuals, or even groups, were not infrequently freed at a certain stage of their career. However, the term "mameluke" still clung to them. To be a mameluke required not only one-time, but not necessarily lasting, servile status, but also implied a certain racial origin and a function, primarily military but frequently extended to administration, indeed to governing. A mameluke could rise to the highest positions in society, and then it was not unknown for his offspring to retain some of his role and his rank. The normal connotations of "slavery" are not appropriate here.

Such mamelukes are first associated with the Abbasid caliphs of Baghdad in the early ninth century. The Arab tribal armies, the creators of the first Islamic empire, that of the Umayyads, had been disbanded, and the Abbasids' claim for political and religious

ABOVE: A romantic European portrayal of a mameluke horseman, an example of the outmoded warrior that charged the French squares at the Battle of the Pyramids (July 1798). Painting by Luigi Mayer published in 1805. ASHMOLEAN LIBRARY, OXFORD

ABOVE: Many handbooks were written for the mameluke army to illustrate exercises of horsemanship and military skills. Polo was regularly played on the special hippodromes (maidan), also with military purposes in mind. BRITISH LIBRARY INDIA OFFICE COLLECTION

leadership was not unchallenged. Mameluke guards gave them a fresh power base, untainted by existing interests, and this provided the continuing rationale for their use: young Turkish men and others, imported, taught to be good Muslims, and trained in their natural martial arts, would subsequently remain loyal only to the patron who had given them Islam and their position in the regime. This proved to be no more true for the Abbasid caliphs and many subsequent Islamic rulers than it had been for the Roman emperors, similarly isolated amongst their German praetorian guards.

The mameluke system was inextricably linked with the centuries-long military and political prominence of Turks in Islamic history. From ninth-century Baghdad the system expanded geographically to almost all regions and spread from the caliphal court to the courts of the sultans and the lesser princes of the politically disintegrated Abbasid empire, where it became largely self-perpetuating. The Seljuk sultanate, created by the westward migration of free Turkish tribespeople, maintained the use of mamelukes.

In Egypt the system reached one of its highest stages of development. The regime inaugurated by the mamelukes of the Ayyubids is known as the Mameluke sultanate, in which successors came from the widest possible "family" of blood descent or mameluke affiliation. Up to the late fourteenth century most mamelukes in Egypt were of Kipchak Turkish origin, imported by specialized traders from the steppes north of the Black Sea through a chain of markets. During the fifteenth century Circassians from the Caucasus predominated. However, there were always other ethnic groups represented, including Europeans. Once in Cairo the new mamelukes were bought chiefly by the sultan or his officers, the emirs. The sultan's mamelukes entered the barracks in the Citadel for training. On its completion they were "passed out" in batches and provided with equipment. Literacy and the bases of Islam were taught, and some mamelukes became respected scholars and authors. Training standards and discipline declined, however, and not infrequently, the mamelukes plundered and terrorized the civilian population.

The whole ruling military edifice was supported by a system of allotment of, mainly, agricultural revenues. A number of villages or a village, even a share in one, was assigned, theoretically without rights of ownership, to an emir, depending on his rank. The number of troopers he had to maintain for the state, conventionally 100, 40, 20, or 10, was a function of his rank and the size of his fief. The troopers of great emirs could well be mamelukes they had purchased from the slave markets, but mamelukes were expensive and many troopers of other emirs belonged to that "hinterland" of the mameluke state, the descendants of mamelukes.

A feature of this system was the way in which mamelukes formed discrete groupings for social and political action, based on such criteria as a shared upbringing and training in the barracks or in an emir's household, or a shared master and manumitter. These shared experiences created strong bonds. In particular, the mamelukes of sultans were distinguished collectively and individually by a term derived from their ruling titles. Those groups, unless actively disbanded or redistributed, tended to survive as troublesome factions under successive reigns.

give religious legality to the sultans who arose through realpolitik.

There was an initial period of experimentation and instability, which included an event rare indeed in Islamic history, namely in 1250 the elevation to power of a woman, Shajar al-Durr, the Turkish widow of the Ayyubid sultan al-Salih. The state was then established on a firm base by the iron-handed and vigorous reign of the sultan Baybars (1260–77).

The Mameluke sultanate, with Cairo as its capital and the imposing Citadel as its administrative seat, long held its position as the leading Islamic power in the world and a major center of Sunni learning and literature. Syria, parts of Mesopotamia and Asia Minor and, for a while, Cyprus became subject to it. The mamelukes also expanded Egyptian control southward toward Nubia. Ambassadors from Byzantium and from European states flocked to the court, and many travelers have recorded their amazement at Cairo's thriving commerce, its fine buildings, and its vast population. As at the height of the Fatimid period, owing to the geographical position of Egypt and the prestige of the regime, the Far Eastern transit trade in spices and other luxury goods was channeled through Egypt's markets at the hands of enormously rich spice merchants.

RIGHT: *A mosque lamp inscribed for Sultan al-Nasir Muhammad. The mosques and other religious buildings of mameluke Cairo were lit by such handsome glass oil lamps, hanging above the worshipers and students. This shape is typical, and most bear the name and titles of the sultan or emir for whom they were made.*
ASHMOLEAN MUSEUM, OXFORD

Egyptian control of the transit trade and excessive exploitation led Europe to seek an alternative sea route to its sources in the Far East and brought the Portuguese to the mouth of the Red Sea and into the Indian Ocean. Still, for a long time there was no real decline in the value of the trade through Egypt.

The internal history of the mameluke period was dominated by the factional fighting of the great emirs (the Sultan's officers), from whose ranks the sultans emerged. Many of them maintained huge households, patronized the arts and crafts and rewarded literary productions in their honor, and used the wealth they amassed to build grand religious buildings and mausolea for their own mortal remains. The endowment of such institutions and the associated religious personnel was the main aspect of their patronage of the ulema, the professional religious classes, with whom the rulers of Egypt from Ayyubid times onward consciously tried to establish a mutually beneficial relationship. The ulema gained pensions and salaries, a developing career structure, a bureaucratic and judicial role, and enhanced prestige, whereas the mameluke elite gained legitimacy from this connection with the upholders of the *Sheria* and benefited from the way the ulema mediated their rule to the indigenous population.

The rulers showed the common tendency to overtax and thus ruin the agriculture and industry of the country. Population decline, particularly from the great plagues of the fourteenth century, and the resultant reduction of the mamelukes' revenues from the land increased this tendency. Throughout this premodern period the ultimate response of a not infrequently oppressed peasantry was to flee its lands, give up a settled life, and become nomads or, as often as not, bandits. The strength of Bedouin forces and the pressure they could assert on the settled areas, even on towns, grew very great at times and obliged the government to make them gifts and concessions.

The Mameluke sultanate, after a long period of steadily increasing rivalry, fell to the Turkish dynasty, the Ottomans, and the cannon and handguns of their

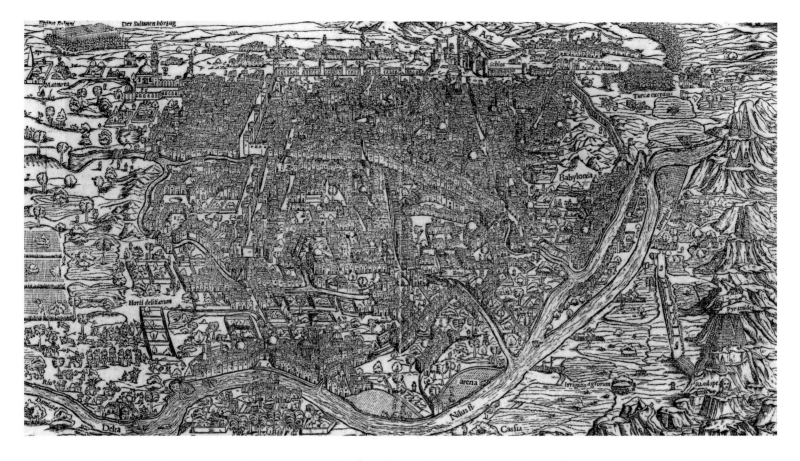

soldiers, the Janissaries in 1517. The last Mameluke sultan, Tuman Bey, was hanged from the Zuwaila gate. Once again Egypt ceased to be the center of empire, and Cairo had to accept the role of provincial capital. Egypt was ruled by a governor (Pasha) and a Janissary garrison, and much of its wealth went to feed the sultan's treasury at Istanbul. The mamelukes did not disappear from the scene, for the practice of importing white slaves into the country did not cease. In fact, over the Ottoman centuries mamelukes steadily gained in power and

ABOVE: *A view of Cairo from Sebastian Münster's* Kosmographie *published in 1574. From the fourteenth century on, increasing numbers of European pilgrims to Jerusalem also visited Cairo, and left interesting accounts, sometimes illustrated by bird's-eye views, which developed a surprising degree of accuracy in topographical detail.* GERMAN ARCHAEOLOGICAL INSTITUTE, CAIRO

LEFT: *The French expedition under Napoleon Bonaparte dramatically introduced Egypt to modern European thought and technology. Nelson's destruction of the French fleet in 1798 in Aboukir Bay doomed the expedition, but before their withdrawal in the following year the French defeated, also at Aboukir, a seaborne Ottoman force. Painting by L. F. Lejeune.* VERSAILLES NATIONAL MUSEUM/PHOTO R. M. N.

MAMELUKE KORANS

The Koran, the sacred scripture of Islam, was inevitably the main subject for most arts of the book — such as calligraphy, nonfigural decoration, and fine binding — developed by Muslims. In the mameluke period sumptuous copies, written in various styles and embellished with geometric and vegetal designs, were deposited by sultans and other notables in religious establishments as permanent charitable donations (*waqf*).

RIGHT: Illuminated page containing sura (verse) 2 ("The Cow"), c. 1367–69. NATIONAL LIBRARY, CAIRO/ ALEXANDRIA PRESS, LONDON
FAR RIGHT: Right-hand frontispiece, c. 1367–69. NATIONAL LIBRARY, CAIRO/ALEXANDRIA PRESS, LONDON

BELOW LEFT: Half of a double frontispiece, c. 1369–72, made for a mameluke emir, Arghun Shah al-Ashrafi. NATIONAL LIBRARY, CAIRO/ALEXANDRIA PRESS, LONDON
BELOW RIGHT: Right-hand frontispiece, Cairo, 1356. NATIONAL LIBRARY, CAIRO/ALEXANDRIA PRESS LONDON

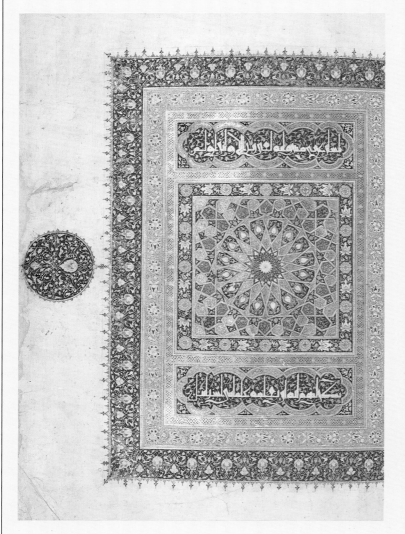

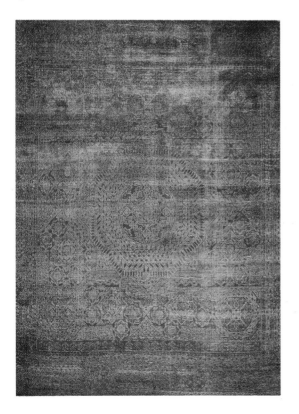

influence, some of them managing to establish themselves as more permanent dynastic "houses." The Pashas sent out from Istanbul became powerless in their own domain, and the Ottoman central government also lost control over the Janissaries. In Egypt, as elsewhere, the latter allied themselves with various urban interests, and their personnel increasingly came to be enlisted locally. Their political influence and military effectiveness waned. Apart from the perennial factional fighting of the mameluke *beys* (provincial rulers), as they were now called, the seventeenth and eighteenth centuries offer a story of shifting alliances between the *beys*, the Janissary forces, the ulema, the urban guilds, and the great merchants, and of the various groups' attempts to maximize their control of the resources of Egypt and to dominate its politics.

In the second half of the eighteenth century, several mameluke *beys*, Ali Bey al-Kabir, Murad Bey, and Ibrahim Bey, were able to monopolize power and make themselves the absolute rulers of Egypt, cutting off even the residual tax remittances to the Ottoman treasury. A full-scale expedition, planned to restore imperial control, was initially successful, but in 1787, when a new conflict with Russia opened, it was withdrawn. The career of these *beys* foreshadowed the much greater one of Muhammad Ali in the nineteenth century.

GREAT CAIRO

Jane Jakeman

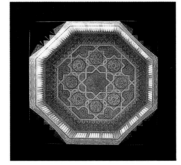

CAIRO IS REALLY a number of separate cities that have been linked up over the centuries. There are monuments of each age in various areas of the present city, nuclei in a connective tissue of streets and dwellings.

The mosque of Amr ibn al-As to the south of the modern city was the first in Egypt, founded by the commander of the victorious Arab army in 641–42, not far from the remains of the Byzantine settlement. It was a modest structure like many early mosques, based on Muhammad's house at Medina, where there was an open rectangular courtyard in which the faithful gathered.

Nearly two centuries after its foundation, Amr's mosque was enlarged to its present great size. Although it has subsequently been rebuilt many times, the mosque retains many Greco-Roman columns reused by early Arab builders. Cairo had limestone quarries in the nearby hills, but decorative and hard stones had to be brought considerable distances. Early Islamic architecture in Cairo relied heavily on stucco as a decorative material — this could easily be made from local lime, gypsum, and sand — and luxury materials such as marble were used and reused by successive generations.

The reason for the enlargement of the mosque of Amr must have been the success of the surrounding city of Fustat, which enjoyed the most sophisticated urban fabric of its time. The markets of Fustat sold every conceivable commodity, including rarities such as crystal, ivory, tortoise-shell, and porcelain so fine you could see your hand through it. The rambling streets, some so narrow that lamps had to be kept burning even in daylight, were laid with crushed stone and watered daily to keep down the dust. The city's dwellings had abundant water supplies and efficient sanitation was achieved with a complex system of pits, channels, and flues. Buildings rose to four or five stories, which might house one family or several in separate apartments. There was a central water supply and a lavatory for each floor. As the excavator of Fustat, George Scanlon, has said, "It was sanitation which brought out the genius in the Fustat architect."

Those who could not afford a whole house could rent rooms in an apartment block, which might have shops and storerooms on the ground floor. Food was usually bought from street vendors, and there were many public bath houses, so kitchens and bathrooms were unusual.

Privacy was the key note in all housing: entry was usually through a

TOP: A restored skylight inside the Qait Bey mosque–madrasa. The original foundation deed still survives, describing the rich ceilings of carved and inlaid rare woods, such as camphor. Like Sultan Hasan, this is still a functioning mosque. JAMES H. MORRIS

ABOVE: The vast white space of the courtyard of the mosque of Ibn Tulun, built 876–79, presents a powerful contrast with the bustle of the city outside the walls. In the center of the courtyard is a small, domed fountain where worshipers could perform their ablutions before prayer. THE IMAGE BANK/GERARD CHAMPLONG

OPPOSITE: A mihrab, or niche indicating the direction of Mecca, in the mosque–madrasa of Sultan Hasan (built 1356–63). JAMES H. MORRIS

turning passageway, and family life was carefully shielded from public gaze. The harem, or family rooms, was separate from the public areas and concealed behind window screens of beautiful fretted woodwork (*mashrabiyya*) that made for coolness. An added aid to keeping the house cool was a local invention, the wind scoop, which rose up through the roof, facing north to catch the prevailing winds and channel them down through the house. Originally a pharaonic invention, such devices were found on houses at el-Amarna and shown on Theban tomb paintings.

Domestic housing was usually built of brick: stone was for mosques and palaces. In wealthy houses, the reception halls and fountains were clad with marble and the woodwork might be inlaid with ivory: rich textiles would add to the atmosphere of luxury. Although various areas of the city became fashionable at different times, the basic arrangements of the Fustat house, planned around a courtyard with a fountain or cistern and with private quarters on the upper floors, would be typical of domestic architecture throughout Cairo until Western influence arrived in the nineteenth century.

Fustat was destroyed in 1168 as a result of a "scorched-earth policy" against threatening Crusaders, and although it was rebuilt it never recovered its former glory. Other mosques were built elsewhere, but Amr's kept its venerable status.

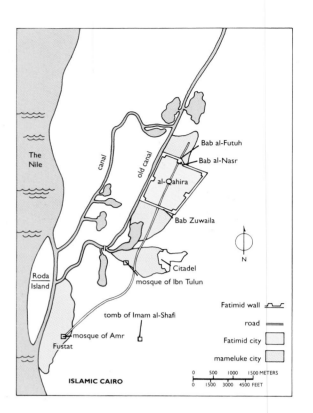

ISLAMIC CAIRO

The mosque to the north of Fustat sponsored by Ahmad ibn Tulun, at first governor in the name of the Abbasid caliphate but later a rebel, is indisputably a work of architectural genius and one of the great buildings of the world. Massive yet simple, it has survived largely intact from its foundation in 876–79. The transition from hectic urban bustle to the tranquility of a mosque courtyard, a theme of Cairene architecture, is at its greatest here. The style, brick covered with white stucco generating stark

RIGHT: Like other traditional ways of cooling a house, such as the courtyard fountain and the wooden window screens or mashrabiyya, *the wind scoop has almost disappeared in Cairo. This picture, taken last century, shows the hoods (in the foreground) angled to catch the prevailing north wind, at the tops of air shafts that led down and funneled the breeze through the house. Rooftop life was a pleasant feature of old Cairo; as well as the wind scoops, there were often seats and gardens at roof level, where the cool air of evening could be enjoyed.*
GRIFFITH INSTITUTE,
ASHMOLEAN MUSEUM, OXFORD

ORNAMENTAL WOODWORK

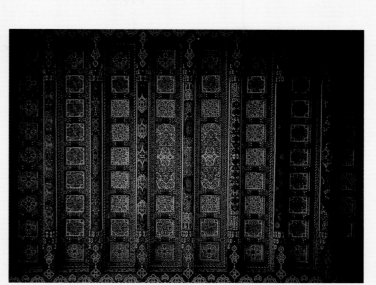

Wood inlaid with elaborately arranged pieces of bone, ivory, or mother-of-pearl has always been a much-admired craft. As early as the fourteenth century AD, scholar Ibn Khaldun wrote that craftworkers in wood needed the skill of geometricians; Euclid, he said, was a carpenter.

ABOVE: This beautifully painted ceiling is from a fourteenth-century foundation, a religious building erected by the great emir Shaykhu, who, during the Black Death of 1349, gave charitable aid, including washing the bodies of the dead. JANE JAKEMAN

LEFT: The streets of Cairo were once lined with windows like these, near the city gate known as Bab Zuwaila. JANE JAKEMAN

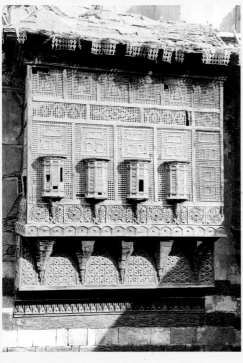

In the *Thousand and One Nights*, Ali Baba's cave of treasures contains rare woods, "heaped up like kindling for the fire." The story reflects the way in which Egyptians could count wood among precious objects; it has always been scarce in Egypt and much has had to be imported. Scented woods such as sandalwood, cedar or camphor are listed in royal inventories along with jewels and gold. Rare woods were worthy of the skills of the finest craftsmen, who developed clever ways of using small pieces of wood fitted together, so that nothing was wasted. *Mashrabiyya* were windows formed of screens of turned and carved wood; they allowed the breezes to blow through, and jars of sherbet or water might be placed on shelves inside to cool. The occupants of the house could look out and enjoy watching the life of the street below, while retaining their own privacy.

LEFT: Elaborate mashrabiyya windows photographed in Cairo sometime before 1874. GRIFFITH INSTITUTE, ASHMOLEAN MUSEUM, OXFORD

RIGHT: Centuries old doors at the mosque known as the "Blue Mosque" because of its blue tile-work show venerable scars inflicted by wind, storm, and time. JANE JAKEMAN

outlines, is an import from the capital of the Abbasid dynasty, Samarra, in Iraq. The giant minaret rises helter-skelter like that of the Great Mosque in Samarra; later Cairo minarets were slim towers, and were built to be thinner and higher as the centuries went on.

An aqueduct was built at about the same time as the mosque, to bring water

from the river. Islamic architects and engineers have always excelled at hydraulics, and the annual flooding of the Nile and the best possible conservation of its waters remained as great a concern as it had been in ancient times. One of the oldest Islamic buildings is the Nilometer (861) on the island of Roda. It is in fact a deep circular pit with tunnels connecting to the river and a graduated scale of markings so that the water level, signifying the vital difference between plenty and famine, could be measured.

Like the mosque of Amr, that of Ibn Tulun was a center of urban life. Around it was Ibn Tulun's now-vanished city, where his son created a famous garden, the classic adjunct to an Islamic palace. In this one, amidst channels and fountains, were tree trunks sheathed with gilt, and in front of the palace, the "Golden House," was a lake filled with mercury where the master floated on an air bed. Nothing now remains but this description: city and palace decayed, and the center of power shifted away with the arrival of the Shiite Fatimid dynasty, which invaded from North Africa.

Their general, Jawhar, in 969 laid the foundations of the Fatimid city, al-Qahira, from which the modern "Cairo" is derived, in an almost-empty area alongside the canal leading to the Red Sea. The new city's brick walls enclosed an area about half a square mile (1 km²) that was intended as a private world from which the populace was excluded: they were to remain in Fustat and enter the new city only to serve the new masters.

RIGHT: *Plan of the combined mosque, madrasa and mausoleum founded by Sultan Hasan, built 1356–63. The foundation is arranged around an open courtyard, but with more covered area than the Ibn Tulun type of mosque.*

FAR RIGHT: *Plan of the mosque of Ibn Tulun, built 876–79. The mosque is of the open courtyard type.*

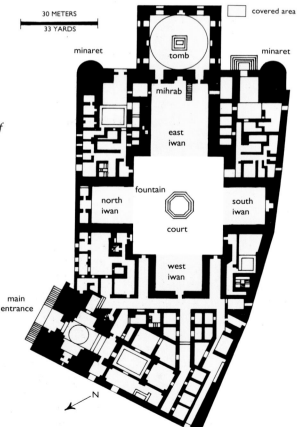

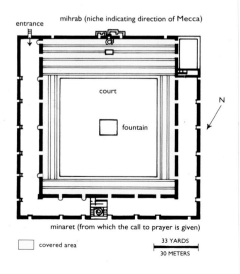

Al-Qahira was very unusual among medieval cities in being a planned town, in contrast to Fustat, with a layout that is still recognizable. A main street ran between two palaces, one for the residence of the caliph and one for service. The first mosque, al-Azhar, founded in 970, was also (and still is) a teaching foundation and probably the oldest university in the world.

The Fatimid walls were extended by the general Badr al-Jamali (the area is described in Naguib Mahfouz's novels). Badr al-Jamali's three tight-fitting ashlar (dressed stone) gates, Bab al-Nasr and Bab al-Futuh to the north and Bab Zuwaila (built 1087–92) to the south, look extremely militaristic and may have deterred would-be rebellious citizenry, but they would not have hindered a serious invader. Nevertheless, they provided a splendid backdrop for the ceremonial of the Fatimid caliphs, who rode in glittering processions in and out of them. Bab Zuwaila was also the scene of public executions, and pieces of the malefactors were nailed to it as a warning to the populace.

The power base moved once again with Saladin's conquest of Egypt, to the Citadel, which became a complex of palaces and barracks. Yet, in spite of the change of dynasty and of religious orientation from Shiite to Sunni, the Fatimid city retained great prestige: the Mameluke sultans rode along the same processional route as the caliphs had, extending it to the Citadel, and competed to found religious buildings on the sites of the two palaces and along the route. The buildings reflected the military successes of the sultanate: Sultan Qalaun's hospital and college (founded in 1284–86) had a mausoleum for its founder built on a plan similar to that of the Holy Sepulcher in Jerusalem. Next door, his son, al-Nasir, installed the portal of a Crusader church, brought from Acre, in the doorway of his pious foundation (1295–1303).

The madrasa, or college, had been introduced by Saladin's dynasty. It allowed for the teaching of the four rites of orthodox Islam, each being allocated a vaulted hall (*iwan*) on one side of a courtyard, giving a cross-shaped ground

plan. The tomb of the founder was often added. These institutions became very common in Cairo, and the madrasas provided residences for students and for mystics and religious teachers. They were maintained by the income from a perpetual trust set up by the founder, whose tomb would thus be surrounded by the continuing prayers of the beneficiaries.

Sultan al-Nasir especially had a mania for building of every kind — as well as madrasas, he built aqueducts, canals,

LEFT: David Roberts's 1838 painting of the mosque–madrasa founded by Sultan Hasan. THE PROVOST AND FELLOWS OF ETON COLLEGE

BELOW: The superbly carved stonework dome of the Qait Bey foundation (built 1475) in the northern cemetery. Like that of Sultan Hasan, this combined a mosque, a madrasa, and a mausoleum, but on a smaller, jewel-like, scale. JAMES H. MORRIS

BELOW: Cairo is the world's greatest medieval city and its minarets convey its long history. JAMES H. MORRIS

THE CITADEL

It is a paradox that the most prominent feature of the venerable city of Cairo is a nineteenth-century building, the mosque of Muhammad Ali. Though the mosque is comparatively modern, the site reaches deep into Cairo's past. The Citadel, created in part out of the monuments of ancient Egypt, was originally the work of Saladin, who began building it in 1176 as part of a line of fortification to protect the whole area including both the old city of Fustat and the newer Fatimid city of al-Qahira. The walls and towers of Saladin and his Ayyubid successors survive in the northern part of the Citadel, which was built on a spur of the Muqattam hills, using blocks brought from the small pyramids at Giza. Saladin took great trouble with the water supply, including an aqueduct, which brought water raised up from the Nile with water wheels, and a well dug by Crusader prisoners that tapped a water supply deep within the rock under the fortress. Saladin intended his walled city as a potential refuge rather than a permanent ruler's residence, but his Ayyubid successor al-Malik al-Kamil took up residence there in 1207–08, and it was a royal residence from then until the last century.

Al-Nasir's lavish rebuilding and additions (1313–38) destroyed the palace, mosque, and

library Saladin had built within the walls but extended the fortifications and hydraulics, digging cisterns in the rock for additional water storage. Over 40 pharaonic columns of red granite were brought from Upper Egypt for al-Nasir's own mosque and palaces. In the Citadel he built his famous "Striped Palace,"

LEFT: Inside the mosque of Muhammad Ali, built 1824–48. This mosque is of the type introduced by the Ottomans: the central area is completely covered over, so a feature of the building is its glittering artificial lighting. JAMES H. MORRIS

ABOVE: The mosque of Muhammad Ali has slender minarets 270 feet (82 m) high. AUSTRALIAN PICTURE LIBRARY/STEVE VIDLER

of alternating courses of brown and black stone. It was one of several gorgeous buildings described by al-Zahiri, an Arab writer, in the fifteenth century:

> The Multicolored Palace is composed of three main buildings used for official ceremonies. They are covered with marble of different colors, and the ceilings are painted in gold and blue and decorated with various paintings. The Great Hall has nothing in the world to equal it; it stands alone and is separated from al-Qasr al-Ablaq [Striped Palace]; it is surmounted by a very high beautiful green dome. That is where the royal throne is kept. This dome, which is of the most beautiful architecture inside and out, rests on marble columns. [translation by Gaston Wiet]

Here the sultan's court signaled the wealth and power of Egypt to the world.

The Citadel was a self-contained world, with barracks that could accommodate 12,000 men, harems for each of the sultan's four wives, and gardens. The principal wife occupied the "Columned Hall," built by the

LEFT: The alabaster-clad mosque of Muhammad Ali forms a striking contrast with the rough medieval walls and towers of the Citadel below. HORIZON/SUSANNA BURTON

ABOVE: "Joseph's Hall," shown here in Luigi Mayer's illustration, was the name mistakenly given to the remains of the palace of al-Nasir, for which many ancient columns were reused. "Joseph" here refers to Saladin, one of whose names was "Yusuf," the Arabic version of Joseph. ASHMOLEAN LIBRARY, OXFORD

LEFT: A view inside the Citadel, showing the fourteenth-century mosque of Sultan al-Nasir (on the right of the picture), by Luigi Mayer, published in 1805. Under the threshold of the mosque can be seen the remains of a pharaonic obelisk reused by the Islamic builders. ASHMOLEAN LIBRARY, OXFORD

Sultana Shajar al-Durr ("Tree of Pearl") in the mid-thirteenth century. Al-Nasir was a notable lover of horses, and his buildings included lavish stables for his favorites.

All that survives of al-Nasir's constructions is his mosque in the traditional courtyard style. Like the mosque of Amr, it reused Ptolemaic, Roman, and Christian columns. The rest of al-Nasir's buildings were swept away in the last century to make way for the palace and mosque of Muhammad Ali; all the rulers of Cairo, mamelukes and Ottomans, had meantime made their embellishments and depredations. Muhammad Ali also made additions to the fortifications, rebuilding the southern section, where the mamelukes murdered in his coup d'état were trapped in the defile behind the Azab gate. In his mosque is his own tomb, hung with green velvet. The mosque itself is in the Ottoman style, contrasting with the severe medieval lines of the earlier mosque of al-Nasir next to it. The later mosque is built to a different plan, with a vast dome covering the central prayer area, four smaller domes at each corner, and four semi-domes at each side. It was modeled on the Mosque of Sultan Ahmad (the Blue Mosque) of Istanbul, but its architect, Yusuf Bushnaq, was Greek.

The Citadel, like the pyramids, is much painted, much photographed, familiar and yet constantly astonishing. The delicate minarets and lush dome of the mosque and the harsh, angular, heavy-towered fortress below make one of the world's most extraordinary architectural contrasts; the lustrous alabaster cladding of the mosque responds to every change in light.

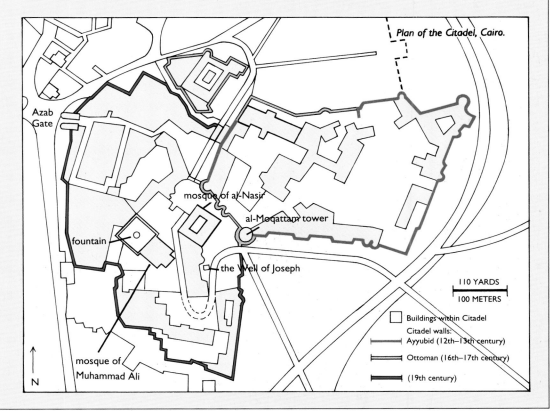

Plan of the Citadel, Cairo.

Azab Gate

mosque of al-Nasir

al-Moqattam tower

fountain

the Well of Joseph

mosque of Muhammad Ali

N

110 YARDS
100 METERS

☐ Buildings within Citadel
Citadel walls:
▬ Ayyubid (12th–13th century)
▬ Ottoman (16th–17th century)
▬ (19th century)

water wheels, palaces, and mosques — and his emirs seem to have competed to get monuments into awkward leftover spaces, fitting them in with ingenuity. Characteristic Cairo scenes were forming: vistas of tightly packed winding streets accented by domed monuments, flights of steps, towering portals, and minarets with spikes to hold lamps.

The madrasa could function as a mosque and sometimes still does, as for example that founded by Sultan Hasan (built 1356–63), from which services have been broadcast on Egyptian television. This building exemplifies the high style of mameluke Cairo, with lavish decoration of gilding and marble inlay, and exquisite stalactite (*muqarnas*) vaulting dripping above its huge doorway. Around the walls are Koranic inscriptions carved in stone or molded in stucco, picked out with gold and rich coloring — a characteristic feature of religious foundations. Although the gilding and colors have mostly worn off, Sultan Hasan's madrasa has been lovingly restored.

Successive sultans tried to outdo their predecessors with lavish building and elaborate decoration. Sultan al-Muayyad even resorted to stripping the brothels of Cairo for marble to embellish his mosque (built 1415–22) near Bab Zuwaila.

As well as these royal religious foundations, there were shrines of humbler individuals. In the southern cemetery lies the famous shrine (1211) of

Imam al-Shafi, a theologian and founder of one of the four Islamic rites. Around his splendid mausoleum are tombs of local people, with as long a history as the architecture of caliphs and sultans. Some of the oldest and specially beloved tombs are those of women.

Another cemetery, farther north, developed later. It contains both vast complexes that housed hundreds of devotees and the (by comparison) small "jewel" of Sultan Qait Bey's tomb and madrasa (built 1472–74), decorated with the most exquisite examples of every craft. The cemeteries have always been well visited, and they may represent a continuation of an old Egyptian tradition, the retreat into the desert for prayer and meditation. In time of plague or famine, the populace of Cairo streamed out into the desert foundations and tombs to pray for relief.

The dusty-domed sprawling cemeteries are as distinctively Cairene as the street scenes. The stone domes, whether in desert or in city, are triumphs of the stone mason's craft, with intricate fluting and carving, perfectly planned and executed, and often sited so as to create a dramatic focal point in a street or a courtyard.

An attractive benefaction to the city street was the *sabil*, or public fountain, where water was cooled by running over a marble slab and protected by a grille. It was a charity especially favored in the Ottoman period (1517–1798) and displays the elaborate architectural style of that time on a miniature scale. The mosques favored by the Ottoman conquerors were unlike the traditional Cairene versions with their open rectangular courtyards; instead they covered the central prayer area with a dome. The Ottomans brought with them, for both domestic and religious building, their taste for tiled decoration. The "Blue Mosque" (mosque of Aqsunqur), originally dating from 1346–47, got its name because of the tiles with characteristic colors of indigo and turquoise with which the Ottoman additions of 1622 were embellished. The baroque taste of the Ottomans, evident in Istanbul, is reflected in Cairo in official and private buildings from the eighteenth century.

The city of the nineteenth century was built closer to the Nile, extending over to the west bank and onto the islands in the river. It incorporated Western-style boulevard architecture, including large commercial buildings, villas and garden suburbs, and wide and straight streets for those who bowled along in carriages.

Egyptian independence has allowed the modern architect to choose from the inheritance of Egypt's own past to produce an inspired reworking of tradition or just pastiche. The difference may depend on whether the architect is prepared to use traditional materials and methods as well as designs, as did Hassan Fathy, who has many followers. Some of Fathy's work, however, made unsuccessful use of tradition, for example, in basing rural village architecture on upper-class urban housing. Much more successful were commissions such as the studio for the artist Hamid Said at el-Marg (1942), but Fathy's work, because of its appreciation by the intelligentsia, has been open to criticism as being "mameluke chic." His use of traditional materials has met with much opposition. Fathy reintroduced mud-brick vaulted architecture, which he

first observed in pharaonic granaries at the Ramesseum (the temple of king Ramesses II, 1279–1213 BC, on the west bank opposite Luxor) and later saw at the Coptic monastery of St Simeon at Aswan and found still being constructed in Nubian villages. Beautiful and simple though this architecture is, its use of local materials and labor made it so quick and cheap to build that it met with great hostility from contractors working for a percentage of the total cost.

The great pressure of tourism has emphasized commercial architecture, with vistas of skyscraper hotels along the Nile. The best of these is probably the Ramses Hilton, with a distinctive triangular shape and a color darkened to resemble sandstone. In civic building, the latest is a grandiose opera house (1988), by the Japanese architect Koichiro Shikida. The new subway system, with spacious concourses and platforms, probably contributes more to the quality of life and has made some reduction in the frantic traffic of the newer city. But still, the narrow streets of old Cairo are cool and breezy, temptingly shady in the heat.

LEFT: The new Opera House in Cairo is a gift from the people of Japan to the people of Egypt. The old Opera House, on a different site, was burned down in 1971. The new one is a vast and lavish, but curious, building, as an opera house is so characteristically a Western feature: grand opera is not a part of traditional Arab culture. Statues based on ancient Egyptian themes, carved from Egyptian porphyry, were commissioned especially for the building as gifts from the British government. PETER CLAYTON

BELOW: Traditional bricks of mud and straw are quick and cheap as a building material and are still extensively used. AUSTRALIAN PICTURE LIBRARY/ZEFA

LEFT: The house Fathy planned for the artist, Hamid Said, in 1942 is on the traditional plan around a courtyard, and is made of local mud brick, easily built up into the domed and vaulted studio and living areas. Many artist and architect friends met regularly here sitting in the cool courtyard to discuss issues of the day. "We are in great need of reintroducing human scale, human reference and musicality in architecture." [Hassan Fathy] ACADEMY EDITIONS, LONDON

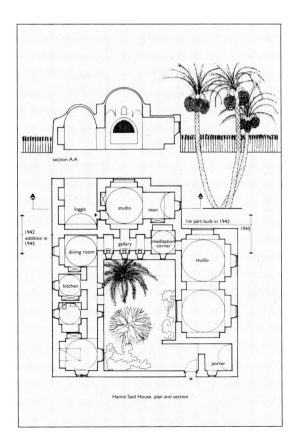

section A.A

1942 addition in 1945
1942
1945
1st part built in 1942

loggia
studio
iwan
dining room
gallery
meditation corner
kitchen
studio
porter

Hamid Said House. plan and section

EGYPT IN THE MODERN WORLD

Penelope C. Johnstone

THE STORY OF Egypt through the nineteenth and twentieth centuries is one of increasing tension between East and West, traditional and modern. This tension appeared first in military terms, then in science and technology, in religion, and in the life of the people.

Egypt's dream of independence from the Ottomans seemed near to realization when disaster struck from the west. General Napoleon Bonaparte, commander of the French army, eager for conquest further afield, perceived Egypt's potential importance for communications, and in 1798 he invaded. The Egyptian army was defeated, and mameluke rule came to an end. Thus the Egyptians were brought face-to-face with an alien civilization and life-style supported by superior fighting power, and the system was unable to offer any effective opposition.

The Egyptian people were hostile to the occupying army, and a British sea blockade increased the army's difficulties. In 1801 the French withdrew. French interests had not been only military: the expedition included a number of scientists who produced an encyclopedic *Description de l'Égypte* and initiated some progress in medicine, for instance. The departure of the French, hastened by British intervention, gave the

Egyptians only temporary respite; their experience of French domination had opened the door to Western influence and involvement, which, over the years, were to be dictated largely by Egypt's strategic importance to the West. The key figure of the early nineteenth century was Muhammad Ali. When he died in 1849 he was succeeded by members of his family, thus inaugurating hereditary rule: Ibrahim, Abbas I, Said, Ismail, and Tawfiq in turn increased both the national debt and foreign influence, mainly because of trade treaties that favored Britain. The Suez Canal project to link the Mediterranean with the Red Sea was initiated by a French diplomat, Ferdinand de Lesseps, and financed jointly by the French and Egyptian governments. The canal was completed in 1869, but by 1875 the khedive (viceroy) Ismail was so heavily in debt that he sold his shares to the British, who from then on had a considerable stake in Egypt and its security.

The internal financial and political situation worsened until the sultan in Istanbul was compelled to depose and exile Ismail, in favor of his son Tawfiq. Just then, Ahmad Urabi, an army officer, headed a military rising against the ruler and in opposition to European influence; subsequent riots brought about

TOP: Ismail Pasha was khedive (viceroy) of Egypt from 1863 until 1879 when he was replaced by his son Tawfiq. This was at the order of the sultan in Istanbul, partly at the instigation of the British and the French, who considered Ismail an incompetent ruler. MARY EVANS PICTURE LIBRARY

ABOVE: The opening of the Suez Canal, on 17 November 1869, was a prestigious moment for Egypt and for the khedive, Ismail, although by then Egyptian funds for the project were almost exhausted. MARY EVANS PICTURE LIBARY

OPPOSITE: The revenue from ships such as this freighter passing through the Suez Canal forms a sizeable proportion of Egypt's national income. THE IMAGE BANK/DAVID W. HAMILTON

the country: agriculture, railways, and public services were expanded, and the first Aswan Dam was constructed between 1898 and 1912. Under the British, however, there was a total failure to understand Egyptian resentment and desire for independence; the "Denshawi incident" in 1906, a clash between British soldiers and Egyptian villagers, many of whom were afterwards severely punished, was long remembered as a symbol of foreign oppression.

The next consuls-general, Sir Eldon Gorst and Lord Kitchener, in turn continued Cromer's efforts to improve the economy. Egyptian opposition to British rule was becoming more vocal and organized, with the rise of a National party led by Mustafa Kamel. At the outbreak of the First World War in 1914, Kitchener was replaced by Colonel Sir Reginald Wingate; Egypt was declared a British protectorate and was an important military base for the British.

By 1919 the Ottoman empire had gone for ever; but Egyptian claims for independence, voiced by Saad Zaghlul of the Wafd party, did not receive a fair hearing. Lord Allenby was appointed high commissioner, Zaghlul was exiled, and British policy continued as before, making only grudging concessions. However, 1922 saw the formal end of protectorate status: a British declaration granted independence to Egypt, retaining in Britain's favor responsibility for the defense of Egypt, protection of foreign interests, security of communications (notably the Suez Canal), and the Sudan. In 1923 the Egyptian constitution was proclaimed, and Khedive Ahmad Fuad became King Fuad I. Zaghlul returned as prime minister in 1924, but the next few years saw constant changes in government, reflecting the conflict between the king, the people, and the British. In 1936 the Anglo-Egyptian Treaty gave Egypt greater autonomy, though British troops remained in the canal zone; in 1937 the Montreux Convention admitted Egypt as a full member of the League of Nations.

During the Second World War Egypt was again a center of British military activity. The Egyptians were insulted and appalled by the British attitude and their

intervention by the British and the French, and in 1882 a British army defeated Urabi's forces at Tell el-Kebir. Thus began a period of occupation, hated by the Egyptians but viewed by the British as the only way to restore stability to the country — and thus guarantee repayment of Egypt's debts to foreign powers — and to protect the Suez Canal, vital to British interests in India.

The British consul-general, Lord Cromer, encouraged the development of

MUHAMMAD ALI

ABOVE: *Muhammad Ali rose from army commander to supreme ruler of Egypt, subject to nominal control by the sultan. His main contribution to Egypt's future was his encouragement of education and economic development.* MARY EVANS PICTURE LIBRARY

Muhammad Ali was an army commander of Albanian origin who was recognized as viceroy in 1805 and gradually asserted Egypt's independence. In 1811 he arranged for the massacre of the leading mamelukes, who had been attempting to regain power, and he tried briefly to extend his rule into Syria. Muhammad Ali's plans for Egypt focused on economic development. He improved irrigation with Nile barrages, canals, and greater cultivation of cotton. In the educational and scientific field, he helped Egypt to acquire the new sciences of the West by sending students to train in Europe and establishing training institutions in Egypt. He modernized the army and its equipment, and initiated a program of shipbuilding; he kept the economy in his own hands, with control over both income and exports, to provide for the upkeep of the army and consolidate his own power.

RIGHT: *The mosque built by Muhammad Ali, with its ornate interior and striking silvery domes, is the focal point of the much older Citadel that overlooks the historic heart of Cairo.* THE IMAGE BANK/PAUL TRUMMER

highhanded tactics, exemplified in their dealings with the young King Farouk.

After the war British negotiators gradually acknowledged Egypt's rights; the agreement of 1946 between Ernest Bevin, British foreign secretary, and Ismail Sidki, then Egyptian prime minister, brought about an improvement in relations. In 1947 British troops were withdrawn from the cities to the canal zone. The general atmosphere, however, was one of unrest and discontent. The demand arose for complete evacuation of all British troops.

LEFT: *King Farouk with seventeen-year-old Narriman Sadeq, his new wife, 19 May 1951. Farouk's personal life and political conduct made him increasingly unpopular, and just over a year later, in the Revolution, he was deposed and exiled.* TOPHAM

About this time the Muslim Brethren, who since the 1930s had been a constant source of friction and opposition to the authorities, became more vocal and often violent. Their leader and founder, Hasan al-Banna, was assassinated in February 1949, but government attempts to suppress the movement were unsuccessful because of its strong religious character and consequent popular appeal.

Meanwhile, events in neighboring Palestine were coming to a head, with the ending of the British Mandate in 1948. When the state of Israel was declared, Egyptian and other Arab armies invaded the areas claimed by the new state, confident of sweeping the Israelis into the sea. Despite overwhelming numerical superiority, the Arab forces were heavily defeated. This blow to Arab pride was felt deeply by the Egyptians, who soon uncovered numerous contributory causes for their defeat — corruption in the army, weak government, favoritism in high places, and purchases of obsolete arms — all of which implicated the king and his advisers and friends.

In 1951 discontent against the British was growing. In January 1952, riots aimed primarily at British property spread to all foreigners in Egypt, particularly Jews. The resentment against the king finally erupted when the "Free Officers" group in the army instigated the July 1952 revolution, in which Farouk was deposed and exiled. The stated aim of the Free Officers was to "cleanse" the army and reform the government; they stressed the importance of Islam in the foundation of a new society. One of the brains behind the revolution was a young officer, Gamal Abdel Nasser. The nominal leader of the new "Revolutionary Command Council," Brigadier Muhammad Naguib, became president and prime minister, but Nasser, his deputy, soon became more influential and in 1954 took over both the prime ministership and the presidency.

The revolution had voiced the grievances of the people, some of which the new government began to address.

The British were persuaded to withdraw their troops, schools and health centers were established, and to help agriculture and industry the project of the Aswan High Dam was planned. Nasser pursued a nonaligned policy, which meant in effect that, since the West was suspicious if not hostile, he had to obtain arms and economic aid from the Soviet bloc. In 1958 he tried to strengthen his emerging position as leader of the Arab world by bringing about political union with Syria. The United Arab Republic, in which Egypt was undoubtedly the stronger partner, lasted only three years.

Relations with the West worsened, aggravated by the US refusal of aid for the Aswan High Dam project, and in July 1956 Nasser announced the nationalization of the Suez Canal, a move that aroused startled reactions among the countries concerned. Britain, France, and Israel held clandestine consultations that led to the Israeli invasion of Sinai. British and French planes bombed military targets; Port Said was captured. International outrage was instant and fierce, and within two months the French and British withdrew. The United

Nations sent a special force to supervise the ceasefire; in 1957 the canal was reopened to shipping. Nasser had won a moral victory.

Nasser enjoyed great popularity; his was a complex character, proud, genuinely concerned for the welfare of his people, but stubborn, delegating with difficulty, and increasingly isolated as a result of his suspicion of foreign powers and even of his own colleagues. Much of his antagonism toward the West was caused by his reaction to what he considered (often justly) to be insulting or disrespectful attitudes on the part of Western leaders.

By 1967 Arab–Israeli tension was again mounting. Nasser closed the Straits of Tiran, at the lower end of Sinai, to Israeli shipping; Egypt made a defense agreement with Jordan. Threatened on all sides, the Israelis struck back: on 5 June they attacked Egypt's air force, a move that effectively won them the war. They

ABOVE: Lake Nasser, formed by the waters of the Nile held back by the Aswan High Dam, now covers a wide area of former dry land. It has increased Egypt's irrigation and its hydro-electric capacity, but there have been some adverse effects downstream. THE IMAGE BANK/GUIDO ALBERTO ROSSI

LEFT: The monument to Soviet–Egyptian friendship at Aswan commemorates the Soviet Union's assistance in building the Aswan High Dam. In 1971 a Soviet–Egyptian friendship treaty sought to consolidate their mutual interests. THE IMAGE BANK/TOM OWEN EDMUNDS

BELOW: Egyptian forces on the Sinai front, 22 May 1967. Tension was mounting, and the Egyptians thought that their preparations made them secure against Israeli attack. Soon after, the June war proved them wrong. POPPERFOTO

ABOVE: *Anwar Sadat (right) with Menachem Begin. Lengthy negotiations between Egypt and Israel, steered by US president Jimmy Carter, culminated in the signing of a peace treaty in 1979.* MAGNUM/JEAN GAUMY

Egyptians who took the initiative, crossed the Suez Canal on 6 October, and advanced into Sinai, but they were soon driven back. The 22 October ceasefire came after heavy losses on both sides, but the "Ramadan" or "Yom Kippur" war (as it was known to Arabs and Israelis respectively) was seen by Egypt as a victory. For the first time Israel had been taken by surprise and was seen to be no longer invincible.

Sadat took a less belligerent attitude than Nasser, with encouragement from the US secretary of state, Henry Kissinger; in 1977 he went to Jerusalem to attempt direct negotiations with Israel. After meetings between Sadat, Menachem Begin, the Israeli prime minister, and US president Jimmy Carter at Camp David, a peace treaty was signed in 1979. An Arab country was officially at peace with Israel.

Although this brave — or rash — move by Sadat brought an end to fighting and meant the return of Sinai, it was rejected angrily by other Arab countries; Egypt was expelled from the Arab League, whose headquarters were moved from Cairo to Tunis. Other factors also caused increasing unrest, especially among the Muslim Brethren, a small group of whom assassinated President Sadat at a military parade in October 1981.

His place was immediately taken by Hosni Mubarak, his vice-president since

advanced into Sinai, and in the campaign thousands of Egyptians were killed. Nasser made a much-publicized offer to resign, but by popular acclaim the offer was refused, and he continued as head of state until his death in 1970, when Anwar Sadat succeeded him as president.

Sadat continued many of Nasser's policies but was more liberal and less suspicious of others, and gradually Egypt's rather isolated and pro-Soviet position was moderated, with the *infitah* (opening-up) policy. Sadat ordered Soviet advisers to leave the country, and a new law encouraged foreign investment.

The Arab–Israeli struggle again came to a head in 1973: this time it was the

RIGHT: *President Hosni Mubarak speaking in parliament, 24 January 1991. Under Mubarak's firm leadership Egypt has consolidated its position as a leading Arab nation. It sent a force to fight in the coalition to liberate Kuwait.* GAMMA/FRANK SPOONER PICTURES

MODERN EGYPTIAN LITERATURE AND TRADITIONAL CAIRO

Cairo has provided both educational opportunities and an intermittent theme for modern Egyptian writers. Al-Azhar, the mosque and university at the heart of old Cairo, can stand as a symbol of traditional Islamic education and values. In 1961 modern subjects were added to its curriculum, and in 1969 women students were admitted for the first time.

The tension between tradition and modernity can be seen in the life and work of the reformer Muhammad Abduh (1849–1905), who studied traditional Islamic sciences at al-Azhar, later took up political journalism, and believed that education based on Islamic principles could use and adapt the best of European science and civilization. He taught at al-Azhar, and toward the end of his life was grand mufti (chief religious and legal adviser). His lectures on Koranic interpretation, later published as the *Manar* commentary, stress the need for Muslims of every epoch to interpret their scripture in the light of contemporary circumstances.

In literature the same tension is apparent. Egyptians' first acquaintance with Western writing was through translations, of varying quality, and the first Arabic novels and plays were somewhat dependent on European models. Poetry began to show changes in outlook, though religious subjects were still treated. Two of the best-known nineteenth-century poets, Barudi and Shawqi, both wrote on the Prophet Muhammad and Islam; Shawqi's *Farewell to Lord Cromer* expressed the pent-up anger and resentment of the Egyptian people against foreign domination.

Taha Husayn's (1889–1973) autobiography (translated into English) shows the odyssey of a clever, blind village boy, through the corrupt and inadequate village school system, to al-Azhar and its traditional methods, to Paris for Western education, and back again to Egypt, where he became a writer and worked within the Egyptian educational system. By 1950 he was minister of education. Taha Husayn wrote on the life of the Prophet, as did several of his contemporaries, drawing his inspiration from early Arabic literature; he is well known as a literary critic and historian.

Tawfiq al-Hakim (1899–1987) wrote numerous stories and essays, and many of his plays are on social and political themes. *The Sultan's Dilemma*, set in the Middle Ages, contains a warning for any ruler (Nasser, in this case) not to meddle with the law. In *Song*

ABOVE: *Naguib Mahfouz in a Cairo cafe. While much has changed, the traditional streetside cafe remains a meeting place for men to discuss politics, exchange stories and anecdotes, and watch the world go by.* AUSTRAL/SYGMA

of Death a son returns from studying at al-Azhar to find that he is expected to commit murder to revenge his dead father; when he refuses, he is himself killed, for defying family and village tradition. *Memoirs of a Country District Attorney*, a novel, gives a scathing account of the abuse of justice. *The Return of Consciousness* is more overtly political, being an account and criticism of the Nasser regime, through al-Hakim's perception of the leader whom he watched in his progress from army officer to absolute ruler.

Drama is represented also by a lively folk theater. More popular still are numerous films, some of high quality, which have helped to make the Egyptian dialect and way of life familiar to a large part of the Arab world.

A novel by Yahya Haqqi (born 1905), *The Lamp of Umm Hashim*, conveys vividly the attraction of Cairo and familiar places. The focus is on a poor, overcrowded area, Sayyida

ABOVE: *Nawal el-Saadawi, in* The Hidden Face of Eve *and other writings and novels, has described the sometimes desperate situation in the less developed parts of the Arab world. As a doctor, Saadawi herself has witnessed extremes of poverty, where women, deprived of education and protection, inevitably suffer most.* SAUDI RESEARCH

LEFT: *Muhammad Abduh, religious reformer and scholar (1849–1905).* SAUDI RESEARCH

Zaynab, and the mosque where the lamp, thought to have healing powers, hangs. The hero, Ismail, sent to England to study medicine, returns as a skilled eye surgeon, and is at first appalled by the superstition and backwardness from which he had himself escaped. Eventually he comes to terms with his background and recovers his faith, and settles in a poor area of Cairo to work for the betterment of his people.

Cairo is minutely observed in the novels of Naguib Mahfouz (born 1911), who won the Nobel Prize for Literature in 1988. He studied Islamic and Western philosophy at Cairo University. His novels are full of social observation and comment. His trilogy follows a family through three generations up to the Second World War. *Children of Gebelawi*, set in Cairo, is an allegory of human religious experience. *The Thief and the Dogs* is a psychological study of Saeed, who rejects the advice of his old sheikh and in seeking revenge sets out on a path that leads to violence and his own death. Naguib Mahfouz, in a particularly poignant and vivid way, evokes the image of Cairo as a religious and national symbol, representing Egypt's problems as well as its stability in the face of Western and secular invasion.

RIGHT: *Egyptian soldiers praying beside their tank in the Saudi desert, 6 September 1990, in the build-up to the Gulf war. Sadam Hussein promoted himself as an Arab and Muslim "hero," a view that was not shared by his opponents, who included many devout Muslims.*
AUSTRAL/SYGMA

BELOW: *The Iraqi invasion of Kuwait in 1990 caused the flight of thousands of Egyptians (some of whom are seen here at Ruweished on the Iraq–Jordan border), who had been working abroad and sending home much-needed remittances to their families. Their return to Egypt led to increased hardship and economic pressure.*
AUSTRAL/SYGMA

1975, a less colorful and volatile man than his two predecessors. His earlier military career gave him a realistic outlook, and he had a firm grasp of government policy. Persons imprisoned by Sadat were gradually released; the economy was guided by practical rather than ideological motives. Relations with Israel were kept muted and those with other Arab states encouraged; Camp David was thus tacitly accepted, and Egypt was readmitted to the Arab fold. Large sums in aid were received from the United States, while in 1983 trade and cultural agreements were signed with the Soviet Union. In the same year a five-year plan was launched, encouraging economic development of a practical nature.

Massive problems are still faced by Egypt, where an essentially rural population is flocking to the capital. Health, education, housing, and transportation are priorities; government welfare schemes are still supplemented by vast amounts of overseas aid, government and private. The magnificent new subway system and the building of new overpasses have slightly eased the transportation problem in Cairo. New universities produce more trained graduates, who then may have to wait years before finding their (guaranteed) government employment. Increasing pressure from Muslim Brethren and their sympathizers means that more Copts are finding advancement blocked, and many of the best qualified emigrate. Tourism has led to the building of more hotels and facilities, and thus employment for those with suitable skills. This part of the economy is affected when incidents such as the 1977 or 1986 riots or the 1990–91

LEFT: *The expressway system in Cairo, near the Nile. Over the past quarter century, increased population and vehicles have led to overcrowding and traffic jams. The situation has been partly relieved by building overpasses.* THE IMAGE BANK/DEREK BERWIN

Gulf crisis cut off the tourist stream and decrease confidence abroad. At such times, when many expatriate Egyptians return home, cash remittances to their families end, and there is an increase in the unemployed.

Overpopulation is one of the most immediately noticeable problems of a country that has a superb climate, good natural resources, and a mixed population providing a large work force — too much of which is undertrained or unskilled. Still, the people overall have an immense zest for life. Their sense of humor, long history, and strong national identity help them face the future with optimism and the equanimity of *ma shaa Allah* ("as God wills").

ABOVE: *The Cairo Metro, built in the 1980s by French construction contractors has somewhat eased the problems of getting across the city from north to south. It is kept remarkably clean, and there is usually a "ladies only" carriage at the front of each train.* AUSTRAL/SIPA

LEFT: *View of Cairo with the tall, slim Cairo Tower —a modern landmark in the commercial and tourist center —in the center of the picture. The patterning of its circular structure recalls palm trunks and its shape is in marked contrast to the ancient symbol of Egypt, the pyramids.* THE IMAGE BANK/GUIDO ALBERTO ROSSI

FAMILY LIFE IN MODERN EGYPT

Fayza Haikal

DIFFERENCES BETWEEN SOCIAL classes in Egypt can be much greater than elsewhere. Urban communities struggle to keep up with the rest of the world, yet in some rural areas time froze centuries ago and started only recently to flow again. "Oriental" and "Occidental" conceptions and ways of life intermingle, and differences in education, income, and standards of living are tremendous. Yet, in spite of this diversity, all Egyptians have a common substratum, a collective and very old culture. Economic problems and changes brought about by modernization affect the family directly, but customs and principles learned in the family define society and help to hold it together.

The current economic situation in Egypt is difficult, and the international crises that have shaken the world have had deep repercussions. There is not enough investment to provide work opportunities for a population of around 57 million inhabitants. Greater Cairo alone houses more than 12 million people; other big cities such as Alexandria, Mansoura, Tanta, Minia, and Asyut attract most of the rest. Housing is insufficient and precarious, or overly expensive, and green zones are lacking in populated areas. The

government faces overpopulation, unemployment, poverty, inflation, and illiteracy. Young people are willing to work abroad for a while or even to emigrate for better salaries, because they feel that they can neither help nor be helped at home. By Western standards or according to Western statistics, in a similar situation chaos, political instability, a high rate of criminality, and extremist, possibly violent, movements would be expected. Yet in Egypt all these remain marginal; there is no famine or organized crime. Security in the streets is noticeable, and there is no real lack of commodities, even though some are too expensive for the masses. Bread is still subsidized, and people continue to live and even keep smiling in their overcrowded cities.

How do they do it? When they are asked, they usually answer that it is *baraka*, the blessing of God, that helps them. As long as you have *baraka* you live well, and in order to keep *baraka*, people have to live in harmony with their society and with the principles of God. Ptahhotpe, an Egyptian sage of the third millennium BC, said that "God is the dispenser of wealth," and the presence of God has been felt in Egypt's daily life throughout history. In another

ABOVE: The traditional way of baking bread. Egyptians of all social classes enjoy the characteristic round, flat loaves of unleavened bread that are often the main element in the diet. STOCKSHOTS/P. BORTHWICK

ABOVE: Huge elaborate tents are put up to provide a temporary shelter from the sun on many religious and social occasions. Tent-making and tent-erecting is an old and respected profession. JAMES H. MORRIS

RIGHT: Streetsellers offer a variety of food delicacies as well as nonalcoholic drinks. JAMES H. MORRIS

passage of Ptahhotpe's famous "wisdom text," we read:

> If you are a capable man, equip your household;
> Love your wife in your home according to good custom;
> Make her happy while you are alive for she is a field profitable to her Lord.
> ... if you are a wealthy man, beget a son who will make God well disposed.

Attitudes toward marriage have not changed. Free sexual relations are still totally disapproved of. In the Egyptian family, children are welcomed and cherished, and religion has an important place in their education. It is their parents' responsibility to bring them up properly, and parents feel responsible for their children — if they can afford it — until they are fully grown up, educated, and married.

In upper- and middle-class families babies are usually born in hospitals or private clinics where proper care is given to both the mother and the child. In poorer social classes and in rural communities, women still frequently deliver at home, with the help of a midwife. The birth of the child is registered at the Ministry of Public Health so that the baby may get a birth certificate and all the necessary vaccinations and health care in due time. Most neighborhoods have state clinics for that purpose, and television and other

media keep reminding unaware or uneducated parents of their duties toward their infants. Muslim baby boys who are born in clinics are often circumcised during the first week following their birth, and the event often passes unnoticed. In rural societies circumcision can take place a little later, in the first years of a baby's life, and it is still celebrated. Although female circumcision is prohibited by law, some people still practice it. A week after the baby's birth its parents usually have a small feast in its honor to which they invite their relatives and friends, and at which the baby is introduced to society.

The emancipation of women and the high cost of living have led most wives in urban societies to take part-time or full-time jobs. Egyptian by-laws entitle the mother of a newborn baby to take maternity leave. Usually she can have up to three months off and can request a longer leave of absence if she wishes — but this would be unpaid, so most young mothers have to find someone to look after their babies and preschool children while they are at work. There are a limited number of inexpensive state-run nurseries, and big factories or other establishments that hire many women

LEFT: *Visiting an Egyptian market is an enjoyable social occasion, far removed from the impersonal service offered in Western supermarkets. However, nowadays people often do their everyday shopping in local shops that do not differ much from their counterparts elsewhere.* JAMES H. MORRIS

have organized their own. Private, well-equipped nurseries exist in large numbers with fees that vary according to neighborhood and quality. In some poorer social classes, mothers usually leave their babies with relatives, neighbors, or friends. Upper-class expensive nurseries often hire foreign babysitters to teach children the rudiments of a foreign language (English or French), as bilingualism is still common and appreciated in Egypt in wealthy circles.

When children reach the age of six, parents have to select a school for them. There are free state schools, private schools with fees that vary from one institution to another, and "language schools," a leftover from the foreign schools of the pre-1956 era. They are all controlled by the Ministry of Education and are supposed to teach the same curriculum.

Schooling in Egypt, after kindergarten, takes eleven years divided into three stages: elementary, intermediate or primary, and secondary or high school. Each of these stages ends with an official state exam. State schools are entirely free of charge. By law children must go to school until they complete intermediate studies, but, unfortunately, the law is not always enforced. After their intermediate studies, children can go either to high school or to lower technical institutes where they are trained for some

ABOVE: *In villages, washing and even washing up may still take place in the river or a canal, but more and more households are now buying washing machines.* AUSTRALIAN PICTURE LIBRARY/ZEFA

LEFT: *Feluccas and other Nile craft embody the tranquillity and regularity of the traditional ways of life, now fast disappearing. In antiquity, the Nile was the main transport artery but that role has now been taken over by roads.* THE IMAGE BANK/FARRELL GREHAN

profession. In spite of the government's strenuous efforts, not all these schools meet the requirements of the ever-increasing population. Both state and private schools are overcrowded and admission is not easy, particularly to private schools, which try to limit the number of their pupils in order to maintain their academic standards. Selection is often according to contacts and influence. The paucity of premises

ABOVE: *Donkey carts are a frequent sight in the less busy parts of Cairo and in the country, although pickup trucks are taking over. The animals are worked very hard and are owned by some of the poorest members of Egyptian society.* JAMES H. MORRIS

ABOVE: *School facilities are often improvised and few Egyptian school children and university students enjoy a standard of school buildings, libraries, and other equipment comparable to their Western counterparts.* JAMES H. MORRIS

ABOVE: *Egyptian children are remarkably keen to learn even in the simplest surroundings, and students are prepared to work in conditions unheard of in the West.* SONIA HALLIDAY PHOTOGRAPHS

RIGHT: *Children in Egypt enjoy playing as much as children everywhere else in the world, but for many of them, particularly those living in villages and in the poorer parts of cities, adulthood and the serious business of life start very early.* JAMES H. MORRIS

compels certain state schools in overcrowded areas to function all day long and receive up to three shifts of schoolchildren a day, keeping each shift for about four hours. There is an early-morning shift, a mid-day shift, and an evening shift. Instruction is sometimes poor, and most children who can afford it rely on private tutoring at home. Their instruction is supplemented by parents, whose whole lives may become centered on their children's schooling, or by a teacher, sometimes the same one they have at school. Private tuition fees form the most substantial part of most instructors' salaries. The final year at school is the nightmare of all families and a tremendous drain on their finances.

Nobody really approves of this quasi-compulsory system of private tuition, and some parents think that it encourages instructors to teach badly in order to have more private pupils. Others attribute the poor quality of teaching to large classes

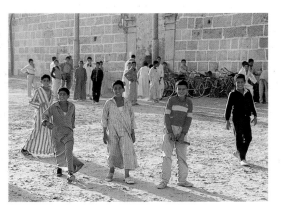

and sometimes also to the poor preparation of the instructor. To avoid private tuition a number of schools teach extra "repetition classes" for weaker pupils. In addition, television programs cover most courses required for the state exams.

As well as these institutions, there are schools run by al-Azhar, the most ancient and revered Islamic institution in Egypt, whose impact on the population is tremendous. These schools, mainly in the provinces and in the crowded urban districts, teach the precepts of Islam and the Koran along with the more secular disciplines.

In the family the children's education is mainly the responsibility of the mother. Even if she chooses to work, it does not relieve her of the obligation to take care of her household. The father may find himself a job in one of the Arab Gulf states, leaving the entire responsibility for the family to his wife. While abroad, the husband is expected to make enough money to support his family so that his wife need not work if she does not want to. His money will serve not only to ensure a better standard of living for his family, but also to save enough for his growing children. His son will need a house and probably a *mahr*, or dowry, that he will present as a gift to his bride; his daughter will need enough money for her *gehaz*, that is, her trousseau and the furniture of her house. In Egypt, furniture is considered the property of the wife and is traditionally brought by her family for the new home.

The absence of a father figure in many homes has had a number of drawbacks. Relative affluence, added to ignorance and unemployment, has facilitated the spread of drug use among young people. Addiction and other problems are tackled at school and in explicit programs on television, and indirectly dealt with through religious teachings, whether in mosques or churches. Moreover, the lessons ulemas (theologians) give in the afternoon in certain mosques are broadcast on television. These teachings undoubtedly affect the conceptions, ideals, and ways of life of a large part of the Egyptian population.

University education in Egypt is free. Pupils who want to pursue university

THE RAMSES WISSA WASSEF SCHOOL

A visitor traveling south from Cairo along the road to Saqqara and Memphis is struck by the number of "carpet schools" advertising their products in bold and often rather unorthodox lettering. The pyramid area has a number of such establishments, and the most famous among them is the Ramses Wissa Wassef School.

Ramses Wissa Wassef was an architect who started a school about 50 years ago that combined children's elementary education with instruction in the art of

ABOVE: Two generations of the same family at work in the school. AUSTRAL/SIPA
ABOVE RIGHT: A former pupil of the school, now a master weaver. AUSTRAL/SIPA

weaving. Children were not asked to follow the well-established and traditional patterns but were encouraged to use their imagination and create their own designs. This was in Cairo, and in 1951 a similar school was created in the village of Harrania and the same experiment was repeated with

a small group of six- to eight-year-old local children, with beautiful results. The school has now diversified its activities but its world-famous tapestries remain its most celebrated products.

ABOVE AND LEFT: One of the Wissa Wassef tapestries, measuring 4 feet 7 inches x 7 feet 3 inches (140 cm x 220 cm). A single tapestry may take several months to complete. AUSTRAL/SIPA

RIGHT: Egyptians are great family people and they enjoy their holidays enormously. Alexandria is the popular holiday resort. THE IMAGE BANK/TOM OWEN EDMUNDS

RIGHT: *Egyptians are great family people and they enjoy their holidays enormously. Alexandria is the popular holiday resort.* THE IMAGE BANK/TOM OWEN EDMUNDS

BELOW: *Women dressed in the traditional Arab fashion can be seen alongside others wearing Western garments in all walks of life and all places, including Cairo University.* MAGNUM/ABBAS

BELOW: *Gezira sporting club in Cairo attracts sportspeople as well as those who just want to relax. The overcrowding of the city and the lack of parks and open spaces are keenly felt.* MAGNUM/S. FRANKLIN

education must pass the *thanaweya amma* (general secondary school) exams, and unless they get the required marks they cannot join the faculty of their choice. To have a university degree today is not necessarily to have craved for knowledge or culture, or to love science and research. Rather, the degree enables its holder to penetrate certain social circles or to become a civil servant. Though generally poorly paid, these posts used to be very much appreciated because they provide security, social contacts, and prestige. Today conceptions of prestige and respectability have changed and although Egyptian universities have accepted 600,000 students for September 1991, most of them will probably not work for the government.

Like the secular national universities, al-Azhar now teaches all subjects in addition to Islamic studies. It draws students not only from Egypt but also from many other African and Asian Islamic countries.

Egyptian young people spend most of their free time in sports clubs. Soccer is the national sport in Egypt, and championships between clubs are organized all year round. These clubs are also meeting places where parents can relax while children play safely. Most of them are equipped with tennis and squash courts, in addition to swimming pools, soccer grounds, and gymnasia.

After graduation begins the hunt for jobs and for independence, and young people begin to experience disillusionment and bitterness. When they want to get married, unless their parents provide them with lodgings, they have to wait for years until they have enough savings to settle down independently. In fact, the paucity of resources and the cost of lodgings cause many engagements to break off, delay many marriages, and produce much frustration.

To keep in touch with and help one's relatives and neighbors is a social priority, and kinship ties entitle people to rely on each other. Relatives are invited to share in joy, and their support is expected in sorrow. In large cities where distances are considerable, traffic difficult, and

EGYPTIAN WEDDINGS

As soon as they can afford it, young men and women get married. In Islam marriage is a social contract. It is celebrated in different ways, according to a family's wealth. Traditionally, the bride is taken to the groom and handed over to him by her parents in a *zaffa* (festive procession). Earlier, particularly in rural areas, the furniture for the new house was carried from the bride's parents' residence to their daughter's in public, accompanied by music and dancing. Because of the expense it entails and also because privacy today is more valued, the furniture is no longer exhibited in the same way. Young couples, however, still show their visitors around their house and take pleasure and pride in displaying their new acquisitions. Most parents today wish to have a *zaffa* at their children's weddings and most young girls dream of it. After the contract of marriage is signed, there usually is a ceremony, which is more or less elaborate, depending on the family's means. The minimum acceptable to mark the occasion is the presentation of a syrup or *sharbat* to the company present at the ceremony, symbolizing a wish for the future happiness of the couple. Guests cannot refuse to drink the *sharbat* even if they have no taste for sweets. In wealthier families the wedding ceremony includes a banquet and, if means and space permit, the famous *zaffa*, which really differentiates a marriage from any

BELOW LEFT: A bridal couple dance at their wedding party. MAGNUM/ABBAS

BELOW RIGHT: In Egypt, the wedding photograph is taken very seriously and preserves much of the formality that has now disappeared in the Western world. MAGNUM/ABBAS

ABOVE: A noisy zaffa on the streets of Cairo often stops traffic and attracts a large crowd of people. JAMES H. MORRIS

other festive gathering and during which all eyes are focused on the bride and groom. The *zaffa* could be compared to the bridal procession inside the church, but in Egypt it takes place in private houses or in hired public places for more space. The procession is accompanied by professional musicians and dancers who slowly lead the bride and the groom, with many pauses, to their *kosha* (a raised platform with specially decorated seats reserved for the couple). Guests will go there in turn to congratulate them on the happy event. At more expensive weddings,

professional musicians and dancers are hired to enliven the feast, and one can often see there the best belly dancers and pop singers in the country. These festivities recall the beautiful banquet scenes depicted in ancient Egyptian tombs, where the tomb owner and his wife are seated among their guests enjoying exquisite food while dancers and musicians are performing for them.

people very busy, ties may be loosening and traditions slowly disappearing, but what remains of them and the sense of responsibility toward one's family are among the factors that consolidate the culture and spare the country even greater problems when social and economic conditions are so difficult.

If birth and marriage are festive occasions where family and friends get together, funerals draw even more relatives. During three whole days people keep coming to the house of the deceased

to comfort the family. Verses of the Holy Koran are chanted, and coffee and food are offered to visitors. The period of mourning and the funerary traditions in Egypt differ noticeably from other Islamic countries. To express their grief, women used to wear black clothes for at least a year. Today, in Egyptian urban society, younger people often reject this custom, stressing that it has nothing to do with Islamic teachings and that black is a depressing color that does not help wounds to heal. In fact, busy urban communities today have little time for emotions! Still, 40 days is considered an acceptable minimum for wearing mourning clothes, since the first 40 days after death have special intensity. Some people believe that the number 40 has a significance dating back to ancient Egyptian mummification practices and although they see no sense in repeating it, they continue to do so. In conservative families, relatives meet in the house of the deceased every Thursday until the fortieth day after the death and go to visit the tomb and present offerings in food and kind to the poor who live around the cemeteries as an act of charity so that God might forgive the deceased any sin committed. They also cover the tomb with flowers and greenery as symbols of regeneration and have verses of the Koran recited near the tomb to comfort themselves and the soul of their cherished dead. These visits to the dead, called *talaa*, "going up to the cemetery," are performed for years afterward, on every religious feast and on the anniversary of the person's death.

In rural communities, manifestations of grief are usually very strong, particularly among uneducated people. During the funerals, women weep loudly and abundantly, and every now and then someone is heard shrieking or calling the departed one with tender names and laudatory epithets. Drums are beaten to call the populace and announce the death, while the cortege follows the shrouded corpse carried on a bier to its final resting place. After interment, close relatives do not wash or wear clean clothes; men do not shave, food is hardly considered, and utter distress is manifested in all possible ways. Funerary

traditions, much of the funerary terminology, cemetery architecture, and even cemetery administration all have their roots in ancient Egypt.

Some people may nowadays be turning to excessive religiosity as a reaction to corruption induced by poverty and to the loosening of traditions caused by the new ways of life introduced with modern technology. The erection of the High Dam at Aswan (completed in 1971), for example, completely altered the environment in rural areas, and the old natural rhythm of life had to change in order to comply with the new methods of irrigation and culture. Tourism, telecommunications, mass media and television programs have brought Western mores and ways of thinking disruptive to society. Returning to traditional "precolonial" costumes may also represent an assertion of "Oriental identity" and "Oriental values." Many people do not see why they should adopt "uncomfortable" Western clothes, and some women believe that they should wear the veil because religion commends modesty. If their grandmothers removed their veils to assert their right to participate in public life, the younger generation seems to consider the veil a protection against undue pestering in that very same public life, where they can now move freely. Today one meets Egyptian women, veiled or not, in all walks of life, assuming top jobs as well as very modest occupations.

Religious feeling is reflected in a noticeable increase in the number of mosques built with funding from private donors. These are really social service centers that generally include a clinic, a nursery, and one or several teaching centers that can be regular elementary schools or can teach reading, writing, and rudiments of various crafts. Their extremely low fees are sufficient for upkeep, since many administrators and professionals are volunteers who donate their time and expertise as an act of religious charity. A number of these mosque centers as well as churches distribute charitable donations to the poorer families of the neighborhood.

Some organizations or wealthy individuals sponsor great *mawaled* (fairs to celebrate the birthday anniversaries of great religious leaders of Islam). At a *mawled* people meet, verses of the Koran and religious hymns are recited, and abundant food is offered. During Ramadan (the month of fasting) many rich people provide food for the poor of their communities; there can be no doubt that in Egypt private religious charity, whether Muslim or Christian, provides as much or more relief than the official state welfare organizations.

The proliferation of religious institutions is matched by equally spectacular growth in the number of restaurants, fast-food shops, nightclubs, and discos. The more expensive public places are frequented by a new society that made its money during the *infitah* years (when there was an opening up of free trade) of the late 1970s and early 1980s, and whose children have no problem getting money and even less spending it. Indeed, Cairo today exhibits more expensive cars than it ever did, and nothing seems to make more money than leisure industries. Contrasts between patterns of life continue to increase as conflicting values compete amidst the crowds, noise, and pollution of big cities. Egypt today is torn between opposites and only history will tell where it is going.

ABOVE: The difference between luxurious hotels and the world outside can be breathtaking, although expensive hotel restaurants and night clubs are by no means patronized only by foreigners. CHRISTINE OSBORNE PICTURES

BELOW: A television set tends to be turned on with little regard for what is being shown or what is going on in front of it, a characteristic that the Egyptians share with people all over the world. MAXIMILIEN BRUGGMAN

CHRONOLOGICAL CHART

Ancient Egyptian chronology has recently been discussed in great detail and often in passionate terms. Nevertheless, the discussion has not yet produced a generally accepted scheme; if anything, the situation is even more complicated (not to put it more strongly) than ever before. This presents difficulties in a collective work because of the diversity of views of individual authors. The chronological scheme adopted here was chosen by the editor of the book and does not necessarily reflect the views of all the contributors. In its general approach it follows, though not slavishly, the following studies:

for the Third Intermediate period, the New Kingdom, and the Second Intermediate period, K. A. Kitchen's *The Third Intermediate Period in Egypt (1100–650 B.C.)* 2nd ed., Warminster, 1986, and the contributions by the same author to P. Åstrom (ed.) *High, Middle or Low?* Parts 1 and 3, Gothenburg, 1987 and 1989 ("high" chronology for the Eighteenth Dynasty, no coregency overlap between the reigns of Amenophis III and IV, and 1279 BC as the accession year of Ramesses II);

for the Middle Kingdom, it retains R. A. Parker's (*The Calendars of Ancient Egypt* The University of Chicago Press, 1950) calculation of the Sothic date (1872 BC) for the seventh year of Senwosret III, but uses the chronological table of D. Franke in *Orientalia* 57 (1988), for the Twelfth Dynasty (recalculating it for Parker's date);

for the Old Kingdom, it follows the scheme in J. Malek and W. Forman *In the Shadow of the Pyramids. Egypt during the Old Kingdom* London, 1986, but uses the corrected date for the beginning of the Ninth and Eleventh (and the end of the Eighth) dynasties.

The dates may be regarded as certain for the Late period. The possible margin of error should not exceed fifteen years for the New Kingdom, some 40 years for the Middle Kingdom, 60 years for the Old Kingdom, and about 100 years for the first two dynasties.

NOTE: From the Twenty-fifth (Nubian) Dynasty onwards, the entries in italics refer to events that took place abroad but were of profound importance for the history of Egypt.

BC   ANCIENT EGYPT

c. **5000–3000 Predynastic period**

c. **3000–2950 "Dynasty 0"**
     including:
     "Scorpion"
     Narmer

c. **2950–2647 The Early Dynastic period**
     First Dynasty
       Aha
       Djer
       Wadj
       Den
       Andjib
       Semerkhet
       Qaa

     Second Dynasty
       Hetepsekhemui
       Raneb
       Ninetjer
       Weneg
       Send
       Sneferka
       Sekhemib-perenmaet (perhaps same as Peribsen)
       Khasekhem = Khasekhemui

2647–2124   **The Old Kingdom (Third through Eighth Dynasties)**

2647–2573	Third Dynasty	
2647–2628	Zanakht	
2628–2609	Netjerikhet (Djoser)	
2609–2603	Sekhemkhet	
2603–2597	Khaba	
2597–2573	Qahedjet	

2573–2454	Fourth Dynasty	
2573–2549	Snofru	
2549–2526	Khufu	
2526–2518	Radjedef	
2518–2493	Khephren	
2493–2488	Khnemka or Wehemka (*reading uncertain*)	
2488–2460	Menkaure	
2460–2456	Shepseskaf	
2456–2454	Thamphthis (*name only known from the historian Manetho*)	

2454–2311	Fifth Dynasty	
2454–2447	Userkaf	
2447–2435	Sahure	
2435–2425	Neferirkare	
2425–2418	Shepseskare	
2418–2408	Raneferef	
2408–2377	Neuserre	
2377–2369	Menkauhor	
2369–2341	Izezi	
2341–2311	Unas	

2311–2140	Sixth Dynasty	
2311–2281	Teti	
2280–2243	Pepy I	
2242–2237	Merenre I	
2236–2143	Pepy II	
2142–2141	Merenre II	
2141–2140	Neitiqert (Queen)	

2140–2134   **Seventh Dynasty**

2134–2124   **Eighth Dynasty**

2123–*c.* 2040 The First Intermediate period (Ninth through mid-Eleventh Dynasties)

2123–2040	Ninth/Tenth (Heracleopolitan) Dynasty *including:*
	Meryibre Akhtoy
	Merykare

2123–c. 2040	**Eleventh (Theban) Dynasty** *(first part)*	
2124–2107	Mentuhotpe I and Inyotef I	
2107–2058	Inyotef II	
2058–2050	Inyotef III	
2050–c. 2040	Mentuhotpe II *(before reunification)*	

c. 2040–1648 The Middle Kingdom
   (Mid-Eleventh through Thirteenth Dynasties)

c. 2040–1980	**Eleventh (Theban) Dynasty** *(second part)*	
c. 2040–1999	Mentuhotpe II *(after reunification)*	
1999–1987	Mentuhotpe III	
1987–1980	Mentuhotpe IV	

1980–1801	**Twelfth Dynasty**
1980–1951	Amenemhet I
1960–1916	Senwosret I
1918–1884	Amenemhet II
1886–1878	Senwosret II
1878–1859	Senwosret III
1859–1814	Amenemhet III
1814–1805	Amenemhet IV
1805–1801	Sobeknofru (Queen)

1801–1648	**Thirteenth Dynasty** *including:*
1738–1727	Neferhotep I
1727	Sihathor
1727–1720	Sobekhotpe IV
1720–1716	Sobekhotpe V
1716–1706	Iaib
1706–1683	Merneferre Ay

1648–1540 The Second Intermediate period
   (Fourteenth through Seventeenth Dynasties)

1648–1540 **Fourteenth, Fifteenth ("The Hyksos") and Sixteenth ("The Lesser Hyksos") Dynasties (contemporary)**

The Hyksos (*according to Josephus*):
   Salitis
   Bnon
   Apakhnan
   Apophis
   Iannas
   Assis

1648–1550 **Seventeenth (Theban) Dynasty** *including:*
   Senakhtenre Teo I
   Seqenenre Teo II
   Kamose

(plus *c.* the first decade of the reign of Amosis of the Eighteenth Dynasty)

1540–1069 The New Kingdom
   (Eighteenth through Twentieth Dynasties)

1540 (1550)–1296 Eighteenth Dynasty
   1540 (accession
   1550)–1525   Amosis

1525–1504	Amenophis I
1504–1492	Tuthmosis I
1492–1479	Tuthmosis II
1479–1457	Hatshepsut (Queen)
1479–1425	Tuthmosis III
1427–1401	Amenophis II
1401–1391	Tuthmosis IV
1391–1353	Amenophis III
1353–1337	Amenophis IV = Akhenaten
1338–1336	Smenkhkare
1336–1327	Tutankhamun
1327–1323	Ay
1323–1295	Haremhab

1295–1186	**Nineteenth Dynasty**
1295–1294	Ramesses I
1294–1279	Sethos I
1279–1213	Ramesses II
1213–1203	Merneptah
1203–1200	Amenmesse
1200–1194	Sethos II
1194–1188	Siptah
1188–1186	Twosre (Queen)

1186–1069	**Twentieth Dynasty**
1186–1184	Setnakht
1184–1153	Ramesses III
1153–1147	Ramesses IV
1147–1143	Ramesses V
1143–1136	Ramesses VI
1136–1129	Ramesses VII
1129–1126	Ramesses VIII
1126–1108	Ramesses IX
1108–1099	Ramesses X
1099–1069	Ramesses XI

1069–c. 715 The Third Intermediate period
   (Twenty-first through Twenty-fourth Dynasties)

1069–945	**Twenty-first Dynasty**
1069–1043	Smendes
1043–1039	Amenemnisu
1039–991	Psusennes I
993–984	Amenemope
984–978	Osochor
978–959	Siamun
959–945	Psusennes II

945–715	**Twenty-second Dynasty**
945–924	Shoshenq I
924–889	Osorkon I
889–874	Takelot I
874–850	Osorkon II
850–825	Takelot II
825–773	Shoshenq III
773–767	Pimay
767–730	Shoshenq V
730–715	Osorkon IV

818–715	**Twenty-third Dynasty** *including:*	
	Pedubaste I	
	Iuput I	
	Osorkon III	
	Takelot III	
	Iuput II	
727–715	**Twenty-fourth Dynasty**	
727–720	Tefnakht I	
720–715	Bekenrenef	

c. 715–332 **The Late Period**
(Twenty-fifth through Thirtieth Dynasties
and the "Second Persian Period")

c. 715–656	**Twenty-fifth (Nubian) Dynasty**	
c. 760–747	*Kashta*	
747–716	*Piye*	
716–702	Sabacon	
702–690	Shebitku	
690–664	Taharqa	
664–656	*Tantamani*	

664–525	**Twenty-sixth (Saite) Dynasty**	
664–610	Psammetichus I	
610–595	Necho II	
595–589	Psammetichus II	
589–570	Apries	
570–526	Amasis	
526–525	Psammetichus III	

525–404	**Twenty-seventh (Persian) Dynasty**	
525–522	Cambyses	
521–486	Darius I	
485–465	Xerxes I	
464–424	Artaxerxes	
423–405	Darius II	

404–399	**Twenty-eighth Dynasty**	
404–399	Amyrtaios	

399–380	**Twenty-ninth Dynasty**	
399–393	Nepherites I	
393	Psammuthis	
393–380	Hakor	
380	Nepherites II	

380–343	**Thirtieth Dynasty**	
380–362	Nectanebo I	
362–360	Teos	
360–342	Nectanebo II	

342–332	**The "Second Persian Period"**	
	(includes the reign of Khababash)	
342–338	Artaxerxes III	
337–336	Arses	
335–332	Darius III	

GRECO-ROMAN AND COPTIC EGYPT

BC

332–305	**Macedonian Dynasty**	
332	Alexander the Great captures Egypt from the Persians	
331	the city of Alexandria founded (7 April)	
323	death of Alexander the Great	

305–30	**Ptolemaic Dynasty**	
305	official establishment of Ptolemy I Soter as king of Egypt (7 November)	
285–246	Ptolemy II Philadelphus	
246–222	Ptolemy III Euergetes I	
222–205	Ptolemy IV Philopator	
217	victory of Ptolemy IV over Antiochus III of Syria at the battle of Raphia	
51	beginning of joint rule of Ptolemy XII Neos Dionysus Auletes, Cleopatra VII Philopator and Ptolemy XIII	
48	Julius Caesar reinstates Cleopatra as queen of Egypt	
34	Mark Antony and Cleopatra proclaim the "Donations of Alexandria"	
31	defeat of Mark Antony and Cleopatra at Actium (September)	
30	Octavian captures Alexandria (1 August); death of Cleopatra (10 August)	

30 BC– AD 395	**Roman Province**	
30 BC	official establishment of Egypt as a Roman province (31 August)	

AD

19	visit of Germanicus to Egypt	
66	Jewish revolt in Egypt	
69	proclamation of Vespasian as emperor at Alexandria (1 July)	
115–17	Jewish revolt in Egypt	
130–31	visit of Hadrian to Egypt	
215	massacre of Alexandrians by Caracalla	
251	persecution of the Christians by Decius	
c. 251–356	life of St Antony, founder of Egyptian monasticism	
270–72	capture of Egypt by the Palmyrenes	
284	accession of Diocletian; starting–point for Coptic era	
297–98	revolt of L. Domitius Domitianus put down by Diocletian	
303	persecution of the Christians by Diocletian	
306	accession of Constantine the Great	
328–73	Athanasius as Bishop of Alexandria	
330	*foundation of the city of Constantinople*	
c. 334–452	life of Shenute, superior of Deir el-Abyad, White Monastery	
371(?)	creation of the Diocese of Egypt	
391	destruction of the Serapeum at Alexandria	
395	*division of the Roman empire*	

395–642 Byzantine Egypt

451	Council of Chalcedon; rejection of Egypt's monophysite doctrine
453	treaty with the Blemmyes
619–28	occupation of Egypt by the Persians
622	*emigration, hijra, of the Prophet Muhammad from Mecca to Medina*
632	*death of Muhammad*
634–40	*Arab conquest of Syria and Palestine*

ISLAMIC EGYPT

639–642 Arabs, led by Amr ibn al-As, conquer Egypt

642	final departure of Byzantine forces from Egypt (29 September); foundation of Fustat
656	*murder of the caliph Othman I*

661–750 *Umayyad Caliphate*

750	*murder of the caliph Marwan II*

750–1258 *Abbasid Caliphate*

762	*transfer of Abbasid capital to Baghdad*
813–33	*caliphate of al-Mamun*
832	al-Mamun's visit to Egypt
838–83	temporary transfer of Abbasid capital to Samarra

868–905 Tulunid Dynasty

868–83	Ahmad ibn Tulun

909 *establishment of Fatimid Caliphate in North Africa*

909–34	*Ubayd Allah (al-Mahdi)*
953–75	*al-Muizz*

934–969 Ikhshidid Dynasty

934–46	Muhammad ibn Tughj
966–68	Kafur (a palace eunuch of the Ikhshidids)

969–1171 Fatimid Caliphate

969	Jawhar conquers Egypt for the caliph al-Muizz and founds al-Qahira (Cairo)
970	foundation of al-Azhar (mosque and university)
996–1021	al-Hakim
1055	*establishment of Seljuk sultanate in Baghdad*
1073–1171	period of the military viziers
1073–94	Badr al-Din al-Jamali
1099	*conquest of Jerusalem by the Crusaders*
1164–1168	Zengid expeditions to Egypt
1168	destruction of the city of Fustat

1171–1250 Ayyubid Dynasty

1171–1193	Saladin
1187	*reconquest of Jerusalem*
1200–18	al-Adil, brother of Saladin
1240–49	al-Salih Ayyub
1249–50	Sixth Crusade of King Louis IX of France
1250	overthrow of the Ayyubids in Egypt, and reign of Shajar al-Durr

1250–1382 Bahri Mamelukes

1258	*Mongol sack of Baghdad and the murder of the caliph*
1260	*mameluke victory at Ayn Jalut, Goliath's Spring, over the Mongols*
1260–77	Baybars
1261	establishment of Abbasid caliphate in Cairo
1279–90	Qalaun
1294–5, 1299–1309, 1309–40	al-Nasir Muhammad
1347–51, 1354–61	Hasan

1382–1517 Burji (Circassian) Mamelukes

1382–89, 1390–99	al-Zahir Barquq
1412–21	al-Muayyad
1468–96	Qait Bey

1517 Ottoman conquest of Egypt

1773	death of Bey al-Kabir
1778–86	Murad Bey
1791–98	Ibrahim Bey

MODERN ISLAMIC EGYPT

1798	Napoleon's expeditionary force lands in Egypt (2 July)
1801	departure of the French army from Egypt
1805–49	Muhammad Ali as viceroy and pasha
1811	massacre of the mamelukes
1849–54	Abbas I Pasha
1854–63	Said Pasha
1863–79	Khedive Ismail
1869	opening of the Suez Canal
1879–92	Khedive Tawfiq
1882	Urabi revolt and defeat at Tell el-Kebir; British occupation of Egypt
1883–1907	Lord Cromer as consul-general
1892–1914	Khedive Abbas II Hilmy
1914–17	Sultan Husein Kamil
1917–36	Khedive Ahmad Fuad (from 1923 King Fuad I)
1922	declaration of independence
1923	Egyptian constitution declared
1936	Anglo-Egyptian Treaty, ending the British military presence in Egypt (except for the Suez Canal zone)
1936–52	King Farouk
1937	Egypt becomes a full member of the League of Nations
1952	revolution of 23 July; King Farouk deposed
1952–54	Muhammad Naguib as president
1954–70	Gamal Abdel Nasser as president
1956	Suez campaign, a military intervention by Israel, Great Britain, and France (19 October – 6 November)
1958–61	United Arab Republic: union of Egypt with Syria
1967	Six Day War (5–10 June); Sinai occupied by Israel
1970-81	Anwar Sadat as president
1971	completion of the High Dam at Aswan
1973	"Yom Kippur" or "Ramadan" War (6–22 October)
1978	Camp David accords (17 September)
1979	peace treaty between Egypt and Israel signed (26 March)
1981	President Sadat assassinated (6 October); Hosni Mubarak as president

Further Reading

The Black Land, the Red Land

Baines, J. and Malek, J. *Atlas of Ancient Egypt* Phaidon Press Ltd, Oxford, 1980

Kees, H. *Ancient Egypt. A Cultural Topography* Faber and Faber, London, 1961

Butzer, K.W. *Early Hydraulic Civilization in Egypt. A Study in Cultural Ecology* The University of Chicago Press, 1976

Rothenberg, B. et al. *Sinai. Pharaohs, Miners, Pilgrims and Soldiers* Joseph J. Binns Publisher, Washington and New York, 1979

Klemm, R. and D. *Die Steine der Pharaonen* Staatliche Sammlung Ägyptischer Kunst, Munich, 1981

Giddy, L.L. *Egyptian Oases. Bahariya, Dakhla, Farafra and Kharga during Pharaonic Times* Aris & Phillips Ltd, Warminster, 1987

Säve-Söderbergh, T. (ed.) *Temples and Tombs of Ancient Nubia. The International Rescue Campaign at Abu Simbel, Philae and Other Sites* Thames and Hudson/UNESCO, London, 1987

An Ancient Civilization

Helck, W. *Geschichte des Alten Ägypten* Handbuch der Orientalistik, 1.1.3. E.J. Brill, Leiden/Köln, 1981

Hoffman, M.A. *Egypt before the Pharaohs* Routledge & Kegan Paul, London and Henley, 1980

Malek, J. and Forman, W. *In the Shadow of the Pyramids. Egypt during the Old Kingdom* Orbis, London, 1986

Wildung, D. *Sesostris und Amenemhet. Ägypten im Mittleren Reich* Hirmer, Munich, 1984

Redford, D.B. *History and Chronology of the Eighteenth Dynasty of Egypt* University of Toronto Press, 1967

Kitchen, K.A. *The Third Intermediate Period in Egypt (1100–650 BC)* 2nd ed., Aris & Phillips Ltd, Warminster, 1986

Rediscovering Egypt

Clayton, P.A. *The Rediscovery of Ancient Egypt. Artists and Travellers in the 19th Century* Thames and Hudson, London, 1982

Dawson, W.R. and Uphill, E.P. *Who was Who in Egyptology* 2nd ed., The Egypt Exploration Society, London, 1972

Drower, M.S. *Flinders Petrie. A Life in Archaeology* Victor Gollancz Ltd, London, 1985

Greener, L. *The Discovery of Egypt* Cassell, London, 1966

Ridley, R.T. "Auguste Mariette: one hundred years after" *Abr-Nahrain* xxii (1983–84): 118–58

Wilson, J.A. *Signs & Wonders upon Pharaoh* The University of Chicago Press, 1964

Life along the Nile

Hayes, W.C. *The Scepter of Egypt. A Background for the Study of the Egyptian Antiquities in The Metropolitan Museum of Art* 2 vols, Harper & Brothers, New York, 1953. Harvard University Press, Cambridge, Mass., 1959

Brovarski, E., Doll, S.K., and Freed, R.E. (eds) *Egypt's Golden Age. The Art of Living in the New Kingdom 1558–1085 B.C. Catalogue of the Exhibition* Boston, Mass., Museum of Fine Arts, 1982

Bourriau, J. *Pharaohs and Mortals. Egyptian Art in the Middle Kingdom* Cambridge University Press and Fitzwilliam Museum, 1988

James, T.G.H. *Pharaoh's People. Scenes from Life in Imperial Egypt* The Bodley Head, London, etc., 1984

Montet, P. *Everyday Life in Egypt in the Days of Ramesses the Great* Edward Arnold (Publishers) Ltd, London, 1958

Lesko, L.H. *King Tut's Wine Cellar* B.C. Scribe Publications, Berkeley, Calif., 1977

Earning a Living

Helck, W. *Wirtschaftsgeschichte des Alten Ägypten im 3. und 2. Jahrtausend vor Chr* Handbuch der Orientalistik, 1.1.5. E.J. Brill, Leiden/Köln, 1975

Janssen, Jac. J. *Commodity Prices from the Ramessid Period. An Economic Study of the Village of Necropolis Workmen at Thebes* E.J. Brill, Leiden, 1975

Janssen, Jac. J., "Prolegomena to the study of Egypt's economic history during the New Kingdom" *Studien zur Altägyptischen Kultur* 3 (1975): 127–85

Posener-Kriéger, P., "Les papyrus d'Abousir et l'économie des temples funéraires de l'Ancien Empire." In: Lipiński, E. (ed.) *State and Temple Economy in the Ancient Near East* i. Orientalia Lovaniensia Analecta, 5. Departement Oriëntalistiek, Leuven, 1979, Pp. 134–51

Kemp, B.J. *Ancient Egypt. Anatomy of a Civilization* Routledge, London and New York, 1989

The Pharaohs and their Court

Brunner, H. *Die Geburt des Gottkönigs. Studien zur Überlieferung eines altägyptischen Mythos* Ägyptologische Abhandlungen, 10. Otto Harrassowitz, Wiesbaden, 1964

Edgerton, W.F., "The government and the governed in the Egyptian Empire" *Journal of Near Eastern Studies* 6 (1947)

Frankfort, H. *Kingship and the Gods. A Study of Ancient Near Eastern Religion as the Integration of Society & Nature* The University of Chicago Press, 1948

Gardiner, A.H. *The Wilbour Papyrus* 4 vols, The Brooklyn Museum and OUP, 1941–52

Posener, G. *De la divinité du Pharaon* Cahiers de la Société asiatique, 15. Imprimerie nationale, Paris, 1960

Trigger, B.G. et al. *Ancient Egypt. A Social History* Cambridge University Press, 1983

The Rise and Fall of Empires

The Cambridge Ancient History 3rd ed. of Vols i, ii, 2nd ed. of Vol. iii, Cambridge University Press, 1970–91

Kitchen, K.A. *Pharaoh Triumphant. The Life and Times of Ramesses II, King of Egypt* Aris & Phillips Ltd, Warminster, 1982

Helck, W. *Die Beziehungen Ägyptens zu Vorderasien im 3. u. 2. Jahrtausend v. Chr* Ägyptologische Abhandlungen, 5. 2nd ed., Otto Harrassowitz, Wiesbaden, 1971

Adams, W.Y. *Nubia. Corridor to Africa* Allen Lane, London, 1977

Vercoutter, J. *L'Égypte et le monde égéen préhellénique. Étude critique des sources égyptiennes. (Du début de la XVIIIe à la fin de la XIXe Dynastie)* Bibliothèque d'Étude, xxii, IFAO, Cairo, 1956

K.A. Kitchen, "Punt and How to Get There," *Orientalia* 40 (1971): 184–207

The World of the Gods

Assmann, J. *Ägyptische Hymnen und Gebete* Die Bibliothek der Alten Welt. Reihe: Der Alte Orient. Artemis Verlag, Zurich and Munich, 1975

Assmann, J. *Ägypten. Theologie und Frömmigkeit einer frühen Hochkultur* Verlag W. Kohlhammer, Stuttgart, etc., 1984

Assmann, J. *Ma^cat Gerechtigkeit und Unsterblichkeit im Alten Ägypten* Verlag C.H. Beck, München, 1990

Hornung, E. *Conceptions of God in Ancient Egypt. The One and the Many* Cornell University Press, Ithaca, NY, 1982

Barucq, A. and Daumas, F. *Hymnes et prières de l'Égypte ancienne* Littératures anciennes du Proche-Orient. Textes égyptiens, Les

Éditions du Cerf, Paris, 1980

Brunner, H. *Grundzüge der altägyptischen Religion* Grundzüge, 50. Wissenschaftliche Buchgesellschaft, Darmstadt, 1983

Sadek, A.I. *Popular Religion in Egypt during the New Kingdom* Pelizaeus-Museum and Gerstenberg Verlag, Hildesheimer Ägyptologische Beiträge, 27. Hildesheim, 1987

The Visual Arts

James, T.G.H. and Davies, W.V. *Egyptian Sculpture* British Museum Publications, London, 1983

James, T.G.H. *Egyptian Painting and Drawing in the British Museum* British Museum Publications, London, 1985

Saleh, M. and Sourouzian, H. *The Egyptian Museum Cairo, Official Catalogue* Verlag Philipp von Zabern, Mainz, 1987

Kozloff, A.P., Bryan, B.M. and Berman, L.M. *Egypt's Dazzling Sun: Amenhotep III and his World* The Cleveland Museum of Art, Ohio, 1992

Smith, W. Stevenson *The Art and Architecture of Ancient Egypt* 2nd ed., revised by Simpson, Wm. K., The Pelican History of Art, Penguin Books Ltd, Harmondsworth, 1981

Monuments of the Mighty

Edwards, I.E.S. *The Pyramids of Egypt* Penguin Books Ltd, London, etc., 1991

Romer, J. *Valley of the Kings* Michael Joseph and Rainbird, London, 1981

Hornung, E. *The Valley of the Kings. Horizon of Eternity* Timken Publishers, New York, 1990

Reeves, N. *The Complete Tutankhamun. The King, the Tomb, the Royal Treasure* Thames and Hudson, London, 1990

Leblanc, C. *Ta set neferou. Une nécropole de Thèbes-Ouest et son histoire* i. Dâr al-Kutub, Cairo, 1989

Invaders and Conquerors

Bowman, A.K. *Egypt after the Pharaohs* 2nd ed., OUP, 1990

Fraser, P.M. *Ptolemaic Alexandria* 3 vols, Clarendon Press, Oxford, 1972

Lewis, N. *Life in Egypt under Roman Rule* Clarendon Press, Oxford, 1983

Lewis, N. *Greeks in Ptolemaic Egypt. Case Studies in the Social History of the Hellenistic World* Clarendon Press, Oxford, 1986

Turner, E.G. *Greek Papyri. An Introduction* Clarendon Press, Oxford, 1980

Monks, Missionaries, and Martyrs

Watterson, B. *Coptic Egypt* Scottish Academic Press, Edinburgh, 1988

Badawy, A. *Coptic Art and Archaeology: The Art of the Christian Egyptians from the Late Antique to the Middle Ages* The Massachusetts Institute of Technology Press, Cambridge, Mass., 1978

Meinardus, O.F.A. *Christian Egypt, Ancient & Modern* Cahiers d'histoire égyptienne, IFAO, Cairo, 1965

Meinardus, O.F.A. *Monks and Monasteries of the Egyptian Deserts* The American University in Cairo Press, revised ed., 1989

Walters, C.C. *Monastic Archaeology in Egypt* Aris & Phillips Ltd, Warminster, 1974

The Sword of Islam

Kubiak, W.B. *Al-Fustat: Its Foundation & Early Urban Development* The American University in Cairo Press, 1987

Lewis, B. "Egypt and Syria," in Holt, P.M., Lambton, A.K.S. and Lewis, B. (eds) *The Cambridge History of Islam* Vol.1: *The Central Islamic Lands* Cambridge University Press, 1970

Wiet, G. *L'Égypte arabe de la conquête arabe à la conquête ottomane 642–1517 de l'ère chrétienne* Vol. 4 of Hanotaux, G. (ed.) *Histoire de la nation égyptienne* Société de l'histoire nationale/Librairie Plon, Paris, 1937

Irwin, R. *The Middle East in the Middle Ages. The Early Mamluk Sultanate 1250–1382* Croom Helm, London and Sydney, 1986

Ayalon, D. *Studies on the Mamlūks of Egypt (1250–1517)* Varorium Reprints, London, 1977

Holt, P.M. *Egypt and the Fertile Crescent, 1516–1922. A Political History* Longmans, London, 1966

Shaw, Stanford J. *The Financial and Administrative Organization and Development of Ottoman Egypt, 1517–1798* Princeton University Press, 1962

Ashtor, E. *A Social and Economic History of the Near East in the Middle Ages* Collins, London, 1976

Lane-Poole, Stanley *The Art of the Saracens in Egypt* Chapman and Hall Ltd, London, 1886

Great Cairo

Aldridge, R. *Cairo. Biography of a City* Macmillan, London, 1970

Behrens-Abouseif, D. *Islamic Architecture in Cairo. An Introduction* Studies in Islamic Art and Architecture. Supplements to *Muqarnas* iii. E.J. Brill, Leiden, etc., 1989

Creswell, K.A.C. *A Short Account of Early Muslim Architecture* revised and supplemented by Allan, J.W., The American University in Cairo Press, 1989

Creswell, K.A.C. *The Muslim Architecture of Egypt* 2 vols, Clarendon Press, Oxford, 1952–59

Parker, R.B. and Sabin, R. *Islamic Monuments in Cairo. A Practical Guide* 3rd ed. revised by Williams, C., The American University in Cairo Press, 1985

Scanlon, G.T., "Housing and sanitation: some aspects of medieval public service," in: Hourani, A.H. and Stern, S.M. (eds) *The Islamic City. A colloquium* Bruno Cassirer, Oxford and University of Pennsylvania Press, 1970

Steele, J. *Hassan Fathy* Architectural Monographs, 13. Academy Editions, London and St Martin's Press, New York, 1988

Egypt in the Modern World

Hopwood, D. *Egypt: Politics and Society 1945–1984* 2nd ed., Allen & Unwin, London, 1985

Little, T. *Modern Egypt* Ernest Benn, London, 1967

Mansfield, P. (ed.) *The Middle East. A Political and Economic Survey* 4th ed., OUP, London etc., 1973

Vatikiotis, P.J. *The Modern History of Egypt* Weidenfeld & Nicolson, London, 1969

Badawi, M.M. *Modern Arabic Literature and the West* The Board of the Faculty of Oriental Studies, University of Oxford, London and Ithaca, 1985

Cachia, P. *An Overview of Modern Arabic Literature* Islamic Surveys, 17. Edinburgh University Press, 1990

Family Life in Modern Egypt

Ammar, H.M. *Growing up in an Egyptian Village, Silwa, Province of Aswan* Routledge & Kegan Paul, London, 1954

Wikan, U. *Life among the Poor in Cairo* Tavistock Publications, London, 1980

Saadawi, N. el *The Hidden Face of Eve. Women in the Arab World* Zed Press, London, 1980

Critchfield, R. *Shahhat an Egyptian* New York, 1978

Hussein, Taha *An Egyptian Childhood* Heinemann, London, 1981

Hussein, Taha *The Stream of Days. A Student at the Azhar* Longmans, Green & Co., London, 1948

Notes on Contributors

M. L. BIERBRIER was educated in Canada and Great Britain specializing in Byzantine history and Egyptology. He has been Assistant Keeper in the Department of Egyptian Antiquities of the British Museum since 1975. He is an authority on the history and chronology of the Ramessid period and the history of Egyptology. He has lectured widely in Britain and elsewhere and taken part in archaeological work in Egypt. His publications include *The Late New Kingdom in Egypt* (1975), *Hieroglyphic Texts from Egyptian Stelae, etc. in the British Museum* Parts 10–11 (1982–87), and *The Tomb Builders of the Pharaohs* (1982).

JANINE BOURRIAU studied Egyptian archaeology at University College, London. She has worked in the Ashmolean Museum, Oxford; the Metropolitan Museum of Art, New York; and the Fitzwilliam Museum, Cambridge, where she became Keeper of Antiquities, 1983–90. Since 1973 she has spent part of each winter in Egypt excavating with the Egypt Exploration Society, first at Saqqara, in the Sacred Animal Necropolis and the New Kingdom Necropolis, and currently at Memphis. On excavations she has specialized in pottery-recording but she has a wide interest in Egypt from the Middle Kingdom to the early Eighteenth Dynasty. In 1988 she expressed this in organising an exhibition, shown in Cambridge and Liverpool, "Pharaohs and Mortals: Egyptian Art in the Middle Kingdom" for which she also wrote the catalogue.

ALAN K. BOWMAN received his BA from the Queen's College, Oxford, in 1966, and his MA and PhD from the University of Toronto in 1967 and 1969 respectively. From 1970–72 he was Assistant Professor of Classics, Rutgers, the State University of New Jersey. From 1972–77 he was Lecturer in Ancient History at the University of Manchester. He has been a student and tutor in ancient history, Christ Church, University of Oxford since 1977. He was a visiting member at the Institute for Advanced Study, Princeton in 1976 and 1982. He is the author of *The Town Councils of Roman Egypt* (1972), *Egypt after the Pharaohs* (1986), and editor of Volumes X–XII of the second edition of the *Cambridge Ancient History*.

WALTRAUD GUGLIELMI received her PhD from the Eberhard-Karls University in Tübingen after studying Egyptology, archaeology, and ancient history. From 1970–79 she was assistant at the Egyptological Institute of the same university, whereafter she taught as Visiting Professor at the universities of Hamburg, Berlin, Trier, and Vienna. In 1991 she was appointed Associate Professor of Egyptology at Eberhard-Karls University. Her main fields of research include ancient Egyptian religion and literature as well as aspects of daily life of the Egyptians.

FAYZA M. H. HAIKAL studied Egyptology at Cairo University and graduated with honors in 1960. From 1960–61 she worked for the Center of Documentation on Ancient Egypt, which was then recording the monuments of Nubia. She was the first Egyptian woman to work on archaeological sites. Given a state scholarship in 1961 to study philology in England, she received her D. Phil. in 1965 from Oxford University and started her career at Cairo University where she taught ancient Egyptian language and religion until 1984, and supervised a number of research students. Currently she is teaching at the American University in Cairo. Her publications include religious papyri from the British Museum, the Louvre, the Vatican, and the Egyptian Museum, Cairo. She is a member of a number of scientific organisations and currently vice president of the International Association of Egyptologists.

JANE JAKEMAN wrote her Master of Philosophy thesis for Oxford University on the religious architecture of medieval Cairo and is currently doing further research on Islamic architecture. She has worked on the staff of the Bodleian and Ashmolean libraries in Oxford.

JAC. J. JANSSEN is Emeritus Professor in Egyptology at the University of Leiden, the Netherlands. Having graduated in history and geography from the University of Utrecht, he taught at various grammar schools whilst taking a second degree, followed by a doctorate, in Egyptology at Leiden. His interest in the socio-economic aspects of history resulted in *Commodity Prices from the Ramessid Period* (1975). He was editor of the *Annual Egyptological Bibliography* for eleven years. With his wife Rosalind Janssen he has written two popular books: *Egyptian Household Animals* (1989), and *Growing up in Ancient Egypt* (1990). His most recent work is an edition of hieratic texts in the British Museum.

PENELOPE JOHNSTONE studied Arabic and Persian at Oxford University and then researched the history of Arabic medicine and herbals (D. Phil. 1972). She did two years' field work in the Palestine–Syria area, the first year at the British School of Archaeology, and a further year of research with the Wellcome Unit for the History of Medicine, Oxford. She spent one and a half years at the Center for Islam and Christian–Muslim Relations, Selly Oak Colleges, Birmingham, and taught Arabic for three years at Manchester University.

C. A. KELLER studied Egyptology and Near Eastern studies chiefly at the University of California, Berkeley, gaining her PhD in 1978. She was Associate Curator of Egyptian Art at the Metropolitan Museum of Art, New York, from 1977–83, when she joined the Department of Near Eastern Studies at the University of California as associate professor. She has excavated and carried out epigraphic work in Egypt and recently completed an in-depth study of the careers and artistic output of the draughtsmen of Deir el-Medina, who drew and painted the royal tombs of the New Kingdom at Thebes.

KENNETH A. KITCHEN was trained in both Egyptology and Semitics, working ever since in Egyptology and other ancient Near Eastern civilisations and their interrelationships. He has visited Egypt sixteen times to work on inscriptions and is the author of numerous works on Egyptology, ancient Near Eastern studies and biblical archaeology. These include: *Ramesside Inscriptions* I–VIII (1969–90), *The Third Intermediate Period in Egypt (1100–650 B.C.)* 2 eds (1972, 1986), *Pharaoh Triumphant. The Life & Times of Ramesses II , King of Egypt* (1983), *Ancient Orient & Old Testament* (1966), *The Bible and its World* (1977), *Suppiluliuma & the Amarna Pharaohs* (1962), and innumerable papers.

ARIELLE P. KOZLOFF was educated at Mount Holyoke College, South Hadley, Massachusetts. Since 1969 she has worked at the Cleveland Museum of Art, Ohio, where she is now Curator of Ancient Art. Her training with works of art continued under the aegis of Egyptologist John D. Cooney, and the museum's director, Sherman Lee. As well as actively building the collection through acquisitions, she has made the museum's fine collections better known through major traveling exhibitions such as "The Gods' Delight: The Human Figure in Classical Bronze," and "Egypt's Dazzling Sun: Amenhotep III and His World."

JAROMIR MALEK studied Egyptology and archaeology at Charles University, Prague. Since 1971 he has been editor of the *Topographical Bibliography of Ancient Egyptian Hieroglyphic Texts, Reliefs and Paintings* at the Griffith Institute, Ashmolean Museum, Oxford. He has taken part in excavations and epigraphic surveys in Nubia, Abusir, and Saqqara. He is Field Director of Epigraphy for the Egypt Exploration Society's expedition to Memphis. He has published a number of specialized papers in Egyptological journals, and is coauthor of the *Atlas of Ancient Egypt* (1980), author of *In the Shadow of the Pyramids* (1986), and coeditor of *A Dedicated Life. Tributes offered in Memory of Rosalind Moss* (1990).

JOHN D. RAY has been Reader in Egyptology at Cambridge since 1977, and is a Fellow of Selwyn College. He is also a committee member of the Egypt Exploration Society. His research and publications concentrate on the Late period in Egypt and on Hellenistic Egypt, the demotic script, and the decipherment of the Carian script from Asia Minor. He is particularly interested in the role played by foreigners and immigrants in ancient Egypt.

D. S. RICHARDS was educated at Queen Elizabeth's Hospital, Bristol, from 1946–53, and Merton College, Oxford, from 1953–57, where he read Honour Moderations in Literae Humaniores and Arabic and Persian for Final Honours School. Since 1960 he has been Lecturer in Arabic at Oxford University. During 1966–67 he was Lecturer in Oriental Studies for Merton College. At present he is Vice-master of St Cross College, Oxford, of which college he is an Official Fellow.

IAN SHAW studied Egyptology at Cambridge University where he received his doctorate. He has excavated at Tell el-Amarna and Memphis, and is currently directing excavations at the Hatnub alabaster quarries in Middle Egypt. He has written a book on ancient Egyptian warfare and translated a history of ancient Egypt from French into English. His current research is on the workers' settlements associated with Egyptian quarries. He is the archaeology correspondent for the *Daily Telegraph* in London and contributes to various scholarly publications. He is now a Research Fellow in Archaeology at New Hall, Cambridge.

COLIN C. WALTERS graduated from Liverpool University in England, and taught Coptic there and later at Oxford University, where he was Lady Wallis Budge Research Fellow in Egyptology. He has excavated in Egypt on a number of occasions and is author of several books including *An Elementary Coptic Grammar of the Sahidic Dialect* (1972) and *Monastic Archaeology in Egypt* (1974).

Acknowledgments

A. K. Bowman, C. C. Walters, D. S. Richards, Jane Jakeman, and Penelope C. Johnstone have written the captions to illustrations in their chapters. The others are by Jaromir Malek, who would also like to thank the staff of the Ashmolean Library in Oxford for their expert help and never failing courtesy.

Index

Page numbers in italics indicate illustrations. Traditional Arabic names appear as written (Muhammad Ali), but modern Egyptian names have been inverted in Western style (Sadat, Anwar).